HIGHER

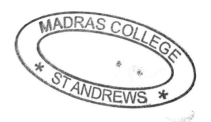

MODERN STUDIES

INTERNATIONAL ISSUES

SECOND EDITION

Frank Cooney
Gary Hughes
Pauline Kelly
& Steph O'Reilly

DYNAMIC LEARNING

HODDER GIBSON
AN HACHETTE UK COMPANY

The Publishers would like to thank the following for permission to reproduce copyright material:

Photo credits

Chapter opener images: **p.1** © frank11 – Fotolia.com; **p.50** © Gang – Fotolia.com; **p.83** © Ignus / stock.adobe.com; **p.132** © Aleksandar Todorovic – Fotolia.com; **p.166** © Rawpixel – Fotolia.com

p.2 © Andrey Popov / stock.adobe.com; **p.3** © Aleksandar Mijatovic / stock.adobe.com; **p.4** (left) © Jürgen Priewe / stock.adobe.com; (right) adaptice / stock.adobe.com; **p.6** (left) © Kitten / stock.adobe.com; (right) © Visions of America, LLC / Alamy Stock Photo; **p.7** © JIM WATSON / AFP / Getty Images; **p.8** © Joebeth Terriquez / EPA-EFE / Shutterstock; **p.10** © Fuse / Corbis / Getty Images; **p.11** (left) © Evan El-Amin / stock.adobe.com; (right) © Chip Somodevilla / Getty Images; **p.13** © AP / Shutterstock; **p.19** © Karl_Sonnenberg / Shutterstock; **p.21** © Democrat Party (United States); **p.22** © Republican Party (United States); **p.23** © Ron Sachs / CNP / Newscom / Alamy Stock Photo; **p.24** (left) © Gabriella Demczuk / Stringer / Getty Images; (right) © Chip Somodevilla / Getty Images; **p.27** © Andres Rodriguez – Fotolia.com; **p.31** © Patsy Lynch / Alamy Stock Photo; **p.32** © Monkey Business – Fotolia.com; **p.34** (left) © Christopher Pillitz / Getty Images; (right) © GIPhotoStock Z / Alamy; **p.36** © Image Source / Getty Images; **p.37** © Renee C. Byer / Sacramento Bee / TNS / Alamy Live News / Tribune Content Agency LLC / Alamy Stock Photo; **p.38** © Joseph Sohm / stock.adobe.com; **p.40** © kritchanut / stock.adobe.com; **p.42** © US Navy Photo / Alamy Stock Photo; **p.53** © By:Lintao Zhang / Getty Images; **p.56** © The Asahi Shimbun via Getty Images; **p.62** © Brian Sokol / Getty Images; **p.63** © Aidan Marzo / SOPA Images / LightRocket via Getty Images; **p.64** © Paul Yeung / Bloomberg via Getty Images; **p.65** © HuiTuan Wang – Fotolia.com; **p.66** © Sovfoto / Universal Images Group / Getty Images; **p.67** © SeanPavonePhoto – iStockphoto via Thinkstock; **p.69** © Lou Linwei / Alamy; **p.71** © Iain Masterton / Alamy Stock Photo; **p.73** © Quirky China News / Shutterstock; **p.74** © Jonathan Browning / Shutterstock; **p.80** © DON EMMERT / AFP / Getty Images; **p.81** © Susan Walsh / AP / Shutterstock; **p.83** © Goddard_Photography – iStockphoto via Thinkstock; **p.85** © Tetra Images / Alamy; **p.89** © Andrea / stock.adobe.com; **p.91** © Eye Ubiquitous / Alamy Stock Photo; **p.92** © Facundo Arrizabalaga / Rex Features; **p.95** © Xinhua News Agency / Shutterstock; **p.97** © Africa Media Online / Alamy; **p.100** (top) © Robin Laurance / Alamy; (right) © Eco Images / Universal Images Group; **p.106** © By:RAJESH JANTILAL / AFP / Getty Images; **p.110** © Gallo Images / Getty Images News; **p.111** © Kim Ludbrook / EPA / Shutterstock; **p.114** © Stock Connection Blue / Alamy; **p.116** (top of left column) © African National Congress; (second in left column) © Democratic Alliance; (bottom of left column) © Economic Freedom Fighters; (top of right column) © Inkatha Freedom Party; **p.117** © Giordano Stolley / Alamy Stock Photo; **p.118** © Gallo Images / Shutterstock; **p.120** © Gallo Images / Shutterstock; **p.136** (left) © Stockbyte via Thinkstock; (right) © Joe Gough – Fotolia.com; **p.138** (left) © mrallen – Fotolia.com; (right) © Syner-Comm / Alamy Stock Photo; **p.139** © Michele Burgess / Alamy Stock Photo; **p.140** © Education Images / Getty Images; **p.143** © Sam Valtenbergs / Getty Images; **p.145** © MIND AND I / stock.adobe.com; **p.146** © National Geographic Image Collection / Getty Images; **p.147** © Ho / Planet Pix Via Zuma Wire / Shutterstock; **p.148** (top right) © somartin – Fotolia.com; (bottom left) © Joe Gough – Fotolia.com; (bottom right) © somartin – Fotolia.com; **p.150** © Michael Kemp / Alamy Stock Photo; **p.154** © African Union / Courtesy of Wikipedia; **p.156** © Unicef; **p.157** © By:PIUS UTOMI EKPEI / AFP / Getty Images; **p.159** © imagebroker / Alamy; **p.160** © www.marysmeals.org.uk; **p.162** (both) © Oxfam; **p.166** © David Sheerin; **p.169** © David Sheerin

Acknowledgements

Extract from "By 2055, the U.S. Will Have No Racial or Ethnic Majority Group." Pew Research Center, Washington, D.C. (23 September 2015) https://www.pewresearch.org/hispanic/2015/09/28/modern-immigration-wave-brings-59-million-to-u-s-driving-population-growth-and-change-through-2065/ph_2015-09-28_immigration-through-2065-17/; Extract from "Hispanics of Cuban Origin in the United States, 2013." Pew Research Center, Washington, D.C. (15 September 2015) https://www.pewresearch.org/hispanic/2015/09/15/hispanics-of-cuban-origin-in-the-united-states-2013/; Extract from "5 facts about illegal immigration in the U.S." Pew Research Center, Washington, D.C. (12 June 2019) https://www.pewresearch.org/fact-tank/2019/06/12/5-facts-about-illegal-immigration-in-the-u-s/; Extract from 'How income inequality hurts America' reproduced from https://money.cnn.com/2013/09/25/news/economy/income-inequality/index.html; Education Week. Map: How Much Money Each State Spends Per Student [Graphic]. (2019). Retrieved November 21, 2019 from https://www.edweek.org/ew/collections/quality-counts-2019-state-finance/map-per-pupil-spending-state-by-state.html; Extract from "5 facts about crime in the U.S." Pew Research Center, Washington, D.C. (17 October 2019) https://www.pewresearch.org/fact-tank/2019/10/17/facts-about-crime-in-the-u-s/; Extract from "Key takeaways on Americans' views of guns and gun ownership." Pew Research Center, Washington, D.C. (22 June 2017) https://www.pewresearch.org/fact-tank/2017/06/22/key-takeaways-on-americans-views-of-guns-and-gun-ownership/; Extract from "China." Pew-Templeton Global Religious Futures Project, Pew Research Center, Washington, D.C. http://www.globalreligiousfutures.org/countries/china/religious_demography#/?affiliations_religion_id=11&affiliations_year=2010; Reprinted from the WHO website, News release, 'Rate of diabetes in China "explosive"', Copyright (2016) from https://www.who.int/macaochina/news/detail/06-04-2016-rate-of-diabetes-in-china-explosive-; Extract from report was written by Africa Check, a non-partisan fact-checking organisation. View the original piece on their website, https://africacheck.org/factsheets/factsheet-south-africas-crime-statistics-for-2017-18/; Extract from 'Afrikaners threaten Christmas violence over loss of their culture' reproduced with permission from the *Guardian*, 1 December 2002; Extract from Center for Strategic and International Studies (CSIS) website, 'Can South Africa Return to the Global Stage?', Richard Calland and Jon Temin, 17 December 2018, https://www.csis.org/analysis/can-south-africa-return-global-stage, reproduced with permission; Avert (last reviewed 25 September 2018) 'Global HIV and Aids statistics' from https://www.avert.org/global-hiv-and-aids-statistics [last accessed 20/11/2019]; Extract from Jubilee Debt Campaign, jubileedebt.org.uk; The materials quoted on the pages 161–162 are adapted by the publisher with the permission of Oxfam, Oxfam House, John Smith Drive, Cowley, Oxford OX4 2JY UK www.oxfam.org.uk. Oxfam does not necessarily endorse any text or activities that accompany the materials, nor has it approved the adapted text; Extract from 'Foreign aid works – it saves lives' reproduced with permission from the *Guardian*, 30 May 2012; Extract from ActionAid website. ActionAid is an international charity that works with women and girls living in poverty; Outcomes taken from SQA website, copyright © Scottish Qualifications Authority; The table on qualitative and quantitative research is copyright © Snap Surveys Limited 2019. Reproduced from www.snapsurveys.com with the permission of Snap Surveys Limited, all rights reserved

Every effort has been made to trace all copyright holders, but if any have been inadvertently overlooked the Publishers will be pleased to make the necessary arrangements at the first opportunity.

Although every effort has been made to ensure that website addresses are correct at time of going to press, Hodder Gibson cannot be held responsible for the content of any website mentioned in this book. It is sometimes possible to find a relocated web page by typing in the address of the home page for a website in the URL window of your browser.

Hachette UK's policy is to use papers that are natural, renewable and recyclable products and made from wood grown in well-managed forests and other controlled sources. The logging and manufacturing processes are expected to conform to the environmental regulations of the country of origin.

Orders: please contact Bookpoint Ltd, 130 Park Drive, Milton Park, Abingdon, Oxon OX14 4SE. Telephone: (44) 01235 827827. Fax: (44) 01235 400454. Lines are open 9.00–5.00, Monday to Friday, with a 24-hour message answering service. If you have queries or questions that aren't about an order, you can contact us at hoddergibson@hodder.co.uk.

© Frank Cooney, Gary Hughes, Pauline Kelly and Steph O'Reilly 2020

First published in 2015 © Frank Cooney, Gary Hughes, Pauline Kelly and Steph O'Reilly

This second edition published in 2020 by

Hodder Gibson, an imprint of Hodder Education,
An Hachette UK Company
211 St Vincent Street
Glasgow, G2 5QY

Impression number	5	4	3	2	1
Year	2024	2023	2022	2021	2020

Cover photo © Lightspring/Shutterstock.com

Illustrations by Integra Software Services Pvt. Ltd., Pondicherry, India and Jeff Edwards

Typeset in Minion Pro 12/15 by Integra Software Services Pvt. Ltd., Pondicherry, India

Printed in Italy

A catalogue record for this title is available from the British Library

ISBN: 978 1510 457799

SCOTLAND EXCEL

We are an approved supplier on the Scotland Excel framework.

Schools can find us on their procurement system as: **Hodder & Stoughton Limited t/a Hodder Gibson.**

MIX
Paper from responsible sources
FSC™ C104740
www.fsc.org

Contents

1 The United States of America — 1

Background — 1
The American Dream — 5
Immigration — 6
The political system — 9
Social and economic inequality — 26
International relations — 42

2 The People's Republic of China — 50

Background — 50
The political system — 51
Human rights — 59
China's economy — 65
Social and economic inequality — 69
International relations — 79

3 The Republic of South Africa — 83

Background — 83
Social and economic issues — 92
The political system — 112
International relations — 125

4 Development issues in Africa — 132

Overview — 132
Social, economic and political factors affecting development — 136
Responses to development issues in Africa — 148
The work of the United Nations agencies and NGOs — 156

5 Assessment — 166

Higher course assessment — 166
The assignment — 167
Research methods — 168
Qualitative and quantitative research — 169

1 The United States of America

Background

The United States of America is the third largest country in the world, in terms of land mass. It covers an area of 9,826,675 km², making it about half the size of Russia and a little smaller than Canada. It is about twice the size of the European Union. It has land borders with two other countries: Canada and Mexico. It is spread over 3000 miles from east to west between the Atlantic and Pacific Oceans.

In June 2019, the United States population reached approximately 329,025,782 people, according to US Census Bureau estimates. That means the US is currently the third most populous country on the planet, behind only China (1.4 billion) and India (1.25 billion).

- The state with the largest population is California with approximately 39.5 million people.
- New York has the highest population of any other US city with an estimated 8.5 million people.

As shown on the map, there are 50 states in the USA. Alaska and Hawaii also make up the 50 states although they are not directly attached to the other states.

1 VERMONT
2 NEW HAMPSHIRE
3 MASSACHUSETTS
4 RHODE ISLAND
5 CONNECTICUT
6 NEW JERSEY
7 DELAWARE
8 MARYLAND

Alaska and Hawaii are not to scale

Figure 1.1 **The states of the USA**

Who makes up the American population?

American society has often been described as a melting pot but it has also attracted other definitions such as 'salad bowl'.

This is due to the number of different ethnic groups and cultures who all make up the American population. There are five main ethnic groups in the USA:

- non-Hispanic white
- Hispanic/Latino
- black
- Asian and Pacific Islander
- Native American.

Ethnic composition of America

The 329 million people making up the population of the United States are categorised into five main ethnic groups outlined above. The population of the US represents over 4.25 per cent of the world's total population. This correlates with the fact that 1 in every 22 people in the world is a resident of the USA.

The US Census Bureau estimates that the population will rise to 417 million by 2060. Figure 1.3 (see page 3) compares the population ratio for the five main ethnic groups in the USA.

Figure 1.2 **The USA is a melting pot of different cultures**

Did you know?

The Hispanic/Latino group is the fastest growing group in the USA. The Pew Research Center has estimated that white people will decrease to under 50 per cent of the population by 2055. It estimates that the population breakdown will be as follows:

Table 1.1 2055 population estimate by ethnic group

White	≈ 48%
Hispanic/Latino	≈ 23%
Asian and Pacific Islander	≈ 12%
Black	≈ 13%

Source: Pew Research Center

White people are known as the majority group as they currently have the largest population in the USA. This is due to the history of white settlers in the USA until the 1920s. These white settlers predominately came from various countries in Europe.

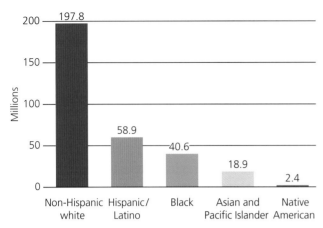

Figure 1.3 **Ethnic groups in the USA, estimated 2018/19**
Source: US Census Bureau

Ethnic minority groups

Hispanic people

There are estimated to be about 58.9 million Hispanic people currently living in the USA, making up over 18 per cent of the population. Hispanic people are the largest minority ethnic group, having overtaken black Americans in number in 2001. Only Mexico has a higher Hispanic population than the United States. The growth of the Hispanic population since then has been mainly due to births in the USA, not immigration from abroad.

Americans with Hispanic or Latino ethnicity are people from Cuban, Mexican, Puerto Rican or Central American, or other Spanish culture or origin.

Around two-thirds (63.3 per cent) of Hispanic people in the USA are of Mexican origin. The other third are from the remaining nine Hispanic origin groups of: Puerto Rican, Cuban, Salvadoran, Dominican, Guatemalan, Colombian, Honduran, Ecuadorian and Peruvian. These ten Hispanic groups differ in terms of numbers who are foreign-born, numbers who are US citizens by birth, and their proficiency in English. There are also differences in terms of their education levels, home ownership rates, income and poverty rates.

Ten US states have more than 1 million Hispanic/Latino residents: Arizona, California, Colorado, Georgia, Florida, Illinois, New Jersey, New Mexico, New York and Texas. An estimated 41 million US residents (13.4 per cent of the population) speak Spanish at home.

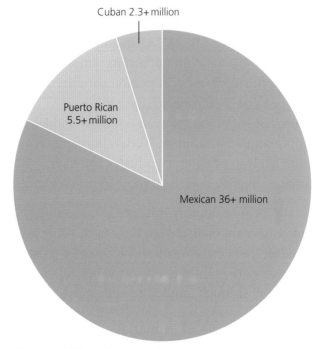

Figure 1.4 **Hispanic population by three main groups**
Source: US Census Bureau

Hispanic people of Mexican origin

Figure 1.5 **The flags of the Unites States and Mexico**

Hispanic people of Mexican origin account for 63.3 per cent of the US Hispanic population, over 36 million people.

The majority of Mexican–Americans are concentrated in the Southwest: California, Arizona, New Mexico and Texas.

The rise of the Mexican–American ethnic groups had resulted in an increasing number of Mexican consulates in various states being opened.

For decades, migrants from Mexico to the USA have largely been low-skilled, unauthorised workers in the agricultural/farming employment sectors. In recent years, migration patterns have changed due to factors including the improvement of the Mexican economy and US immigration enforcement. Today, immigrants are more likely to be college graduates and have stronger English skills than those in prior decades.

Mexicans are primarily Roman Catholic and usually remain dedicated to their faith while in the USA. Mexicans are often family orientated and many are granted green cards (lawful residency) through family ties and connections.

Hispanic people of Puerto Rican origin

Figure 1.6 **The flag of Puerto Rico**

There are approximately 5.5 million Hispanic people of Puerto Rican origin living in the USA, which is more than the population of Puerto Rico itself at 3.1 million. Around two-thirds of the Puerto Rican population was born in the USA and one-third was born in Puerto Rico. Many Puerto Rican–Americans live in the mid-Atlantic area of America – mainly in New York. Anyone who is born in Puerto Rico is considered to be an American citizen by birth, due to the fact that Puerto Rico is a Free-Associated State of the USA, which entitles Puerto Ricans to enter mainland USA to live and work.

Puerto Ricans are increasingly becoming more educated than in previous decades with almost 20 per cent earning a bachelor's degree. It is also estimated that 38 per cent own their own homes. This being said, these statistics are still lower than the US average.

Hispanic people of Cuban origin

Figure 1.7 **The flag of Cuba**

Hispanic people of Cuban origin account for almost 4 per cent of the US Hispanic population. On average, Cubans living in the USA tend to be older than the general US population and than other Hispanic groups. Around 70 per cent of Cubans live in Florida – predominately, Miami. New York is also home to a large proportion of Cubans.

From 1960s onwards, most Cubans entered the USA for humanitarian reasons and to gain political asylum during Fidel Castro's reign. There have been many laws that have been passed through Congress to support Cubans from the oppression experienced in their homeland. Today, Cubans who enter the USA on a visa are eligible for a green card after one year in the USA.

Cuban immigrants are less likely to be proficient in speaking the English language at home than other foreign-born immigrants.

Cubans tend to be better educated than the other Hispanic groups, particularly if they were born in the USA as opposed to being an immigrant. Around 36 per cent of USA-born Cubans aged 25 and above have obtained a bachelor's degree compared with 27 per cent of Cuban immigrants. As far as income levels are concerned, the numbers are higher than for all other Hispanic groups but lower than for the US population as a whole.

Black Americans

Black people account for about 13 per cent of the US population and are the second largest minority ethnic group in the USA. The 40.6 million black Americans are descendants of African slaves brought over to the USA from Africa to work on the plantations of the southern states in the seventeenth and eighteenth centuries. Slightly more than half of this group are concentrated in the states of the south and south-east; the rest are to be found in the industrial cities of the north-east, and in central and Pacific Coast states.

After the Civil War (1861–65), slavery was abolished but black Americans still faced massive political, social and economic inequality, especially in the south. The civil rights movement of the 1960s and subsequent civil rights acts finally gave them full equality. However, poverty and segregation are very much evident in the USA today for black Americans.

Asian and Pacific Islanders

The 18+ million Asian and Pacific Islanders (APIs) account for over 5.5 per cent of the US population and are the third largest minority ethnic group in the USA. They are a diverse ethnic group who have come from countries in Asia such as Korea and China or the Pacific Islands. The majority group are the Chinese population at over 5 million people. APIs are generally well educated and have the highest educational attainment levels and median annual income of all the ethnic minority groups. As a result they also have one of the lowest poverty rates. Just over half of the population aged 25+ have a bachelor's degree or similar diploma. The majority have settled in the cities of the west and south. Hawaii is the only US state in which Asian Americans or Pacific Islanders are the largest racial/ethnic group.

Native Americans

Native Americans account for 1.2 per cent of the total American population. This ethnic group are known as the 'original' Americans. Nearly 5 million Americans identify as Native American or Alaska Native solely or in combination with one or more races. Of them, more than 2 million identify as purely Native American or Alaska Native. In the most recent census figures, the majority tend to live in urban areas. Alaska has the highest Native American population, followed by New Mexico, South Dakota, Oklahoma and Montana. The majority of Native American citizens live on Reservations – these are recognised in US law as foreign territories and are not subject to all of the other laws of the USA.

The American Dream

The Declaration of Independence holds true the principles of the American Dream that everyone is given the chance to reach their potential:

'We hold these truths to be self-evident, that all men are created equal, that they are endowed by their Creator with certain unalienable Rights, that among these are **Life**, **Liberty** and **the pursuit** of **Happiness**.'

Figure 1.8 **The Statue of Liberty**

The search for the American Dream has been one of the most influential 'pull' factors for decades. Many immigrants, including those who are unauthorised, move to the USA to try to make their fortune from the capitalist system, hard work and sheer determination. This has not been the reality for the large majority of immigrants.

The Statue of Liberty symbolises democracy as well as international friendship; it is a colossal symbol of freedom to millions around the world. Its inscription reads:

> 'Give me your tired, your poor,
>
> Your huddled masses yearning to breathe free,
>
> I lift my lamp beside the golden door!'

These words, written by Emma Lazarus in 1883, have come to portray the statue's universal message of hope and freedom for immigrants coming to America and people seeking freedom around the world.

Immigration

Immigration has been a controversial topic in the USA over a number of decades. The fact remains that the United States has more immigrants than any other country. It is estimated that more than 40 million people living in America today were born in another country. Most of the countries in the world are represented in the USA to some degree.

It is difficult to gain a true figure as many people who come to live in the USA do so illegally. Having said this, the Pew Research Center has estimated that in 2007 there were approximately 12.2 million unauthorised immigrants, and 10.5 million in 2017.

Many immigrants, mainly illegal, lack any formal education and therefore seek work as unskilled labourers. They often take the sort of jobs that most native-born Americans refuse to do for the wages offered. For example, much of California's agricultural sector is dependent on thousands of immigrant labourers.

Figure 1.9 **Naturalisation ceremony**

What are the key issues?

The key issues are focused around controlling illegal entry. In the aftermath of 11 September 2001, the influx of illegal immigrants were sometimes thought to have posed a threat to national security. The US business sector claims that immigrants are a necessary workforce for the economy and so supports changes in the law to control entry and to clear up issues surrounding those already in the country illegally. The business sector would like to see illegal immigrants being allowed to remain in the country legally and wants the cap on the number of Temporary Worker Visas to be set higher or removed altogether.

Temporary Worker Visas (also known as the Guest Worker Program) allow foreign workers to reside and work in the USA for a fixed period of time. More than 900,000 of these visa types were granted in 2018.

Others want tougher enforcement of the land borders and existing laws on immigration. For example, some want to extend the fencing that already exists along a part of the US–Mexican border and introduce tougher penalties for businesses caught employing illegal migrants. Despite objections from the Mexican Government, this fence has been extended by 700 miles and is now patrolled by several thousand reserve soldiers of the USA National Guard.

The current president, Donald Trump, believes the USA needs tougher enforcement laws and has implemented some controversial strategies. His policy of 'Buy American' and 'Hire American' is at odds with the concepts of imported goods and foreign workers. Trump has stated that he will amend the Guest Worker Program and many similar programmes as there is an issue with tracking visas and knowing who has left the country when intended. Trump has also expressed his views on the need for a wall on the US–Mexican border. He has said that Mexico should pay for the wall as many illegal immigrants entering the USA are from Mexico. It is estimated that it would cost $20 billion to build the wall.

Immigration and politics

Politicians are aware of the growing immigrant electorate and so are reluctant to annoy and put off potential voters. The Republican Party faces confrontation from its social conservatives and

the business lobby because of the view from some that a harder line is required and that illegal immigrants should be criminalised. At the same time, the Democratic Party is trying to avoid conflict with trade unions who claim that the Guest Worker Programs only drive down wages and cause unemployment for American citizens.

In 2012, President Obama issued the DACA executive order (Deferred Action on Childhood Arrivals) programme. This was to try to help illegal immigrants who were brought to the USA as children to have a chance to live and work in the USA legitimately. There were many requirements such as background checks, evidence of arrival and age upon entering the USA. In addition, they had to renew their application every two years.

Figure 1.10 **Presidents Trump and Obama**

During the 2016 presidential campaign, Donald Trump stated that he intended to reduce both legal and illegal immigration and implement a system based on merits. In January 2017, he issued three executive orders on immigration with the aim of ensuring proper screening and monitoring for people attempting to enter the USA in an attempt to protect American jobs and not allow illegal immigrants to occupy positions. There has been fierce opposition to his plans to end the DACA programme and at the time of writing, the outcome is due to be determined by the Supreme Court.

Trump's zero-tolerance policy

In 2018, President Trump introduced a highly controversial immigration policy that saw the children of illegal immigrants separated from their parents after crossing the southern border. The adults faced criminal charges and were taken to adult detention centers, while the children were taken to shelters run by the Department of Health and Human Services.

Figure 1.11 **Families at the border**

- In the first two months, 2800 families were separated.
- The policy was called inhumane by both the Republican and Democratic Parties.
- Trump was pressured into signing an executive order to cancel the family separation policy.
- US District Judge Dana Sabraw in California banned the separation policy and ordered the administration to reunite families. Separation would only occur if it was deemed that the child/children were not safe with their accompanying adult.
- Many families have still not been reunited.

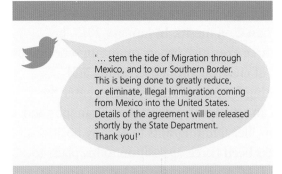

'… stem the tide of Migration through Mexico, and to our Southern Border. This is being done to greatly reduce, or eliminate, Illegal Immigration coming from Mexico into the United States. Details of the agreement will be released shortly by the State Department. Thank you!'

Figure 1.12 **Tweet from Donald Trump discussing immigration, 7 June 2019**

Assignment ideas

American Dream

- The American Dream is no longer a reality for those migrating to the USA.
- Capitalism allows anyone to have the opportunity to achieve the American Dream.

Immigration

- The US Government must adopt tighter border controls to eliminate illegal immigration to the USA.

Show your understanding

1 Write down the following information for the five main ethnic groups in the USA:
   - Population living in the USA
   - Reasons for them migrating to the USA
   - Where they tend to live in the USA
   - Evidence to show how they are progressing as a group, e.g. educational attainment
2 Read the text about the American Dream on pages 5–6.
   a) With a partner, discuss your own interpretation of the American Dream.
   b) Do you think the American Dream exists in the USA? Write down reasons for and against.
3 a) What evidence is there to suggest that illegal immigration may not be as big an issue as it once was?
   b) Write as many points as you can think of under each of these headings: 'Points in favour of immigration' and 'Points against immigration'.
   c) Why do politicians need to be careful how they handle the immigration topic in the USA?
4 Describe the actions taken by President Obama and President Trump on immigration.

The political system

The US Constitution

The US Constitution and system of government was written by the founding fathers, after the 13 colonies gained their independence from Britain in 1783. The then 13 states agreed to devise a new form of government – a **federal state**. Here power would be divided between the national (federal) government and the respective states. A second compromise was to have a Congress made up of two Houses: the **Senate** and the **House of Representatives**. In the Senate there would be equal representation for all states. In contrast, in the House of Representatives there would be representation proportional to the population of each state. Another compromise was to have the president elected indirectly by the people. The citizens would elect the **electoral college** and the latter would choose the president. A **Bill of Rights** would protect the rights of all citizens.

All these compromises and more helped to create the written Constitution of the USA, based on federalism, separation of powers and checks and balances. The Constitution is a set of rules by government establishing how it should be run. The Constitution is the supreme law of the USA, and it defines the relationship and allocation of powers between the Executive, Legislature and Judiciary. This separation of powers or doctrine of shared powers ensures that no one branch of government can dominate and thus protects the fundamental rights of US citizens.

Bill of Rights

The first ten amendments to the Constitution are referred to as the Bill of Rights, which is a series of constitutionally protected rights of citizens. The first two are:

First Amendment Right to freedom of religion, speech and the press, and the right to assemble peaceably, and to petition the government for a redress of grievances.

Second Amendment Right to bear arms in common defence.

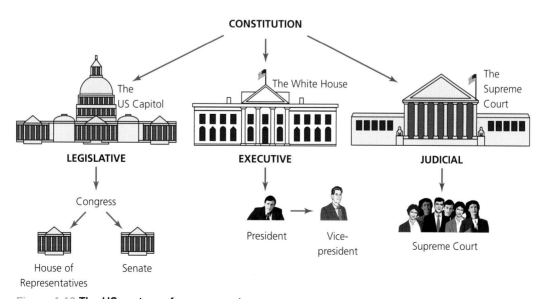

Figure 1.13 **The US system of government**

Figure 1.14 **The US Congress sits in the Capitol building in Washington**

The federal government

The federal government deals with matters concerning collective state issues and also foreign affairs. All powers not allocated to the federal government are retained by the respective states. The 50 states have the right to make their own laws on internal matters.

The federal government has authority over:

- the armed forces
- the post office
- the currency of the USA
- disputes between states
- foreign relations, for example, declaring war.

The separation of powers

The American political scientist, Richard Neustadt, wrote that 'the Constitution had created a government of separated institutions sharing powers', while his UK counterpart,

Professor Samuel Finer, described the Legislature and Executive as being 'like two halves of a bank note – each useless without the other'. This separation of powers or doctrine of shared powers ensures that no one branch of government can become dominant.

The Legislative branch makes laws

Established by Article 1 of the Constitution, the US Congress comprises two chambers: the Senate and the House of Representatives. Congress is the legislative (law-making) and oversight (government policy review) body of the national government. For a law to be made, it has to be passed by both chambers by a simple majority and finally signed by the president. Under the Constitution, each state is entitled to be represented by two senators (each serving a six-year term) and at least one representative (serving a two-year term).

The House of Representatives has several powers exclusively assigned to it, such as the impeachment of federal officials.

The Senate has the sole power to ratify treaties and to approve senior posts such as appointments to the Supreme Court.

The Executive branch carries out laws

The chief executive of the USA is the president. The president is responsible for implementing and enforcing the laws written by Congress. The president appoints the heads of federal agencies, including the Cabinet. Each secretary (Cabinet member) is in charge of a Department of State, which employs thousands of people to do the day-to-day work. The president is elected to a four-year term, and may only be elected to serve two terms.

Figure 1.15 **The White House is the president's official residence**

The Judicial branch interprets these laws

Article 111 of the Constitution establishes the Judicial branch. The Supreme Court is the highest court of the USA and the only one specifically created by the Constitution. Members of the Supreme Court are appointed by the president and confirmed by the Senate. The Supreme Court consists of nine Justices who are appointed for life and are replaced only when they resign, retire or die. In 2009, President Obama appointed the liberal Sonia Sotomayor, with the approval of Congress, to fill a vacancy in the Supreme Court, making her the first Hispanic Justice.

In 2017, President Trump was able to appoint his first Supreme Court Justice successfully following the death of Justice Antonin Scalia. Neil Gorsuch became one of the nine Supreme Court Justices.

In 2018, Trump appointed his second Supreme Court Justice following the retirement of Anthony Kennedy. When Brett Kavanaugh was on the nominee list, three women came forward to say that Kavanaugh had sexually assaulted them in the 1980s. The Republican-controlled Senate Judiciary Committee held a hearing over the allegations, after which it voted for Kavanaugh's nomination to go to Senate for a full vote. Brett Kavanaugh was voted in by 50–48 votes. No criminal charges have ever been brought against Brett Kavanaugh.

Federal courts hold the sole power to interpret the laws. The judges determine whether a law that has been passed is constitutional or not. The Judicial branch determines whether Legislative or Executive acts conform to the Constitution.

In 2019, the Supreme Court issued a decision that overturned 'Nevada v. Hall' (which held that the Constitution does not approve state immunity from lawsuits in another state's courts) and held that the California franchise Tax Board was immune from a lawsuit in Nevada. Basically, the Supreme Court had ruled that no state is immune to a lawsuit in another state and then overruled their action – now states are given immunity from legal action in neighbouring states.

Figure 1.16 **The nine Supreme Court Justices**

1 **John G. Roberts** (Chief Justice) – appointed by President George Bush
2 **Clarence Thomas** – appointed by President George Bush Snr
3 **Ruth Bader Ginsburg** – appointed by President Bill Clinton
4 **Stephen G. Breyer** – appointed by President Bill Clinton
5 **Samuel A. Alito** – appointed by President George Bush
6 **Sonia Sotomayor** – appointed by President Barack Obama
7 **Elena Kagan** – appointed by President Barack Obama
8 **Neil M. Gorsuch** – appointed by President Donald Trump
9 **Brett M. Kavanaugh** – appointed by President Donald Trump

Table 1.2 **The three branches of the US Government**

Legislative branch	Executive branch	Judicial branch
Checks over the Executive branch: • May override presidential vetoes with a two-thirds vote • Has the power over the purse strings to actually fund any executive actions • May remove the president through impeachment • Senate approves treaties • Senate approves presidential appointments Checks over the Judicial branch: • Creates lower courts • May remove judges through impeachment • Senate approves appointments of judges	Checks over the Legislative branch: • Has power to veto legislation • Has ability to call special sessions of Congress • Can recommend legislation • Can appeal to the people concerning legislation and more Checks over the Judicial branch: • President appoints Supreme Court and other federal judges	Checks over the Executive branch: • Judges, once appointed for life, are free from controls from the Executive branch • Courts can judge executive actions to be unconstitutional through the power of Judicial Review Checks over the Legislative branch: • Courts can judge legislative acts to be unconstitutional

What is meant by the 'separation of powers' and 'checks and balances'?

The Constitution outlines the different powers/authority for the three branches of government – Legislative, Executive and Judicial. The Constitution allows each branch to check and balance the others. For instance, the president can veto bills approved by Congress and nominates individuals to the Federal Judiciary; the Supreme Court can declare a law enacted by Congress or an action by the president as unconstitutional; and Congress can impeach and remove the president and Federal Court justices and judges. In November 2019 the House Committee controlled by the Democrats began impeachment hearings against President Trump. He has been accused of using the office of president for political gain. The accusation is that he withheld the delivery of military equipment to Ukraine to put pressure on the Ukrainian president to find 'dirt' on his democratic rival Joe Biden.

The Legislative branch is given the powers to make the laws. The Executive branch is given the power to carry out the laws. The Judicial branch is given the power to interpret the laws. Table 1.2 shows how the branches check and balance each other.

Show your understanding

1 Why is the US Constitution such an important document?
2 Explain how the checks and balances separate and limit the powers of the three branches of government.
3 Describe how power is separated between the three branches of government.

ICT task

Read the paragraph about the Supreme Court Justices. See the list of the current nine Justices on page 11. Choose one of the Justices and carry out research online to write a timeline of their pathway to becoming a Supreme Court Justice. Include:

- their place of birth
- their education – including universities, etc.
- their political affiliation – Democrat or Republican
- different areas of politics they were involved in, etc.
- when they became a Supreme Court Justice.

The powers of the president

Article II of the Constitution sets out the powers of the president. These powers are both defined and limited by the Constitution.

The constitutional powers can be divided into three categories:

1 legislative powers
2 head of state powers
3 executive powers.

Chief legislator

As chief legislator, the president is expected to suggest proposals on laws to Congress. The president can refuse to sign a bill that he or she does not feel is in the best interests of the American people. Article 1 of the Constitution lays down the president's veto power:

'Every bill … shall, before it becomes a law, be presented to the President of the United States; if he approves he shall sign it, but if not he shall return it, with his objections, to that house from which it shall be originated.'

However, Congress has the power to override the veto with a two-thirds majority in both houses.

The president uses the annual State of the Union address to expand the legislative role of the presidency. At the start of each session in Congress, the president outlines important issues that have affected the country. The president discusses the Executive's actions in the past year and the intended actions of the next 12 months in office. At this stage Congress may pass proposed legislation on behalf of the president. In President Trump's 2018 State of the Union address he appealed to Congress: 'Tonight I'm calling on Congress to produce a bill that generates at least $1.5 trillion for the new infrastructure investment that our country so desperately needs.' At the time of writing, the issue is still being discussed and debated in Congress.

Figure 1.17 **President Trump delivering his State of the Union address to Congress in 2018**

The president can also submit an annual budget to Congress with great fanfare – perhaps at a ceremony in the White House. All presidents, even if their party controls Congress, must try to work in a bipartisan way (both parties working together for the good of the people rather than rejecting each other's policies). For example, George W. Bush achieved his education reforms – No Child Left Behind – in 2002 because he worked with leading Democrats such as the late Edward Kennedy to enable the bill to be passed. Barack Obama had hoped to create a bipartisan Immigration Bill in 2013 and this was achieved in the Senate but blocked by the Republican-controlled House of

Representatives. In October 2018, President Trump signed the bipartisan support for the Patients and Communities Act – described by the White House as 'the largest single piece of legislation to address a drug crisis' in the USA.

Head of state

The president is the chief public representative of the USA, embodying a sense of national pride. The presidential role combines the duties that in the UK would be carried out by a monarch and a prime minister. The president and vice president are the only elected members of the government. A president carries out the following duties:

- meets with leaders of other countries
- makes treaties
- appoints ambassadors.

Commander in Chief of the Armed Forces

Article II Section 2 of the US Constitution, the Commander-in-Chief clause, states that: '[t]he President shall be Commander in Chief of the Army and Navy of the United States, and of the Militia of the several States, when called into the actual Service of the United States'.

The questions of whether, and to what extent, the president has the authority to use the military in the absence of a Congressional declaration of war have proven to be sources of conflict and debate throughout American history. Some scholars believe the Commander-in-Chief clause confers expansive powers on the president, but others argue that, even if that is the case, the Constitution does not precisely define the extent of those powers. However, this clause does explain why presidents have far greater international powers than domestic powers.

In 2018, President Trump claimed he would spend billions of dollars to make the American armed forces the 'finest that our country has ever had' and he has used his power as Commander in Chief to

send 6000 active duty troops to the southwestern border, a move that he says will protect the USA from the influx of immigrants from Mexico.

Chief executive

As chief executive, the president is responsible for the implementation of laws and policy: 'he shall take care that the laws be faithfully executed'.

The president has a duty to uphold the decisions of the Supreme Court.

Executive Order The president can use this in certain emergency circumstances. This has the power of law but does not need Congress to pass it.

Power of 'patronage' The president controls the civil service, meaning that he or she can fill government offices. Therefore, the president appoints the top four layers of departments:

- Cabinet
- officials of the Executive office
- heads of independent Executive agencies
- independent regulatory commissions.

Control of Congress

In the USA, where the Executive and Legislature are elected separately, there is no guarantee that the president's party will be in majority in either house of Congress. Nor is it guaranteed that the president will have any control over his or her party in the Legislature.

- President Clinton (Democrat) was more of a 'defensive president' as he faced a hostile Congress dominated by Republicans. He failed to get his Health Bill through and used the president's veto 36 times. The Republican Congress tried to impeach Clinton. The House of Representatives passed two articles of impeachment by simple majority. The Senate conducted the trial and failed to obtain a two-thirds majority that would have removed Clinton from office. (President Nixon resigned rather than face certain impeachment.) Congress can remove the president, but the president cannot remove Congress.

- President George W. Bush (Republican) was more of an 'imperial president'. In his first six years he was allowed to expand the office of presidency, partly due to the fact that his own party controlled both chambers and partly due to the crisis created by 9/11. This all changed when the Democrats regained control of Congress in December 2006. Bush had not used his veto in his first six years; in his last two he used the veto 11 times. Congress overrode four of his regular vetoes, including his veto of the 2008 Food Conservation and Energy Bill.
- President Obama (Democrat) faced a predominately Democratic Congress in his first term and this enabled him to appoint a Hispanic liberal judge to the Supreme Court and to get through his health-care reforms.

However, in the mid-term elections of 2010 the Republicans gained control of the House and then in 2014 gained control of the Senate. After 2014 Obama was described as a 'lame duck president' because he faced both a hostile House and Senate and failed to implement key policy priorities such as new gun control laws and a new immigration bill.

- President Trump (Republican) has 51 Republican and 49 Democrat senators. However, in the House of Representatives, there is a Democrat majority. Trump has used two vetoes from 2017 until May 2019. In 2019, Trump declared a state of emergency in relation to building a wall at the border between the USA and Mexico. The House of Representatives passed a bill which rejected the state of emergency. However, the Senate supported Trump as it has an overall majority of Republicans. Trump faces a hostile House and a more supportive Senate.

Did you know?

The federal budget must be approved in order for government departments to receive the money they need to operate. When the budget is not approved, non-essential government services are shut down and workers are sent home without pay. Workers in essential services, such as security and law enforcement, continue to do their jobs but are not paid during the shutdown. In 2018, President Trump had requested (no less than) $5.7 billion to build a wall on the USA–Mexico border but Democrats in Congress were mainly opposed to the demand and refused to approve the funds, resulting in the longest government shutdown in US history, from 22 December 2018 to 25 January 2019. During this time, 800,000 federal workers were unable to attend their place of work. Trump maintained the wall was required to secure the US border in order to halt illegal immigration but Democrats viewed the wall as being too expensive and ineffective.

Congressional Committees

In the USA, no Executive staff are members of Congress and there is no equivalent of 'Question Time' in the House of Commons, in which members of the UK Government are grilled by the opposition parties. As a former president once wrote: 'Congress in session is Congress on public exhibition, whilst Congress in its committee rooms is Congress at work.' Congressional Committees in the USA are far more independent and powerful than their UK counterparts. Overall, there are 199 committees and subcommittees in Congress.

Standing Committees

Congressional Standing Committees are permanent policy specialist institutions which play a strategic role both in legislation and in overseeing the Executive branch. They are →

permanent legislative panels established by the House of Representatives and the Senate rules. Standing Committees consider bills and issues and recommend measures for consideration by their respective chambers.

Select Committees

Congress can also set up Select Committees to investigate Executive action. The House of Representatives set up a committee to investigate the terrorist attack on the American embassy in Iraq in 2012. The final report was highly critical of President Obama's foreign policy.

Conference Committees

These ad hoc (short-term) committees are set up towards the end of the legislative process. Bills tend to have a House version and a Senate version and members from each chamber try to create an agreed form of the bill. If agreement is reached, the full Congress votes to accept or reject – no amendments can be made.

State government

Powers not assigned to the federal government are retained by each of the 50 states. Each state has its Executive, led by a governor, and all have state legislatures. States collect their own local taxes and can decide on issues such as the use of capital powers (see Table 1.3). The death penalty currently applies in 30 states, with Texas having the highest number of executions. Citizens at the state level can also take part in direct democracy by putting forward proposals to change state laws, which are referred to as ballot measures.

In addition to their exclusive powers, both the national government and state governments share the power of being able to:

- collect taxes
- build roads
- borrow money
- establish courts
- make and enforce laws
- charter banks and corporations
- spend money for the general welfare
- take private property for public purposes, with just compensation.

Table 1.3 **Powers of national and state government**

National government	State government
<ul><li>Print money</li><li>Regulate interstate (between states) and international trade</li><li>Make treaties and conduct foreign policy</li><li>Declare war</li><li>Provide an army and navy</li><li>Establish post offices</li><li>Make laws necessary and proper to carry out these powers</li></ul>	<ul><li>Issue licences</li><li>Regulate intrastate (within the state) businesses</li><li>Conduct elections</li><li>Establish local governments</li><li>Ratify amendments to the Constitution</li><li>Take measures for public health and safety</li><li>May exert powers the Constitution does not delegate to the national government or prohibit the states from using them</li></ul>

Show your understanding

1 Outline the powers of the president.
2 Explain why the Constitution issued the separation of powers.
3 Compare the role of the three branches of government in terms of laws.
4 Describe the workings of committees in Congress. Why is it important that they exist?

5 Outline the powers that states have.
6 Do you think that it is important that states have different laws from each other? Explain your answer. Find out what issues states have different laws for, such as ages for marriage or driving licences.

Assignment ideas

Presidential elections

- The US system for electing the president should rely solely on the popular vote.

Rights and responsibilities of US citizens

Rights of US citizens

Most rights fall into one of three general categories:

- security
- equality
- liberty.

Security

Security means protection from unfair and unreasonable actions by the government. The government, for example, cannot arrest, imprison or punish people or search or seize their property without good reason and without following certain rules. The principle of 'due process of law' protects these rights for all Americans. The due process clause, which is found in the Fifth and Fourteenth Amendments, states that no person shall be deprived of 'life, liberty, or property, without due process of law'. Due process means that the laws must be fair and reasonable, must be in accordance with the Constitution, and must apply to everyone equally.

Equality

The right of equality means that everyone is entitled to the equal protection of all the laws in the USA. That is, all people have a right to be treated the same, regardless of ethnicity, religion or political beliefs.

Liberty

Fundamental freedoms fall into this category. Most of them are spelled out in the Bill of Rights.

Duties and responsibilities of US citizens

US citizens have an obligation to carry out certain duties and responsibilities. Duties are things citizens are required to do; if citizens fail to perform them, they may be subjected to legal penalties, such as fines or imprisonment. Responsibilities are things people should do. We can fulfil these obligations voluntarily. Fulfilling both duties and responsibilities helps ensure that citizens have good government and continue to enjoy their rights.

→

Duties include:	Responsibilities include:	
1 Obeying the laws 2 Paying taxes 3 Defending the nation 4 Serving in court 5 Attending school	1 Being informed about the government and knowing your rights in order to preserve them 2 Participating in government 3 Respecting the rights of others 4 Respecting diversity	In theory these freedoms and rights cannot be taken away from US citizens. However, since 9/11 national security issues can threaten these rights. Both President George W. Bush and President Obama ordered the extra-judicial killing of suspected terrorists around the world and some US citizens have been denied the procedural of the Bill of Rights. The Executive branch of government has claimed the right to search hostile journalists' email accounts or to listen in to their phone calls.

Political participation

In the USA, people may participate in politics in many ways. This is partly due to the federalist system, whereby people have many opportunities to participate in US democracy at federal, state and local levels. They can write to their representative or senator or work for a candidate or political party. They can make presentations to their local school board or city council, or call the police to complain about the neighbour's dog. Turnout at national elections in presidential election years is significantly higher than that for mid-term elections. Propositions/ballot measures are one way that voters can be directly involved in political change (see page 20).

Interest groups

Americans can join interest groups. This is an effective way to put pressure on the government to benefit their individual causes – there is power in numbers, and politicians and political institutions are more likely to take notice of a group and its methods. Lobbyists are hired by interest groups to speak for them. Lobbying and lobbyists may be seen negatively, but the First Amendment states that people have free speech and are allowed to petition the government. Interest groups also use other methods such as social media, protests/demonstrations, letter/email campaigns and petitions.

Protests

The day after the inauguration of President Trump, in January 2017, an estimated 1 million people took to the streets in Washington DC in support of gender equality and women's rights, and to protest against the new president following his inflammatory remarks about women made during the presidential campaign. In many countries in the world, people would be arrested or even killed if they protested against their leader. However, the First Amendment is interpreted as giving people the right to question the government. This is a sign of a functioning democracy as the people have the right to join with fellow citizens in protest or peaceful assembly.

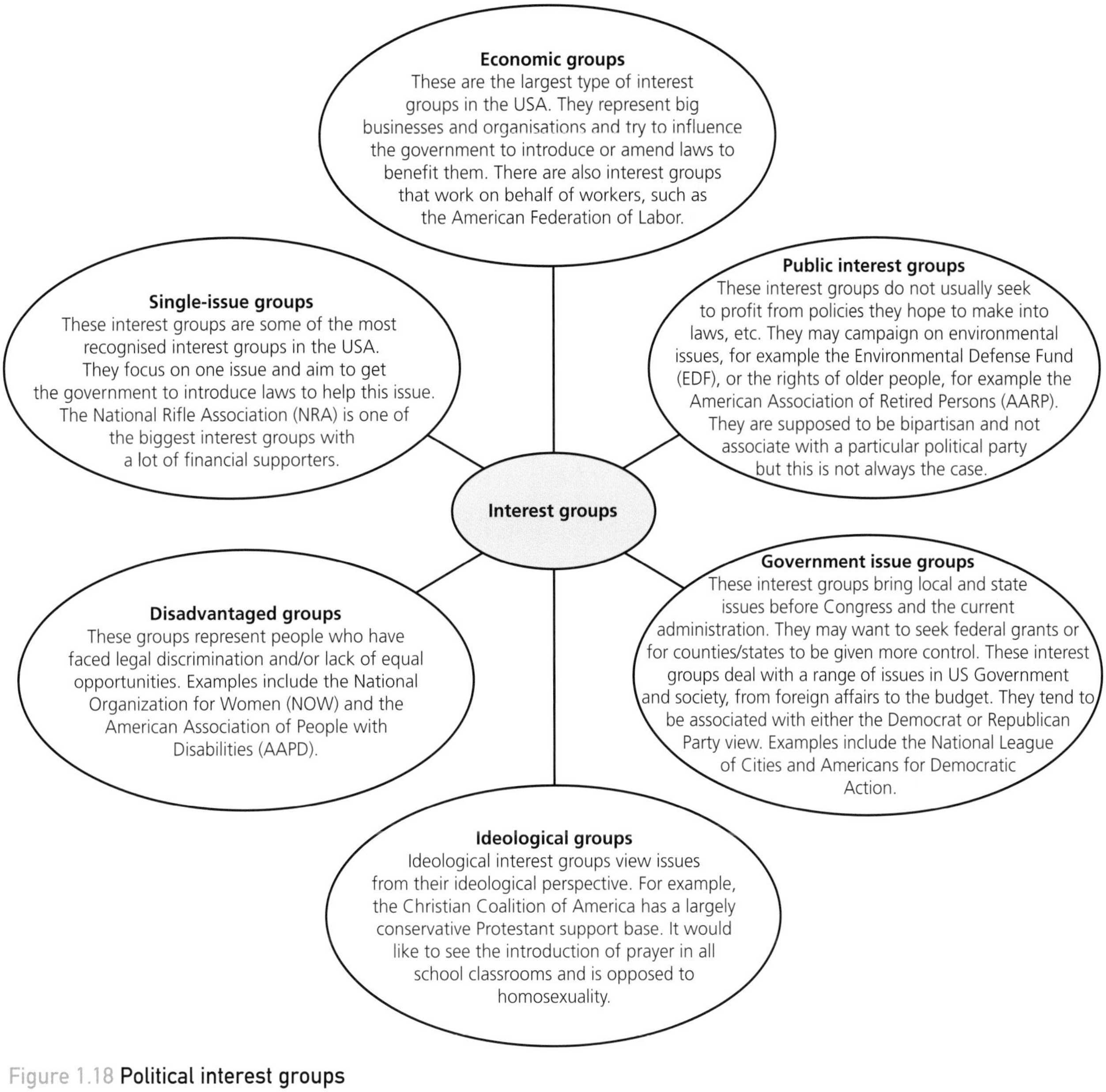

Economic groups
These are the largest type of interest groups in the USA. They represent big businesses and organisations and try to influence the government to introduce or amend laws to benefit them. There are also interest groups that work on behalf of workers, such as the American Federation of Labor.
Single-issue groups
These interest groups are some of the most recognised interest groups in the USA. They focus on one issue and aim to get the government to introduce laws to help this issue. The National Rifle Association (NRA) is one of the biggest interest groups with a lot of financial supporters.
Public interest groups
These interest groups do not usually seek to profit from policies they hope to make into laws, etc. They may campaign on environmental issues, for example the Environmental Defense Fund (EDF), or the rights of older people, for example the American Association of Retired Persons (AARP). They are supposed to be bipartisan and not associate with a particular political party but this is not always the case.
Interest groups
Disadvantaged groups
These groups represent people who have faced legal discrimination and/or lack of equal opportunities. Examples include the National Organization for Women (NOW) and the American Association of People with Disabilities (AAPD).
Government issue groups
These interest groups bring local and state issues before Congress and the current administration. They may want to seek federal grants or for counties/states to be given more control. These interest groups deal with a range of issues in US Government and society, from foreign affairs to the budget. They tend to be associated with either the Democrat or Republican Party view. Examples include the National League of Cities and Americans for Democratic Action.
Ideological groups
Ideological interest groups view issues from their ideological perspective. For example, the Christian Coalition of America has a largely conservative Protestant support base. It would like to see the introduction of prayer in all school classrooms and is opposed to homosexuality.

Figure 1.18 **Political interest groups**

If one man can destroy everything, why can't one girl change it?
I'M WITH HER

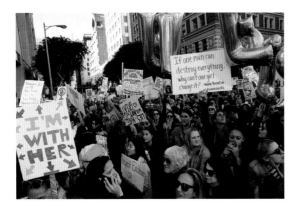

Figure 1.19 **Women's March 2017**

Propositions/ballot measures in the USA

At state level, citizens can make and amend the laws of their respective state by voting on a range of propositions (in the UK the equivalent would be referenda; for example, the September 2014 referendum on Scottish independence or the EU referendum in 2016). Propositions have included setting budget priorities, setting the minimum wage, marijuana use and gay rights.

In California, the most expensive proposition/ballot measure of 2018 was Proposition 8, which would have required dialysis clinics to issue refunds to patients or people paying for the procedures for revenue above certain limits. (Dialysis is a medical treatment for people with kidney issues.) Voters rejected the proposition.

Supporters of ballot measures/propositions argue that they encourage local engagement in decision making and can increase voter turnout. They can hold elected officials to account and can help to overturn unpopular policies. Propositions can also recruit, mobilise and energise citizens and make them feel that their votes really count.

However, critics of propositions argue that they can undermine democracy by enabling well-funded business interests to manipulate the process; for example, gaming and the gun industry. They can also undermine the ability of elected officials to control state finances; for example, in California, Proposition 13 (1978) limited the property tax powers of the state government.

Show your understanding

1. Outline the main rights and responsibilities of US citizens.
2. Outline reasons for having different types of interest groups in the USA.
3. With reference to the 'Protests' section, decide whether the USA is a fully democratic country.
4. Outline the arguments for and against the use of propositions/ballot measures in the USA.

ICT task

Using the website **www.ballotpedia.org** research California's Proposition 8 in 2018. Do you think it should have been passed? Explain your answer.

Research an interest group that operates in the USA that you identify with/share the beliefs of. Write an extended paragraph outlining:

- who they are
- what they support
- why you agree with their cause
- what the government could do to support them.

Political parties

Political parties in the USA are different from those in the UK. They are more state-based than national. Political parties in the USA are decentralised. They do have a national party organisation, but its role is mostly limited to the choice of presidential candidate at their respective national conventions, held every four years.

The USA is often described as a 'two-party system'. This refers to the fact that the Democrat and Republican Parties dominate politics. Most elected officials serving as president, members of Congress and state governors are members of these two main parties.

The Republican Party is the more conservative of the two parties. Yet there are 'moderate Republicans' in the north-east of the country, 'right-wing Republicans' and 'Christian conservatives'. In the 2000 presidential election, George W. Bush popularised the term 'compassionate conservatives'.

The Democratic Party contains both 'liberal Democrats' (such as President John F. Kennedy, who pushed for civil rights for African Americans) and 'conservative Democrats' who are mainly from the south.

However, over the last three decades both parties have become more ideologically based. The large conservative wing of the Democratic Party – mainly from the south – has gradually transferred their support to the more naturally conservative Republican Party. And the liberal wing of the Republican Party – mainly from the north-east – has moved support to the more naturally liberal Democratic Party.

The Democratic Party

Its agenda states that it is 'committed to keeping our nation safe and expanding opportunity for every American'. It ensures that this commitment is reflected by:

- strong economic growth
- affordable health care for *all* Americans
- retirement security
- an open, honest and accountable government
- securing the nation while protecting civil rights and liberties.

Figure 1.20 The donkey, symbol of the Democratic Party

Democratic presidents

- John F. Kennedy
- Bill Clinton
- Barack Obama

Democratic supporters

The Democratic Party tends to gain support from the poorer classes, ethnic minorities, women and people who strongly agree with its liberal views.

The Republican Party

Its agenda states that 'the United States has been blessed with a unique set of individual rights and freedoms available to all.' Republicans share many of the party's main beliefs:

- people can succeed through hard work, family support and self-discipline
- helping through voluntary giving and community support is better than taxation or redistribution
- government should never become too powerful and infringe on the rights of the people
- a commitment to lower taxes
- the armed forces should protect and defend our democracy.

Republican presidents

- Ronald Reagan
- George H.W. Bush
- George W. Bush
- Donald Trump

Figure 1.21 The elephant, symbol of the Republican Party

Republican supporters

The Republican Party tends to gain support from men, the middle and wealthier classes, white people and people with more conservative views.

Presidential elections

One of the most important events in US Government and politics is the election of the president. This event is held every four years and is often compared to a race. It is said that someone is 'running for office' and that the 'presidential race' is on. Choosing presidential candidates can begin more than two years before the actual election.

A nominee needs a majority of the electoral college votes to win the presidency. The race is over as soon as one of the nominees gets one vote more than half, or 270, of the total electoral votes. Although the elections are held in November, the new president does not take office until the following January.

Did you know?

The Constitution allows each state to have as many electoral votes as it has representatives in Congress. The size of the state's population is the basis for the number of representatives. No state has fewer than three electoral votes. This is because each state has two senators and at least one representative in the House of Representatives.

When citizens vote for the president of the USA they are actually voting for the electors nominated from their state, who will cast their votes based on which presidential candidate has won the popular vote.

Presidential election 2016

Figure 1.22 **Donald Trump and Hillary Clinton during the 2016 presidential race**

Following the 2016 presidential election, Donald Trump became the 45th president of the United States. Trump officially accepted the Republican Party's nomination for US presidency on 22 July 2016. His running mate was Governor Mike Pence. Hillary Clinton (former First Lady to Bill Clinton) was officially nominated on 26 July at the Democratic Convention. Her running mate was Senator Tim Kaine.

Although Hillary Clinton received about 2.9 million more votes in the popular vote, Donald Trump won overall victory in the electoral college vote – winning 30 out of 50 states.

The Republicans gained a majority in the House of Representatives with 240 seats. The Democrats lost overall control with only 195 seats.

The Republicans gained a majority in the Senate by two seats – winning 51 seats and the Democrats winning 49 seats.

Voting patterns

Voter turnout in the 2016 presidential election was 61.4 per cent, meaning a record 137.5 million Americans voted. There are many factors that influence a person's voting preference, such as gender, age or geographical area.

Table 1.4 **2016 election results**

Candidate	Party	Electoral college vote	Popular vote
Donald Trump	Republican	304	62,980,160
Hillary Clinton	Democratic	227	65,845,063

Source: US Federal Election Commission

Table 1.5 **Voting by ethnicity and gender in 2016 presidential election**

	White (%)	Black (%)	Hispanic (%)	Asian (%)	Men (%)	Women (%)
Clinton	37	89	66	65	41	54
Trump	57	8	28	27	52	41

Source: Exit Polls 2016

Presidential election 2012

332 Obama   270 to win   Romney 206

In the US presidential election of 2012, the Democratic nominee, President Barack Obama, and his running mate, Vice President Joe Biden, were re-elected to a second term, defeating the Republican nominee, former Governor of Massachusetts Mitt Romney, and his running mate, Representative Paul Ryan from Wisconsin.

Overview of results

The gender vote was split between the two candidates: Obama won 55 per cent of the female vote and Romney won 52 per cent of the male vote. Obama once again won the ethnic minority vote. Young voters favoured Obama, but less so than in 2008.

Table 1.6 **Presidential election results, 2008 and 2012**

Results: 2008	Votes	Won
Barack Obama	69,492,376	53.0%
John McCain	59,946,378	45.7%
Others	1,703,390	1.3%

Results: 2012	Votes	Won
Barack Obama	62,611,250	50.6%
Mitt Romney	59,134,475	47.8%
Others	1,968,682	1.6%

Table 1.7 **Voting by ethnicity and gender in the 2012 presidential election**

	White (%)	Black (%)	Hispanic (%)	Asian (%)	Men (%)	Women (%)
Obama	39	93	71	73	45	55
Romney	59	6	27	26	52	44

Source: National Election Pool, a consortium of ABC News, Associated Press, CBS News, CNN, FoxNews and NBC News

The Congressional Black Caucus

Figure 1.23 **The Congressional Black Caucus**

'Since its establishment in 1971, Members of the Congressional Black Caucus have joined together to empower America's neglected citizens and to address their legislative concerns. For more than 40 years, the CBC has been committed to utilizing the full Constitutional power, statutory authority, and financial resources of the government of the United States of America to ensure that everyone in the United States has an opportunity to achieve their version of the American Dream.'

Source: The Democratic Caucus

The Congressional Black Caucus (CBC) is an organisation representing the African American members of the United States Congress. The Black Caucus consists of all the black members of the House of Representatives. This group can prove influential when passing a bill through this chamber. There were 46 African American members of the House of Representatives in the 114th Congress and if their votes were cast together they could deliver over 20 per cent of the votes required. The Black Caucus provides a united front and requires that both Democrats and Republicans vote together.

The Congressional Hispanic Caucus

There were 34 CHC Members in the 114th Congress.

Figure 1.24 **The Congressional Hispanic Caucus**

'The Congressional Hispanic Caucus (CHC) was founded in December 1976 as a legislative service organisation of the United States House of Representatives … The CHC addresses national and international issues and crafts policies that impact the Hispanic community … The Caucus is dedicated to voicing and advancing, through the legislative process, issues affecting Hispanics in the United States, Puerto Rico, and the Commonwealth of the Northern Mariana Islands.'

Source: The Congressional Hispanic Caucus

2018 mid-term elections

In the 2018 mid-term elections, the Democrats increased their majority in the House of Representatives by having 235 out of a possible 435 seats. The Republicans kept their control of the Senate by having 53 out of a possible 100 seats after the mid-term election. These results, when compared to the 2016 presidential election, saw the Republicans gain more control of the Senate but lose control of the House of Representatives.

Show your understanding

1 Using the information in this chapter, describe a typical Democrat supporter and a typical Republican supporter.
2 Compare the election results from the 2012 and 2016 presidential elections. Include statistics in your answer.
3 With reference to the Caucus groups, describe the ethnic minority representation in the Congress elected in November 2016.
4 Describe the activities of the Black Caucus and the Hispanic Caucus groups.
5 In what way did the results of the 2018 mid-term elections differ from the 2016 presidential election?

12-mark question

'Analyse the different political opportunities that exist for people to influence decision making.'

The youth vote

Around 45 per cent of young people aged 18–29 voted in 2012, down from 51 per cent in 2008. In the 2016 presidential election, 46.1 per cent of young people aged 18–29 voted – this was the only age group to report increased turnout compared to the 2012 presidential election.

Why youth voting matters

- Voting is habit-forming: when young people learn the voting process and vote, they are more likely to do so when they are older. If individuals have been motivated to get to the polls once, they are more likely to return. So, getting young people to vote early could be key to raising a new generation of voters.
- Young people are a major subset of the electorate and their voices matter. According to Circle (Center for Information and Research on Civic Learning and Engagement), an estimated 23.7 million young voters participated in the 2016 presidential election.
- Young people's participation can influence election results.
- Involving young people in election-related learning, activities and discussion can have an impact on the young person's household,

increasing the likelihood that others in the household will vote. In immigrant communities, young voters may be easier to reach, are more likely to speak English (cutting down translation costs), and may be the most effective messengers within their communities.

There have been numerous campaigns over the years to encourage the youth to vote in the USA, as highlighted below:

> There have been numerous campaigns over the years to try and encourage young people to register and vote in the USA:
>
> - Rock the Vote – campaigning in all presidential elections for the past 25 years
> - Vote or Die – 2004 presidential election
> - Declare Yourself – 2008 Presidential election.
>
> These campaigns are backed and supported by celebrities and politicians during presidential elections. Many celebrities will use their social media platform to associate and support a particular political party. The main aim is to encourage young people to register to vote in the hope that they will use it during the election.

Assignment ideas

Voting in elections

- Eligible 18-year-olds should automatically be registered to vote in presidential elections.

Show your understanding

1 Describe the ways in which the youth are encouraged to vote in US presidential elections.
2 Explain why the 'youth vote' is important in the USA.
3 Research a campaign that tried to encourage the youth in the USA to vote, e.g. 'Rock the Vote', 'Vote or Die' or 'Declare Yourself'.

Social and economic inequality

Social factors	Economic factors
Education	Poverty/low income
Health	Unemployment
Housing	
Family structures	
Crime and justice	

The USA is one of the most affluent countries in the world, with a leading system of higher education; it is also the world's most industrialised country but has one of the most uneven distributions of wealth. Americans face inequalities and the gap between rich and poor is not only widening but also affecting other social and economic factors.

The Economic Policy Institute reported that, in 2015, families in the top 1 per cent of earners in the USA made more than 25 times what families in the bottom 99 per cent did.

In 2019, Gabriel Zucman, an economics professor at the University of California, declared that 'US wealth concentration seems to have returned to levels last seen during the Roaring Twenties … when the top 0.1 per cent richest adults' share of total household wealth was close to 25 per cent'. The high concentration is similar to that in China and Russia.

> According to a number of sources, in 2017 the USA ranked sixth out of 38 OECD countries in income inequality based on 'market incomes' – that is, before taking into account the redistributive effects of tax policies and income-transfer programmes such as social security and unemployment insurance. (For comparison, the UK ranked ninth.)

'It's not just income inequality. It's lifespan inequality, education inequality and declining economic growth.' (CNN Money)

Education

Educational attainment, which represents the level of education completed (i.e. a high school diploma or equivalency certificate, a bachelor's degree or a master's degree), is an important socio-economic indicator. Obtaining a higher education can be a major step towards better occupational and economic outcomes. Too many of America's most disadvantaged children grow up without the skills needed to thrive in the twenty-first century. Inequality persists, whether in educational attainment between income groups or racial/ethnic groups or across geographic locations. Low levels of performance among the most disadvantaged create long-term problems, particularly in an economy in which higher skill levels are more and more valued and the wages available to less-skilled workers are diminishing.

It is widely understood that the single best predictor of future financial success is educational achievement, yet educational opportunities seem to be sorely lacking for all but the families at the top of the income ladder in the USA.

College tuition costs

According to the World University Rankings, the USA is one of the most popular countries for higher education – and also the most expensive. Tuition fees can range from $5000 to $50,000 per year depending on university and course. The average rate is estimated at $33,215 per year. These fees do not include accommodation, bills, books or resources. Average debt (for fees alone) after studying for a typical four-year degree is $132,860. It costs more for a student to study outside of their home state than to study 'in state'.

Figure 1.25 **College graduation in the USA**

Government response

Educational reform is a common topic for politicians and many presidents and their administration have proposed legislation on reforms. When he became president in 2008, Obama promised to invest in early education and billions of dollars went into the Head Start and Early Head Start federal programmes that promoted pre-school education for low-income families. Part of the Head Start programme provided nutrition to poorer pupils. The Obama Government also invested heavily in high school education through the Race to the Top programme, which created over 300,000 new teachers with performance-related pay. The American Recovery and Reinvestment Act 2009 invested $30 billion towards college scholarships for poorer families.

Under Trump, the White House website states that 'Our Nation's elementary and secondary education systems are falling behind the rest of the world. The Administration supports an agenda that provides school choice for parents, better prepares students to compete in a global economy, modernizes an antiquated federal student aid system, and holds higher education institutions more accountable to students and taxpayers alike.'

Fact file

US parents are given the option to send their children to a **public school**, which is a typical state run/funded school. According to the National Center for Educational Statistics (NCES), the majority of young people attend a public school in the USA. **Charter schools** are publicly funded but are not operated by local school districts. They operate the same free education and open admission as public schools (i.e. entrance is not determined by test results) but their 'charter' (the legally binding contract under which they operate) means they may follow different rules, such as running longer school terms or being able to hire uncertified teachers. **Private school** is an option for parents who are able to pay fees for their children to receive an education. Private schools offer students a range of experiences as they are predominately funded through tuition fees. Students are taught in smaller classes, benefit from better technology, and tend to show high attainment levels. Previously, most private schools were Catholic (but accepted students of all religious backgrounds) but today more and more have no religious affiliation. Some states have a high number of **homeschooled** children.

Generally, states and taxes fund public schools and this leads to inequalities across the country. Affluent states tend to spend more per head than poorer states. Some states may prioritise other spending areas over education. Vermont spends approximately $20,000 per student per year to fund schools whereas Utah spends less than half of this per student. Students who are fortunate to live in more affluent areas will benefit from the higher proportions of funds that are given to schools. This could ultimately lead to a better life with a higher educational attainment and better employment opportunities.

Educational attainment differs between ethnic groups as a result of location, public or private education and language barriers.

The number of students in each type of education in 2018 was as follows:

Public schools – 50.7 million (2.8 million were charter schools)

Private schools – 5.8 million

Homeschool – 1.6 million

In 2016, the NCES recorded that it was the first year that the **majority** of public school children were from minority ethnic groups – meaning that white students now accounted for less than half of the students who attended public schools. Public schools differ in terms of funding and graduation statistics depending on their location. White students tend to be concentrated in suburban and rural areas whereas students from minority ethnic groups tend to attend schools in cities and towns. Charter schools have a higher ratio of students from minority ethnic groups.

Table 1.8 Attendance at public, charter, Catholic private and non-religious private schools by ethnicity

	Public school	Charter school	Catholic private school	Non-religious private school
White	48.9%	33%	66%	65%
Hispanic/Latino	25.9%	27%	8%	9%
Black	15.5%	32%	16%	8%
Asian and Pacific Islander	6%	4%	6%	10%
Native American	1%	1%	1%	1%

Source: National Center for Education Statistics

NCES also stated that when it came to the ethnic composition of students who attended private schools in the USA, there was a larger majority of white students than all of the other minority groups combined.

In 2017, more than 85 per cent of students graduated from public high schools.

Table 1.9 Percentage of students who graduated from public high school, 2017, by ethnicity

	Graduated from public high school (%)
Asian and Pacific Islander	91
White	89
Hispanic	80
Black	78
Native American	72

Source: National Center for Education Statistics

Proclamation on National Charter Schools Week, 10 May 2019

During National Charter Schools Week, we recognize the important contributions public charter schools make by providing American families with the freedom to choose high-quality education options that meet their children's needs. For more than a quarter century, charter schools – tuition-free public schools of choice – have been incubators of educational innovations, while being accountable for student achievement and outcomes. Today, what began as a grassroots movement now flourishes in 44 States, the District of Columbia, Guam, and Puerto Rico, with more than 7,000 schools serving approximately 3.2 million students.

Charter schools empower families to pursue the right educational fit for their children, helping ensure that there are paths to the American Dream that match the needs of students striving to achieve it. The unique needs of students, rather than address or family income, should determine where they learn. My Administration is committed to reducing the outsized Federal footprint in education and to empowering families, as well as State and local policymakers and educators, with the flexibility to adapt to student needs.

Public charter schools work for students, teachers, and communities. The Center for Research on Education Outcomes found that charter schools better serve low-income students, minority students, and students learning English than neighboring public schools. The success of our Nation's public charter schools in helping students of all backgrounds thrive and in addressing the needs of local education confirms what Americans have always known: those who are closest to students know best how to prepare them to reach their full potential.

Nothing better proves the value of and need for charter schools than the ever-growing demand from students and families. Although charter school enrollment has increased at least sevenfold in the past 18 years, more than one million students remain on charter school waiting lists today. A recent survey found that 59 percent of parents would prefer to send their child to a different type of school than the one to which they have been assigned.

Because of the success of and demand for public charter schools, each year since taking office, I have proposed to increase and improve funding for them as a key part of my Administration's ambitious efforts to expand every family's access to all types of high-quality education opportunities. In my fiscal

➔

year 2020 budget request, I called on the Congress to increase funding for the Federal Charter Schools Program to $500 million, an increase of $60 million over the current level.

No matter where they live or how much their parents earn, all children deserve access to education that enriches their minds. This week, we celebrate all the students, families, teachers, administrators, and community leaders who support public charter schools and education freedom. We reaffirm our commitment to expanding every family's access to high-quality education opportunities and to supporting educational excellence and innovation for the benefit of every student and for the continued prosperity of our great Nation.

NOW, THEREFORE, I, DONALD J. TRUMP, President of the United States of America, by virtue of the authority vested in me by the Constitution and the laws of the United States, do hereby proclaim May 12 through May 18, 2019, as National Charter Schools Week. I commend our Nation's successful public charter schools, teachers, and administrators, and I call on States and communities to help students and empower parents and families by supporting high-quality charter schools as an important school choice option.

IN WITNESS WHEREOF, I have hereunto set my hand this tenth day of May, in the year of our Lord two thousand nineteen, and of the Independence of the United States of America the two hundred and forty-third.

Source: www.whitehouse.gov/presidential-actions/proclamation-national-charter-schools-week-2019/

Making college affordable

As discussed above ('College tuition costs'), the US has one of the most expensive college tuition systems in the world. In June 2014, President Obama signed a new Presidential Memorandum directing the Secretary of Education to propose regulations that would allow an additional almost 5 million federal direct student loan borrowers the opportunity to cap their student loan payments at 10 per cent of their income. The memorandum also outlines a series of new executive actions aimed to support federal student loan borrowers, especially vulnerable borrowers who may be at greater risk of defaulting on their loans.

President Trump sought to address the problem with the following Executive Order issued in March 2019:

'The financial burden of higher education on students and their families is also a national problem that needs immediate attention. Over the past 30 years, college tuition and fees have grown at more than twice the rate of the Consumer Price Index. Rising student loan debt, coupled with low repayment rates, threatens the financial health of both individuals and families as well as of Federal student loan programs …

Institutions should be transparent about the average earnings and loan repayment rates of former students who received Federal student aid. Additionally, the Federal Government should make this information readily accessible to the public and to prospective students and their families, in particular.

This order will promote greater access to critical information regarding the prices and outcomes of postsecondary education, thereby furthering the goals of the National Council for the American Worker established by Executive Order 13845 of July 19, 2018 (Establishing the President's National Council for the American Worker). Increased information disclosure will help ensure that individuals make educational choices suited to their needs, interests, and circumstances. Access

→

to this information will also increase institutional accountability and encourage institutions to take into account likely future earnings when establishing the cost of their educational programs …

[The Secretary of Education shall] make available, by January 1, 2020, through the Office of Federal Student Aid, a secure and confidential website and mobile application that informs Federal student loan borrowers of how much they owe, how much their monthly payment will be when they enter repayment, available repayment options, how long each repayment option will take, and how to enroll in the repayment option that best serves their needs …'

Executive Order on Improving Free Inquiry, Transparency, and Accountability at Colleges and Universities, 21 March 2019

Figure 1.26 **President Trump signing a bill**

Show your understanding

1 Outline the ways in which education can be linked with low-income employment.
2 Why is entry to college/university education difficult for those experiencing social inequality even if they have the grades?
3 Describe the educational situation of each ethnic group, which schools they attend and how many graduate from high school, etc.?
4 What are the main features of charter schools in the USA?
5 Outline the actions taken by President Trump to make the cost of fees and the repayments system more transparent.

Health

Unlike the UK, the USA does not have a National Health Service (NHS) that is free to use. American citizens currently pay for their medical bills through private medical insurance: they have to pay for their health care. Medical insurance finances a person's health-care expenses. The majority of American citizens have private medical insurance coverage, primarily through an employer; many others obtain health insurance through programmes offered by the Government – Medicaid or Medicare.

Low-wage workers may receive no health insurance, sick pay or pension plan through their employer. If a person cannot afford to miss work because they are unwell, or if they cannot afford to pay for preventative medicine to treat a problem, their condition can worsen and they may end up using the emergency room because they have no other choice.

Some individuals do not have health insurance at all; there were approximately 42 million Americans (13.4 per cent) who were uninsured in 2013. This figure had fallen to 28.5 million (8.8 per cent) in 2017.

Medicaid and Medicare are two government programmes that provide medical and health-related services to specific groups of

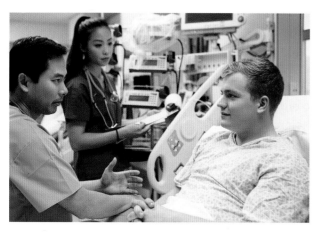

Figure 1.27 **US citizens must pay for their health care**

people in the USA. Although the two programmes are very different, they are both managed by the Centers for Medicare and Medicaid Services, a division of the US Department of Health and Human Services.

- Medicaid is a means-tested health and medical services programme for certain individuals and families with low incomes and few resources. In 2017, 19.3 per cent of citizens were covered by Medicaid.
- Medicare is a federal health insurance programme that pays for hospital and medical care for elderly patients and certain Americans with disabilities. In 2017, 17.2 per cent of citizens were covered by Medicare.

Who experiences inequalities?

The main people who will experience inequalities in health are the uninsured American citizens. According to the US Census Bureau, the uninsured tended to be 19 to 64 years old and male, with less than a high school education and/or a low income. The following groups also face inequalities:

Young people (2017)

- The percentage of children under age 19 who were uninsured was 5.4 per cent.

- In 2016, only 92 per cent of Hispanic children had coverage for some part of the year, compared with 96 per cent of non-Hispanic white children and 95 per cent of black and Asian children.

Ethnic groups (2017)

- 6.3 per cent of white people were uninsured.
- 7.3 per cent of Asian people were uninsured.
- 10.6 per cent of black people were uninsured.
- 16.1 per cent of Hispanic people were uninsured.

Immigrants

Most of the uninsured (75 per cent) are US citizens, and 25 per cent are non-citizens. Uninsured non-citizens include both lawfully present and undocumented immigrants. Undocumented immigrants are not eligible for federally funded health coverage, but legal immigrants can qualify for subsidies in the employment industry or private health care and those who have been in the country for more than five years are eligible for Medicaid.

Low-income groups (2017)

- The majority of uninsured people had a high school diploma at most.
- 26.9 per cent of uninsured people did not have a high school diploma, compared to 11.8 per cent of the population as a whole.
- People without health insurance were much more likely to live in poverty than those with health insurance.
- Around 33 per cent of uninsured workers worked in service positions, compared to around 20 per cent of the population as a whole.

Government response

The Affordable Care Act (ACA), known as 'Obamacare', was passed by Congress and signed into law by President Obama on 23 March 2010.

The Affordable Care Act

The law helps you by bringing down health-care costs and making sure your health-care dollars are spent wisely. Insurance companies will now be accountable to their customers for how they are spending premium dollars, and how much they are raising rates. Plus, the new law will help lower costs through new tax credits and new marketplaces where insurers will have to compete for your business.

Small business tax credits

Small businesses have long paid a premium price for health insurance – often 18 per cent more than larger employers. The tax credit will benefit an estimated 2 million workers who get their insurance from an estimated 360,000 small employers who will receive the credit in 2011 alone.

The health-care law builds on what works in our health-care system. And it fixes what's broken by providing you with more health insurance choices and better access to care.

Coverage for young adults

Under the law, most young adults who can't get coverage through their jobs can stay on their parents' plans until age 26 – a change that has already allowed 3.1 million young adults to get health coverage and given their families peace of mind.

Coverage for Americans with pre-existing conditions

Before the law, many Americans with pre-existing conditions were locked or priced out of the health insurance market. More than 50,000 Americans with pre-existing conditions have gained coverage through the new Pre-Existing Condition Insurance Plan. This temporary programme makes health coverage available and more affordable for individuals who are uninsured and have been denied health insurance because of a pre-existing condition. In 2014, insurance discriminating against anyone with a pre-existing condition will be illegal.

Source: https://obamawhitehouse.archives.gov

It became law on 1 October 2013. The Act promises 'comprehensive reforms that improve access to affordable health coverage for everyone and protect consumers from abusive insurance company practices'.

President Trump has been very vocal with his feelings about 'Obamacare'. Under his administration, the White House website reads: 'Obamacare is hurting American families, farmers and small businesses with skyrocketing health insurance costs'. The Trump administration introduced the American Health Care Act 2017. While there are some similarities and some policies from Obamacare remain the same, there are some updates and changes:

- '**Under Obamacare** most people are required to purchase coverage on their own unless they get qualified coverage through an employer or another source. Those who go without qualifying health insurance for more than two consecutive months risk a penalty on their federal taxes. Obamacare also required employers with more than 50 full-time workers (or the equivalent in part-time workers) to provide coverage to their employees or risk penalties.'

- '**Under the American Health Care Act** no one would be required to purchase health insurance, and there would be no tax penalty for going uninsured. However, in an effort to discourage people from allowing their coverage to lapse, a one-year 30% surcharge may apply when you re-enroll in coverage after a significant gap. Employers would no longer be penalised for not providing health insurance to employees.'

- '**Under Obamacare** older people can be charged up to three times more than younger people for coverage under the same health insurance plan (this is described as a 3:1 cost ratio).'
- '**Under the American Health Care Act** a 5:1 ratio would apply, meaning that older people

can be charged up to five times more than younger people for coverage under the same plan.'

Source: www.ehealthinsurance.com

Assignment ideas

Health care

- The USA should offer free universal health care to every American citizen.

Housing

Figure 1.28 **The difference between poor and rich housing areas in the USA**

Home ownership

In the USA, buying a home is the key to achieving the American Dream. Around 42 per cent of the net worth of all households consists of equity in their homes – this means that, for most Americans, their homes are their single largest asset. Home ownership provides families with the means to invest in education, business opportunities, retirement and resources for the next generation.

However, the banking crisis of 2008 and the collapse of the housing market created a turning point, resulting in misery for millions of people. In the economic boom prior to 2008 many low-paid workers were able to buy their own homes. But with the collapse of house prices and

the economic recession of 2008 onwards, many householders realised that their homes were worth much less than their mortgages and many suffered unemployment. As a result, since 2008 almost 11 million homes have been repossessed, 3.5 million more home owners are behind in their payments, and another 1.5 million homes are in the foreclosure process.

The percentage of Americans who own their homes has fallen from 69 per cent in 2004 to about 65.23 per cent in 2019.

According to the US Census Bureau, figures for the home ownership rate for the first quarter of 2019 are as follows:

- White home owners were highest at 73.2 per cent.

- API and Native American home owners were second at 56.9 per cent.
- Hispanic home owners were third at 47.4 per cent.
- Black home owners were lowest at 41.1 per cent.

In the first quarter of 2019, the largest group of homeowners were people aged 65+. Of this group, 78.5 per cent own their own home. The group with the smallest rate of home ownership, at 35.4 per cent, is the under 35s.

Homelessness

In 2018, a report from the Department of Housing and Urban Development (HUD) found that just under 553,000 people were homeless: 17 out of every 10,000 people in the country. Approximately 65 per cent of them stayed in sheltered accommodation.

California (129,972 people), New York (91,897), Florida (31,030), Texas (25,310) and Washington (22,304) together have half of the homeless people in the USA. Unsurprisingly, the problem is far more visible in urban areas and the 50 largest cities in the country account for 51 per cent of the country's homeless people.

Government response

The Department of Housing and Urban Development plays a crucial role in providing affordable homes and shelter and support to the homeless and to those in need, such as the elderly and the sick. Its mission statement is 'to create strong, sustainable, inclusive communities and quality affordable homes for all'. On 11 March 2019, the Trump Administration announced its proposed 2020 budget for HUD: 'a $44.1 billion spending plan that expands resources to prevent/end homelessness; invests record funding to reduce lead and other home health and safety hazards; and preserves rental assistance to HUD-assisted households'. In 2011,

Congress allocated $46 billion to the agency.

The HUD claims to be advancing economic opportunity for low-income families through:

- home ownership
- workforce training
- educational advancement
- health and wellness programmes.

How has the HUD achieved this?

In 2018, the HUD announced the first 17 EnVision Centers in communities around the country, providing information on their website. 'Located on or near public housing developments, EnVision Centers will be centralized hubs that serve as an incubator to support four key pillars of self-sufficiency – (1) Economic Empowerment, (2) Educational Advancement, (3) Health and Wellness, and (4) Character and Leadership.'

In 2018, HUD's Federal Housing Administration (FHA) 'served nearly 669,000 mostly first and low- to moderate-income, single-family homebuyers through home loans; supported the production and preservation of 121,600 multifamily units; and provided $2.45 billion in insurance for hospital and residential care facilities'.

The HUD 'continued to implement the expansion of the Moving To Work demonstration program from 39 to 139 public housing authorities across the country, encouraging innovative, locally-designed strategies for housing choice, self-sufficiency, and economic opportunity for low-income families'.

In 2018, it expanded its Book Rich Environments Initiative 'to provide more than 400,000 new books to low-income children in 37 HUD-assisted communities across the country'.

In 2018 the HUD 'awarded over $2 billion in Continuum of Care (CoC) program grants, $270 million in Emergency Solutions Grants

(ESG) program funds, and $43 million in funding for Youth Homelessness Demonstration Program (YHDP) grants to communities working to end homelessness'.

Crime and law

The analysis of crime in the USA is generally measured by violent crime and property crime. According to the Pew Research Center, violent crime has been on the decline over the past 25 years. In 2017, it was reported that violent crime was down 49 per cent from 1993. Statistical analysis found that many Americans still feel that crime is an issue and that 68 per cent of the population felt that crime in 2017 had been worse than in the previous year.

Figure 1.29 **A prisoner inside a US federal prison**

Most crimes that are committed in the USA take place in inner-city areas. Many different factors can contribute to making certain cities dangerous to live or work in within the USA. There can be issues with armed robberies, lack of police funding, gang-related violence and much more that contributes to the lack of safety within city limits.

Who makes up the prison population?

In 2019, the Federal Bureau of Prisons released data outlining the number of ethnic minorities in prison. According to the statistics, there is an overall higher majority of ethnic minority inmates than white inmates:

Table 1.10 **Prison population**

	Number of inmates
White	105,813
Black	67,685
Hispanic	58,530
Native American	4,075
Asian	2,708

Source: www.bop.gov/about/statistics

The Bureau of Justice and Statistics has stated that black and Hispanic populations are over-represented in US prisons. When you compare the percentages in the population as a whole to that of inmates there is a huge difference. Black people have more than five times the imprisonment rate of white people.

Death row

There are currently 29 states in which capital punishment is legal. According to the Death Penalty Information Center, 25 people were executed in the USA in 2018. There were 42 death penalty sentences granted in 2018.

In October 2018, there were 2721 people on death row.

Table 1.11 **Ethnicity of inmates on death row**

White	1,144	42.04%
Black	1,130	41.53%
Hispanic	366	13.45%
Asian	52	1.91%
Native American	28	1.03%
Unknown at this issue	1	0.04%

Of the 2721 inmates on death row, 2666 (97.98 per cent) are male and 55 (2.02 per cent) are female.

Source: www.naacpldf.org

Racial issue?

Figure 1.30 **Stephon Clark**

Police shooting of Stephon Clark

On March 2018, Stephon Clark was shot and killed by two police officers.

Stephon was a black man living in California and he was shot and killed by two white police officers. Stephon was in his grandmother's garden and was unarmed at the time.

This was another story of a high-profile police shooting of a black unarmed man by white police officers.

In March 2019, both police officers were acquitted of murder after a year-long investigation.

Use of guns

The *Washington Post* has created a database called Fatal Force to record every fatal shooting by police in the USA. In 2018, police fatally shot and killed 992 people. As of June 2019, it is estimated that the figure is 425. Out of the 425 people, 85 are white, 56 are black, 44 are Hispanic, 9 are categorised as 'other' and there are 231 people whose ethnicity is unknown.

Gun ownership

The USA has the highest rate of gun ownership in the world. Many gun owners believe that they are exercising the right outlined in the Second Amendment, the 'right to bear arms'. On average, approximately 96 people are shot and killed every day in the USA. It is very difficult to gain an accurate record of how many people own guns in the USA as many are obtained illegally. The Pew Research Center stated that in 2017, at least 42 per cent of people said that they lived in a house with someone who owned a gun.

Mass shootings

It is undeniable that the USA has more gun violence than any other developed country. Data from Gun Violence Archive reveals there is a mass shooting nine out of every ten days on average.

On 1 October 2017, 58 people were killed and 800 people were injured at a music festival in Las Vegas. This is one of the deadliest mass shootings in US modern history.

In December 2012, a mass shooting at Sandy Hook Elementary School shook the nation and the world: 20 children and 6 teaching staff were killed. There was a call for gun reform in the USA. The message was 'never again'. Since then there have been 2117 mass shootings, resulting in 2389 people being killed and 8805 wounded.

Fighting for gun reform

'Moms Demand Action for Gun Sense in America is a grassroots movement of Americans fighting for public safety measures that can protect people from gun violence. Moms Demand Action campaigns for new and stronger solutions to lax gun laws and loopholes that jeopardize the safety of our families. Moms Demand Action has established a chapter in every state of the country and, along with Mayors Against Illegal Guns, Students Demand Action and the Everytown Survivor Network, it is part of Everytown for Gun Safety, the largest gun violence prevention organization in the country with nearly 6 million supporters and more than 350,000 donors.'

Source: https://momsdemandaction.org

Government response

On 16 January 2013, President Obama put forward a specific plan to protect children and communities by reducing gun violence. The plan combined executive actions and calls for legislative action that would help keep guns out of the wrong hands, ban assault and high-capacity magazines, make schools safer, and increase access to mental health services.

However, the Republican-controlled House of Representatives at the time refused to support this modest gun reform and no action was taken. This highlights the limitations of presidential powers.

Gun control reforms

After the shooting at Marjory Stoneman Douglas High School in Parkland, Florida, in February 2018, President Trump said he wanted to strengthen background checks for gun ownership. At times he has appeared to support universal checks that would apply to private sales and gun show sales: 'Very strong improvement and strengthening of background checks will be fully backed by White House. Legislation moving forward', he tweeted a month after the attack. The president also suggested that teachers/staff should be trained to use guns and firearms to protect students in the case of another school shooting, saying the federal government would work with states to provide voluntary 'rigorous' firearms training for 'specially qualified' school personnel. Trump has used mass shootings as examples of situations where a member of the public or staff at a mall, cinema or school would be able to protect themselves and others by killing an active shooter – if they carried a gun.

In 2019, the Democratic-controlled House of Representatives passed a bill on gun control reforms. This would result in tougher background checks for people wanting to buy a gun or firearm. They had stated that they would increase the number of days to carry out these checks from three to ten days. This would include people who buy guns online or from a gun show. President Trump has promised to veto the proposals, arguing they would restrict the rights of gun owners and the legislation is unlikely to pass through the Republican-controlled Senate.

Income and poverty

Figure 1.31 **Children in poverty**

Many people might think that poverty levels in the United States would be lower than most developed countries due to the country's wealth but this is not the case. In 2017, 39.7 million Americans were living in poverty.

The lowest poverty rate was in New Hampshire and the state with the highest poverty rate was Mississippi.

Using data from the US Census Bureau, Children International, an organisation that aims to help children living in poverty, claimed that in 2014, one child in every seven was born into poverty in the United States.

Race and ethnicity

The incidence of poverty among African American and Hispanic people exceeds that of white people by a factor of between two and three. In 2017, the US Census Bureau Income and Poverty report revealed that the following were considered to be living in poverty:

- 21.2 per cent of black people
- 18.3 per cent of Hispanic people
- 10 per cent of Asian and Pacific Islanders
- 8.7 per cent of white people.

Overall, one in every eight Americans lives below the poverty line – this is around $25,000 per year for a family of four to survive on. The black poverty rate is more than double the white poverty rate.

In 2017, people with at least a bachelor's degree were the only group to have an increase in people living in poverty and older groups saw a fall in poverty levels. As previously mentioned, the number of children living in poverty is continuing to increase.

'The U.S. Census Bureau released national poverty data for 2017.

The headline was that 39.7 million people were poor in 2017. This works out to 12.3 percent of the population or 1 in 8 Americans. The good news is that the U.S. poverty rate has fallen since 2010, when it hit 15.1 percent, and is now where it was before the Great Recession.

The bad news is that poverty still exceeds the 11.3 percent rate of 2000 and far too many people are poor in a country that is so rich. Another bit of bad news is that things look even worse if we use what many scholars like myself believe is a better poverty measure.

Who Is Poor?

In 2017, women had higher poverty rates than men and minorities had higher poverty rates than non-Hispanic white people, mainly because women earn less than men and minorities receive lower wages on average than white people. For similar reasons, adults with lower education levels are more likely to be poor.

What's more, having an additional adult able to earn money gives married-couple families much lower poverty rates than households headed by a single woman.

Poverty also varies by age. For those 65 and over, the poverty rate fell from the 1960s until the 1990s, mainly due to more generous Social Security benefits. Since then, it has remained at around 10 percent. The poverty rate for prime-age adults fell until around 1980. After 1980, it fluctuated around 10 percent, rising during recessions and falling during economic expansions.

Child poverty, however, has been relatively high in the U.S. since the late 1970s; it has increased in recent years and now stands at 17.5 percent. For children in a female-headed household, the poverty rate is near 50 percent.'

Source: Steven Pressman, http://theconversation.com

Government response

Figure 1.32 People working in America

'The economy has come roaring back to life under President Trump. The stock market has hit record high after record high, helping more Americans build wealth and secure their futures. Through needed tax cuts and reform, the Administration will bring jobs back to our country. The President is helping U.S. workers by expanding apprenticeship programs, reforming job training programs, and bringing businesses and educators together to ensure high-quality classroom instruction and on-the-job training.'

Source: www.whitehouse.gov

Under President Trump's Executive Order Establishing the President's National Council for the American Worker, the Department of Commerce is asked to appoint and administer a 25-member American Workforce Policy Advisory Board. The Executive Order states:

'This new Presidential Advisory Board will draw upon the knowledge and expertise of its members as we develop and implement a strategy to overhaul America's training policies and practices.

'Members of the Board will include a wide range of stakeholders, including employers, labor advocates, educational and training institutions, and state governments. Together, these experts will offer diverse perspectives on how to resolve workforce issues facing communities and businesses across the country.'

Source: www.whitehouse.gov

In the 2020 budget proposal, President Trump and his administration have proposed cuts to government spending which would have an impact on the poorest Americans.

The Trump administration requested that Congress release $4.75 trillion for the newest budget plan.

The Whitehouse website displays the budget proposal and outlines that military spending is a top priority for the Trump administration. There was a request for an additional $750 billion to be given to the military budget. Trump also requested more funds for border control and $8.6 billion to build a wall between the US and Mexico.

Critics have argued that cuts to government spending have negatively affected Medicaid and other welfare programmes. The suggestion of lowering the inflation rate will alter the true rate of poverty figures in the US as people may no longer be categorised as needing government welfare. This will have a negative impact for people who rely on government assisted programmes such as Medicaid, food stamps and housing issues.

The budget proposal has to be passed by Congress.

Labour force and ethnicity

Labour-market differences within racial and ethnic groups are associated with many factors, not all of which are measurable. These factors include variations across the groups in educational attainment; the occupations and industries in which the groups work; the geographic areas of the country in which the groups are concentrated, including whether they tend to reside in urban or rural settings; and the degree of discrimination encountered in the workplace.

According to the US Census Bureau of Labor Statistics, there was a slight decline in unemployment rates for white and Hispanic people from May 2018 to May 2019, and a slight increase for black and Asian people. Having said this, some ethnic minorities still experience inequalities in the labour market.

Table 1.12 **Unemployment figures in May 2019**

Black	6.2%
Hispanic/Latino	4.2%
White	3.3%
Asian	2.5%

Source: US Census Bureau of Labor Statistics

Earnings

Among the major race and ethnicity groups, Hispanic people and black people continue to have considerably lower earnings than white people and Asian and Pacific Islanders in 2017.

The median household income in 2017 was $61,372.

In terms of household income, Asian and Pacific Islanders were the highest earning group and black people had the lowest earnings in 2017.

Table 1.13 **Household income, 2017**

Asian and Pacific Islander	$81,331
White	$68,145
Hispanic	$50,486
Black	$40,258

Source: US Census Bureau

Other factors

Data for 2017 from the US Census Bureau highlights the effect of educational attainment on income.

Table 1.14 **Educational attainment and average annual salary, 2017**

Less than a high school diploma	$27,597
High school diploma/equivalent	$38,145
Some college education but no degree	$38,695
Bachelor's degree or higher	$67,763
Doctorate degree	$118,903

Government response

Long-term unemployment is falling, but still work to do

President Trump states that his administration is 'helping US workers by expanding apprenticeship programs, reforming job training programs, and bringing businesses and educators together to ensure high quality classroom instruction and on-the-job training.'

On 22 December 2017, President Trump signed the Tax Cuts and Jobs Act. The Act cut the corporate tax rate from 35 per cent to 21 per cent beginning in 2018. The corporate cuts are permanent, while the individual changes expire at the end of 2025. Corporate tax is what big businesses pay and under this Act they will pay less tax.

In July 2018, the Bureau of Labor Statistics reported 6.9 million job openings nationally, with a further 500,000 jobs available in the manufacturing industry.

Show your understanding

1 What evidence suggests that the USA is a violent society?
2 Research mass shootings in the USA. Describe the incidents.
3 Why do most ethnic minorities feel that they are discriminated against in terms of law and order issues?
4 Compare the income, poverty and unemployment experiences of different ethnic groups.

Show your understanding (continued)

Group task

Create groups of three or four students.

Each group should choose one social or economic factor.

Your task is to create a handout of your chosen factor – this will be given to everyone in the class to use as a study aid.

Research your chosen factor and make detailed notes on:

- inequalities and those who experience inequalities
- what the Government is doing to help
- whether any progress has been made.

20-mark question

To what extent does social and economic inequality exist?

International relations

USA world dominance

For over 25 years the USA has been the dominant economic and military power across all continents of the world. From the United Nations to NATO to the G7 group, the US influences global events and has used its military might to take action against states and organisations that threaten the security of the West. Table 1.15 highlights the massive military might of the USA. However, there is a perception today that America's dominance is on the decline. Both the banking crisis of 2008 and the subsequent economic recession have weakened the US economy and have led to many Americans questioning US involvement abroad. The failure to destroy Al-Qaeda and the Taliban, and the rise of ISIS in Syria and Iraq, explain why public approval of President Obama's foreign policy was at an all-time low. The USA also faced the emergence of an aggressive Russia willing to use military force in Eastern Europe and a confident China no longer willing to accept US dominance in Asia. President Trump

promised to 'Make America Great Again' prior to becoming president in January 2017. He also stated that the problems of other countries cannot always be solved by the USA and that it is not America's responsibility.

Table 1.15 **Military spending, 2019**

Country	Spending ($bn)
United States	717
China	177
India	61
Germany	53
Saudi Arabia	51
Britain	49

Source: army-technology.com, 2019

Figure 1.33 **US aircraft carrier, the USS Abraham Lincoln**

USA and the United Nations

The USA played a leading role in setting up the United Nations after the Second World War and this is reflected in its headquarters being in New York. The USA has one of the five permanent seats on the UN Security Council along with Russia, China, France and the UK. The Security Council can impose economic sanctions on a country and can also take military action, such as sending 30,000 UN soldiers to the Darfur region of Sudan. However, all of the permanent members must agree to any action and can use a veto. This can lead to no action being taken by the UN. For example, the USA, the UK and France wished to condemn and take action against the Assad regime in Syria. However, both China and Russia vetoed such a move. This highlights the limits of US influence in the Security Council as it cannot impose its foreign policy objectives.

However, the USA has been far more influential in the humanitarian work of the specialised agencies of the UN such as WHO (World Health Organization). The UN declared the Ebola outbreak in West Africa an international public health emergency and the USA, alongside the UN, has acted swiftly to provide doctors, scientists and military support to tackle the crisis in the countries affected. To date, more than 8000 people have died from the Ebola virus in seven countries.

Table 1.16 **UN budget contribution by selected country 2019: peacekeeping**

Country	Contribution (%)
USA	27.8
China	15.2
Japan	8.6
Germany	6.1
UK	5.8

Source: peacekeeping.un.org

The contrasting foreign policy actions of President Obama and President Trump are reflected in their respective speeches to the UN Security Council (Obama in 2014 and Trump in October 2019).

NATO
Obama

'And these are simple truths, but they must be defended. America and our allies will support the people of Ukraine as they develop their democracy and economy. We will reinforce our NATO Allies and uphold our commitment to collective self-defense. We will impose a cost on Russia for aggression, and we will counter falsehoods with the truth. And we call upon others to join us on the right side of history.'

Trump

'As we rebuild the unrivaled might by the American military, we are also revitalizing our alliances by making it very clear that all of our partners are expected to pay their fair share of the tremendous defense burden, which the United States has borne in the past.'

Iran
Obama

'America is pursuing a diplomatic resolution to the Iranian nuclear issue, as part of our commitment to stop the spread of nuclear weapons and pursue the peace and security of a world without them. And this can only take place if Iran seizes this historic opportunity. My message to Iran's leaders and people has been simple and consistent: Do not let this opportunity pass. We can reach a solution that meets your energy needs while assuring the world that your program is peaceful.'

Trump

'One of the greatest security threats facing peace-loving nations today is the repressive regime in Iran. Not only is Iran the world's number one state sponsor of terrorism but Iran's leaders are fueling the tragic wars in Syria and Yemen. At the same time, the regime is squandering the nation's wealth and future in a fanatical quest for nuclear weapons and the means to deliver them. We must never allow this to happen. To stop Iran's path to nuclear weapons and missiles, I withdrew the United States from the terrible Iran nuclear deal, which has very little time remaining, did not allow inspection of important sites and did not cover ballistic missiles. Following our withdrawal, we have implemented severe economic sanctions on the country. Hoping to free itself from sanctions, the regime has escalated its violent and unprovoked aggression. In response to Iran's recent attack on Saudi Arabia oil facilities, we just imposed the highest level of sanctions on Iran's Central Bank and Sovereign Wealth Fund.'

World poverty and global warming

Obama

'America is committed to a development agenda that eradicates extreme poverty by 2030. We will do our part to help people feed themselves, power their economies, and care for their sick. If the world acts together, we can make sure that all of our children enjoy lives of opportunity and dignity. America is pursuing ambitious reductions in our carbon emissions, and we've increased our investments in clean energy. We will do our part, and help developing nations do theirs.'

Trump

He doesn't mention the Paris Agreement on climate change in his speech, including his plans for the US to withdraw from this.

Arab–Israeli Conflict

Obama

'We recognize as well that leadership will be necessary to address the conflict between Palestinians and Israelis.'

Trump

He doesn't reference resolving the conflict in his speech.

USA and China

In 2013, the new leader of China, Xi Jinping, stated that 'the vast Pacific Ocean has enough space for the two large countries of China and the United States'. China's new confidence is now challenging US dominance of south-east Asia. Tension has always existed between the two countries over the island of Taiwan; when the Chinese Communists gained control of mainland China, the defeated Chinese Government fled to Taiwan and set up their own independent China. The US protects Taiwan and provides it with up-to-date military equipment to deter a mainland attack. There is also tension over Hong Kong, a former British colony, now ruled by China. Recent student demonstrations there in support of free elections could lead to military intervention by China. Neighbouring countries such as Japan and the Philippines look to America for protection. China has territorial demands against these countries, and there is a danger of this leading to military conflict. China has, for example, fuelled anti-Japanese riots in its cities and has challenged Japan's control over uninhabited islets. The US fleet still dominates the Pacific but China has now in service its first aircraft carrier (the US has 11 worldwide). The USA has military bases in South Korea and Japan, and China wishes to challenge US dominance in the region.

Trump has maintained a tough policy towards China and has displayed continual American support to the island of Taiwan by selling up-to-date military weapons and by sending American warships to the area. The leaders of China state that Taiwan must be united with the mainland, by force if necessary.

President Trump has taken action against China's economy by placing massive tariffs on more than $500 billion worth of Chinese-made goods. He stated that 'it [China] has embraced an economic model dependent on massive market barriers, heavy state subsidies, currency manipulation, product dumping, forced technology transfers and the theft of intellectual property, and also trade secrets on a grand scale. The United States lost 60,000 factories after China entered the WTO.' It is clear that China is now the number one economic power in terms of GDP (see Figure 1.34) and that America feels threatened. (A different picture emerges when one compares GDP per person, in China it is only $16,000 and in America $55,000.) However, Trump's action has hurt American exports – General Motors sells more cars to China than it does to American citizens.

In October 2019 the Trump administration boosted its support of human rights by blacklisting 28 Chinese organisations for their involvement in abuses against ethnic Uighurs in China's Xinjiang province. These organisations are now on the Entity List which bars them from buying products from US companies without approval from Washington. (In May 2019 the Chinese telecommunications giant Huawei were placed on the Entity List.)

Table 1.17 **Selected military assets, China and USA**

	China	**USA**
Defence budget 2019 ($ billion)	177	717
Active personnel in 2018 (million)	2.3	1.4
Intercontinental missiles	66	450
Bombers	118	178
Nuclear-powered submarines	3	71
Main battle tanks	9,000	9,500
Aircraft carriers	1	11

Source: adapted from various US military sources

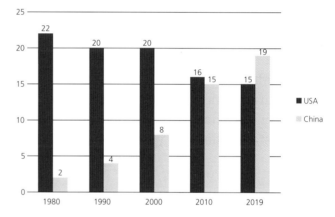

Figure 1.34 **Global GDP % of total**

Source: IMF

USA and NATO

The USA has been the dominant member of NATO (North Atlantic Treaty Organisation) since its inception in 1949. NATO was set up as a political and military alliance to defend the freedom and security of its members. NATO now has 29 members including countries from the former Russian-controlled Eastern Europe (see below). NATO will defend its members from aggression and an attack on one member is regarded as an attack upon them all, as defined in its Article 5. This explains why Georgia and Ukraine are anxious to join as they have both been threatened by Russian aggression. However, in a Fox television interview in 2018, Trump undermined Article 5, NATO's common defence clause, by suggesting that the small nations of NATO, such as Montenegro, could be the cause of a third world war. He stated, 'Montenegro is a tiny country … They're very aggressive people. They may get aggressive and congratulations, you're in world war three.'

Over the last 20 years, the US and its NATO allies have played an important role in crisis management and peacekeeping in areas such as the former Yugoslavia and Afghanistan. NATO troops have played their part in the defeat of the Islamic State in Syria and Iraq. The countries of NATO invoked Article 5 to assist America after the September 2001 terror attacks. Trump has criticised NATO's European members for not contributing their proper financial contribution. European countries have responded by increasing their financial contributions in each of the last three financial years.

The expansion of NATO

The new members of NATO are:

- Albania
- Bulgaria
- Croatia
- Czech Republic
- Estonia
- Latvia
- Lithuania
- Montenegro
- Poland
- Romania
- Slovakia
- Slovenia.

Russian aggression

Under President Putin, Russia is now determined to challenge US and NATO's dominance in Eastern Europe. In 2008, Georgia sent troops into South Ossetia (part of Georgia) to crush rebel groups. Putin sent in Russian forces to eject the Georgian forces from South Ossetia and Abkhazia. The area still had not been returned to Georgia, with pro-Russian rebels remaining in control. The USA, NATO and the European Union (EU) condemned this invasion and provided Georgia with $6 billion in humanitarian aid. Aware of the lack of action by the West, Putin raised the stakes and set out to effectively partition Ukraine and destabilise the country. Obama in his address to the Security Council described the situation as follows:

'After the people of Ukraine mobilized popular protests and calls for reform, their corrupt president fled. Against the will of the government in Kyiv, Crimea was annexed. Russia poured arms into eastern Ukraine, fueling violent separatists and a conflict that has killed thousands. When a civilian airliner was shot down from areas that these proxies controlled, they refused to allow access to the crash for days. When Ukraine started to reassert control over its territory, Russia gave up the pretense of merely supporting the separatists, and moved troops across the border.'

The USA and the EU have imposed economic sanctions on Russia, which has weakened the Russian economy. NATO troops have stepped up military exercises in Eastern Europe and the USA has reassured Poland of NATO's support if Russia violates its territory. Putin's objective has been achieved: Crimea has been taken from Ukraine, and Russian troops control part of eastern Ukraine. Meanwhile, the USA and NATO are helpless. Their leaders and citizens do not wish to engage in military conflict in a far-off country, and Putin is aware of this.

USA and international terrorism

America's response to 9/11 in 2001 was to mobilise the international community and launch a 'war on terrorism'. Iraq was invaded by coalition forces and its leader, Saddam Hussein, executed. Afghanistan was also invaded to root out Al-Qaeda and to remove the Taliban Government. All this was quickly achieved but neither of these countries enjoyed peace. Democracy failed to take roots in either country and civil war took place. When Obama became president in January 2009, he stated, 'we will kill Bin Laden. We will crush al-Qaeda'. The former was achieved in May 2011 when American special forces killed Bin Laden and numerous drone attacks wiped out 30 top leaders of the group. Obama also carried out his promise to take all troops out of Iraq and to begin a gradual reduction from Afghanistan; however, by the time US troops withdrew from Iraq over 4000 of their comrades had been killed.

However, fast-forward to 2015 and US foreign policy objectives of bringing peace and stability to the region were in ruins. Obama failed to act in Libya in 2011, leaving it to Libya's European partners to use air power to enable the rebels to depose the dictator Gaddafi. Extremist groups used the chaos in Libya to seize huge stockpiles of weapons to start conflict in Syria. This new fundamentalist group ISIS (Islamic State of Iraq and Syria) has launched a 'holy war' to set up their Islamic state in Syria and northern Iraq. Obama responded by co-ordinating US-led coalition airstrikes to push back ISIS.

ISIS were finally defeated in 2018 with the Kurdish forces playing an important role in this victory. However, to the shock and dismay of the international community, President Trump announced in October 2019 that he was withdrawing all American troops from north-eastern Syria. This enabled Turkish troops to attack Kurdish forces in this area as the presence of US troops deterred such a move (Turkey regards Kurds as terrorist, as Turks in Turkey want an independent Kurdish state). The withdrawal was heavily criticised by the Kurds who accused Trump of betrayal. The Turkish army quickly overran the Kurdish forces and this enabled Russian troops to intervene to organise a cease-fire. The Kurdish state was obliterated leaving Russia the dominant power. Trump's action was heavily criticised by fellow Republicans as weakening US influence in the area and as betrayal of a loyal ally.

Has President Trump weakened the international influence and status of the USA?

President Trump won the 2016 election with the slogan of 'making America great again'. Three years on, the consensus within the US State Department and the international community is that Trump's words and actions have weakened the international influence of the USA. Trump would argue the following actions are proof of making America great: through his historic meeting with Kim Jong, he has persuaded North Korea to agree to the dismantling of their nuclear programme; he confronted the threat from Iran by abandoning President Obama's nuclear agreement with Iran and imposing sanctions; he persuaded the other members of NATO to increase their financial contributions; he withdrew America from the Paris Agreement on climate change; and he firmly supported the right-wing Israeli Government of Benjamin Netanuahu by moving the US embassy to Jerusalem and officially condoned Israel's annexation of the Golan Heights.

NATO and the EU

Trump has weakened America's influence in Europe by referring to the EU as the 'foe' and by placing tariffs on selected EU products such as Scotch whisky.

Ukrainegate

Trump has been accused of soliciting foreign interference in the 2020 elections for his personal political interests. He has not denied asking the president of Ukraine to help find incriminating evidence against a political rival, the former Democrat vice president Joe Biden. Congress had authorised $400 million to help Ukraine combat the threat of Russian-backed rebels in the east of the country. Trump blocked these funds being allocated before contacting the Ukrainian president for his 'assistance'.

'In the course of my official duties, I have received information from multiple US government officials that the president of the US is using the power of his office to solicit interference from a foreign country in the 2020 US elections. This interference includes, among other things, pressuring a foreign country to investigate one of the president's main domestic political rivals.'

(Extract released by the House Intelligence Committee from the nine-page document submitted by an intelligence officer)

Arab-Israeli conflict

Trump has abandoned the long-standing US policy of playing the 'honest broker' in the peace process between Palestinians and Israelis. His unconditional friendship towards Israel has undermined any US proposals to resolve the conflict.

Iran

Trump has ended the agreement with Iran over its nuclear capabilities and has imposed sanctions. This has led to Iran attacking Saudi Arabian oil fields and a massive increase in international tension in the area.

China

In his presidential campaign in 2016, Trump stated that China was a bigger problem than Jihadi terrorism. He has highlighted their currency manipulation and unfair trade with the West. However, his unilateral actions against China in imposing tariffs and sanctions has resulted in a trade war with China which has disrupted international commerce and shaken global economic confidence without improving the US economy.

North Korea

John Bolton, former national security adviser to President Trump has contradicted the administration statement that Kim Jong Un is willing to give up his nuclear weapons. His view is that it was all well and good for Trump to visit and negotiate with North Korea, however it has been detrimental to American security and influence in the region. Trump has cancelled the annual large-scale joint military drills with South Korea as a concession to Kim Jong Un. In response North Korea has continued to carry out the firing of several missiles over the Sea of Japan in defiance of the ban imposed by the United Nations and his promises to Trump.

United Nations

Trump's withdrawal from multilateral agreements such as the Paris Agreement on climate change, his attacks on UN specialised agencies and his criticism of long-standing allies has weakened US influence in the United Nations. According to a 2019 policy paper by the European Council on Foreign Affairs: 'The two most severe challenges to the multilateral order today are the relative decline of American power, and the emergence of China as a rival power to the US in global organisations. Over the last decade, there has been an observable decline in America's capacity to shape multilateral affairs.'

How foreigners view the US: Pew Research Center, February 2019

This poll highlights growing international public concerns about America's role in world affairs. Many believe the US is doing less to help solve major global challenges than it used to. In Germany, just 10 per cent of people have confidence in Trump. Below is a summary of issues raised:

- Another country's power and influence pose a major threat to our country:

USA	45% (in 2008, under Obama, it was only 25%)
Russia	36%
China	35%

- 70 per cent lack confidence in President Trump to do the right thing in world affairs.
- 75 per cent say the US is doing less these days to address global problems.
- 39 per cent rated US as the world's leading economic power compared to 34 per cent who placed China first.

Show your understanding

1 What evidence supports the view that the USA is the world's superpower?
2 Why is there a perception today that US domination is on the decline?
3 Describe US involvement in international organisations such as the UN and NATO.
4 What action has the US taken against international terrorism?
5 To what extent is China a threat to US dominance in south-east Asia?
6 Read Obama's address to the UN Security Council and list the problems faced by the international community and the actions taken by the USA.
7 Compare the foreign policy priorities and actions of Presidents Obama and Trump as outlined in their respective addresses to the UN Security Council.
8 Outline the evidence that supports and opposes the view that under President Trump there has been a decline in America's international influence.

20-mark question

To what extent has a world power you have studied had influence in international relations?

2 The People's Republic of China

Background

The People's Republic of China has the largest population in the world (1.415 billion), with one in five people in the world living in China. Geographically, it is a very large country, the fourth largest in the world behind Russia, Canada and the USA, with an area of 9,596,961 km². China's population is split between urban and rural areas and it has a very diverse population in terms of wealth, language and culture. The country is bordered by 14 other countries: Afghanistan, Bhutan, India, Kazakhstan, Kyrgyzstan, Laos, Mongolia, Myanmar (Burma), Nepal, North Korea, Pakistan, Russia, Tajikistan and Vietnam. The way in which the country has developed is a direct result of its geography. Most of its major cities lie along the eastern seaboard, ideal for shipping China's produce around the world. Its major geographical features include the world's tallest mountain (Everest) and two major rivers (the Yangtze and the Yellow River). China's main ethnic group is the Han Chinese who make up 91.6 per cent of the population. The other 8.4 per cent is made up of over 55 other minority groups.

China has experienced remarkable economic growth over the last 35 years and in 2011 China's economy became the second largest in the world. It is now challenging American dominance in south-east Asia. The Chinese Communist Party (CCP) came to power in 1949 under Chairman Mao and it has ruled China ever since.

Figure 2.1 **China**

Fact file

China

Capital: Beijing

Population: 1.415 billion people

Main language: Mandarin

Major government ideology: Communism based on teachings of Karl Marx, a nineteenth-century German political philosopher

Religions: Buddhism, Christianity, Islam and Taoism

Currency: Yuan

GDP: $11.2 trillion

The political system

China's political system differs enormously from that of the UK. Instead of the representative democracy that we have, China has a very authoritarian, communist government, which permeates every aspect of people's lives. China is ruled by the Chinese Communist Party, which has ultimate political control over its citizens and allows for no real form of political opposition. Although the CCP tolerates the existence of other political parties, they must be ideologically similar to the CCP and there is little representation of other political ideas. The CCP has been in control of China since 1949, and its strict communist regime is founded on the principle of strong state intervention, based on the communist teachings of the political philosophy of Karl Marx, whereby the CCP dominates every aspect of people's lives – what they watch on television, what they can access on the internet and which religion they can practise freely.

The Chinese Communist Party

Political parties in China work very differently from those in the UK. Despite the fact that the CCP is the largest political party in the world with 98 million members, it is a very exclusive organisation that only allows admission after several years of a lengthy application process. Around 7 per cent of China's population are members of the CCP. The first taster of the CCP is often in primary school, where children are encouraged to join the Young Pioneers of China. This ensures that children are introduced to the Chinese communist ideology from an early age. Thereafter, adults who wish to join the CCP must complete substantial written applications, pass interviews and exams that test their political ideology and suitability, be sponsored by a current member of the party and serve a full year's probationary period. Gaining party membership often comes down to who you know, as this elite group usually admits people to the CCP who have family connections. Indeed, the current leader of the CCP, Xi Jinping, has been nicknamed as a 'Princeling', as he has managed to ascend to a position of power within the CCP because of his own family connections to the party: Xi Jinping's father was Xi Zhongxun – one of the Communist Party's founding fathers. As a direct result of this type of admission, the party is largely unrepresentative of China as a whole; only a quarter of the CCP are under 35 and only one-third of members are female. Selection to the CCP from within means it is very difficult for ordinary citizens to infiltrate the party.

Many people still wish to join the CCP, as it is seen by many as a ticket to success in communist China. In 2017, many university students applied to join the party (indeed 45 per cent of the new intake to the CCP that year were students); a far cry from 30 years ago when students protested against Communist-Party rule in Tiananmen Square.

Joining the Communist Party in China is attractive as members are usually guaranteed better government jobs, which are crucial to being economically successful in China. The vast influence that the party has in society ensures that members have access to the best schools for their children and better health care. The privileges of party members are taken much further than occupational benefits, however; there are many reports of corruption being rife within the CCP, including claims that officials accept bribes as common practice. At the 19th National Party Congress in 2017, President Xi Jinping reaffirmed his commitment to tackling corruption. He described corruption within the party as 'grim and complicated to tackle'.

The influence of the CCP in China extends much further than that of the political parties within the UK. The CCP controls exactly what is taught in schools, which includes a vast history of the CCP and China's political greatness. It also censors the internet to a large extent, blocking major sites like Facebook and ensuring that Chinese people have no anonymity on micro-blogs like Twitter. The different levels at which the party functions ensures there are always local village representatives, meaning the CCP is aware of what is happening in every area of society.

The CCP is very insular and all major political decisions are made by CCP officials without the influence of the public. Xi Jinping has been nicknamed the 'Chairman of Everything'; he is the general secretary of the CCP, the president of China, chairman of the Military Commission and the leader of Internet Security. It is the party's job to appoint and promote all its government officials, the majority of whom come from the CCP itself. Underneath Xi Jinping in terms of influence is the seven-member Politburo Standing Committee or PBSC, which acts like the president of the USA's Cabinet. The head of the PBSC is China's premier, Li Keqiang. Most of the PBSC's work is carried out in private, and this is where the majority of the major political decisions for China are made. This group effectively runs China. Underneath them in terms of power is the 25-member Politburo (which includes the seven members of the PBSC), which is the CCP's decision-making body.

National Party Congress

Roughly once every five years, the CCP holds a National Party Congress (not to be confused with the National People's Congress – China's parliament) where major political decisions made by the CCP are announced and where the

Figure 2.2 **The structure of the CCP**

policies for China for the next five years are announced – the Five-Year Plan. At the 19th Party Congress in October 2017, a major new ideological plan was launched called 'Xi Jinping's Thought on Socialism with Chinese Characteristics for a New Era'. It is at this meeting that the members of the Politburo and PBSC are chosen.

The CCP has several major institutions:

- The Politburo Standing Committee (PBSC)
- The Central Committee of Politburo
- The Central Military Affairs Commission.

The Central Military Affairs Commission

In an authoritarian communist country, the army plays a vital role in national security and policing the nation. The army has maintained order recently during protests from former army veterans who are angry about poor pensions and during protests in Tibet. China is a country with nuclear weapon capabilities and where the CCP is permitted, by the Central Military Affairs Commission (CMAC), to control China's armed forces and nuclear weapons. At the 19th Party Congress in 2017, Xi Jinping highlighted the need to overhaul the military to make it stronger and more loyal to the CCP. He stated that the ideological foundation of the People's Liberation Army (PLA) is its 'absolute loyalty to the Chinese Communist Party'. As part of the military overhaul, the CMAC has been reduced from eleven to seven members in order for Xi Jinping to maintain tighter control and loyalty. It is the CMAC's job to make decisions regarding army deployment, appointing high-ranking military personnel and arms spending. The CCP holds ultimate power over the CMAC, as Xi Jinping is also the chairman of the CMAC. Many have observed that the Government and the army in China are one and the same thing, as all army personnel are members of the CCP and pledge allegiance to serve the party.

'Xi Jinping's Thought on Socialism with Chinese Characteristics for a New Era'

At the 19th Party Congress (2017), Xi Jinping announced a new political ideology called 'Xi Jinping's Thought on Socialism with Chinese Characteristics for a New Era' or 'Xi Jinping's Thought' for short. The ideology aims to do three main things – strengthen the power that Xi Jinping and the CCP have over the Chinese people, increase China's political power worldwide and extend China's economic dominance.

- **Strengthening political power** – As part of this new doctrine, Xi Jinping has begun to strengthen his political power by getting rid of the presidential term limit, meaning that there is now no limit to the amount of time he can serve as leader. This, along with the military overhaul already mentioned, strengthens Xi's political influence and ensures that he oversees the party, military and state and internet security.

- **Increasing political power worldwide** – Huge increases in military spending of around 7 per cent a year have helped China to strengthen its position as a world power. Official figures for 2017 show China's military spending at around $151.4 billion (the USA's spending was approximately $523 billion). Investment in the army has seen an increase in nuclear spending, naval resources and the number of missiles. China's aim is to offset America's influence over islands in the South China Sea. Xi Jinping has taken steps to ensure that the CCP's influence permeates every aspect of society. Xi's economic plans in many other countries worldwide have led to deeper political co-operation and can be used as a political bargaining chip by the Chinese in order to negotiate better trade deals.

- **Extending China's economic dominance** – Xi Jinping has also pledged to invest $1 trillion into economic trade deals and infrastructure projects. He has invested in a new programme called the 'One Belt, One Road' project, which aims to develop infrastructure projects including a 260-mile railway system across eight countries and building $46 billion worth of power plants. Xi Jinping aims to invest in projects across 60 countries as part of the next Five-Year Plan, including $10 billion worth of railway projects in Africa and Laos and the Hinkley Point C nuclear power plant in Britain.

Figure 2.3 Xi Jinping, China's president

Show your understanding

1 Create a diagram of the main institutions within the Chinese political system.
2 Explain how China's political system differs from our own.
3 Describe the process Chinese citizens must undertake to join the CCP.
4 Briefly explain the structure of the CCP and explain who holds the real power.
5 Outline what is meant by Xi Jinping's 'Thought on Socialism with Chinese Characteristics for a New Era'. Give examples of what it includes.

Structure of the national government

As we have already mentioned, the Chinese political system is a communist system dominated by the CCP. It has a system of 'collective leadership' whereby the president (currently Xi Jinping) and the seven members of the Political Bureau Standing Committee have different ranks and roles within the Government, and power is shared to a small extent. It can be argued that President Xi Jinping is more of a 'one-man band' than his predecessor, Hu Jintao, as Xi is in charge of the CCP, the army and internet security. Although there is a State Constitution, which outlines how the government of China should share powers and observe people's rights, party members and government officials are encouraged instead to abide by the party's Constitution as their supreme code of conduct, which means people's rights are often overlooked. The Constitution of China can be overruled in practice by the CCP on any decision and there are many protests for the Constitution (as it is on paper) to be upheld. The national government consists of the State Council, the president and the National People's Congress.

Branches of government

Legislative: National People's Congress
Executive: State Council, president, vice president and premier
Judicial: Supreme People's Court

Figure 2.4 **The three branches of central government in China**

The National People's Congress

The Congress meets for around ten to fourteen consecutive days every year in March. In 2018 there were 2980 delegates, making the National People's Congress (NPC) the largest parliament in the world. These delegates are elected for a five-year period, and their main job is to approve laws and the appointments of senior party officials. Of the 2980 members, 2119 are from the CCP, once more confirming the CCP's dominance in Chinese politics. According to Articles 57 and 58 of the Chinese Constitution, the NPC is 'the highest organ of state power', which can 'exercise the legislative power of the state' (make laws). However, in practice this is not the case. The NPC merely approves or 'rubber-stamps' laws that have been made by the PBSC and the Politburo. The NPC has its own Standing Committee of 150 officials who meet once every two months. This group is made up of retired government officials and representatives from the eight 'democratic parties' and they appoint the new state president and vice president.

The State Council

The State Council is made up of around 35 members and is led by China's premier, Li Keqiang (also a member of the PBSC). The council meets monthly and is in charge of carrying out party policy at all levels. It often prepares draft laws, which are sent to the NPC. The State Council also has members from each of the Government departments for internal politics, national defence, finance and the economy. It is in charge of managing China's Five-Year Plan and the budget.

Supreme People's Court

China's Supreme Court is unlike a Western Supreme Court. In theory, the Supreme Court is the highest judicial administration in the land with the power to protect the rights of citizens. In practice, however, this is not the case, and the court mainly works to represent CCP interests by outlining controls on the people. It currently has around 340 judges.

Local politics in China

Having looked at the national government, it is also important to look at the other administrative levels within the country. Chinese politics at a local level is very complex. Because of China's sheer size and massive population, the CCP also has officials on regional and local levels to ensure it always has ultimate control and that its policies are implemented. There are four levels of government administration: national, provincial, protectorate and county. All major decisions are made at national level and 'trickle down' through these lower levels of government. There are local village elections in which Chinese people can choose their local representatives. The lowest level is the Village Committees.

Village Committees

In the 1980s, official Village Committees (VCs) were introduced at a grass-roots level. They are elected every three years and consist of a handful of members made up of a chairperson, vice chairperson and representatives. This allows Chinese people to vote on a local level and to stand as a candidate for election. Women are also playing a larger role within these committees and are supposed to be guaranteed equal representation,

although this is still not the case in practice. However, this makes China no different from countries like the USA and the UK, where women are still vastly under-represented. Voters are now supposed to be granted a secret ballot, aimed at reducing bribes, corruption and election-related violence. According to Article 2 of the Villagers' Committees Law, 'the Villagers' Committee is the primary mass organisation of self-government, in which the villagers manage their own affairs, educate themselves and serve their own needs and in which election is conducted, decision adopted, administration maintained and supervision exercised by democratic means'.

However, the village party secretary is the most important person within the village and is always a member of the CCP overseeing the work done by the VCs. Village Committees therefore have little real power, although they are often involved in the running of village schools and enforcing family planning regulations. This is the only level at which people can vote directly in Chinese politics. Even at village level, there are often 'irregularities' within the votes cast and some people are suspicious of the way in which the votes are counted. Also, CCP officials can step in at any time to oversee elections as they have the ultimate power within the political process. Local politics in China is rife with corruption – in 2018, 39 village leaders were sacked from their positions in the Guandong Province because of links to criminal gangs.

In the Western world, many may argue that Chinese democracy is not as transparent and legitimate as it should be. Western observers are sceptical about the CCP's motivations for allowing local village elections. Many have noted that this move has been to merely justify and legitimise the CCP's leadership; allowing people to vote for the CCP makes people feel that they have been involved in the political process and it is perceived therefore to be fairer.

Checks and balances on government

By Western standards, it may seem that the Chinese political system does not meet with our concept of what a democracy should be. Limited human rights, discussed later in the chapter, along with a lack of choice over which political party to vote for and being unable to choose your national representatives, means that the Chinese Government can rule with very few checks and balances and limited scrutiny from the people. Although China does have a written Constitution, which outlines the rights of all people, the Government is not held accountable by the people, who are heavily restricted in their right to protest. Indeed, it is not a government for the people or by the people, but instead a government the people must obey.

However, it would be naive not to recognise the changes to China's political system that have made it more democratic in recent years at the local level. Local village elections add an element of democracy that has allowed villagers to choose their village leaders and co-operate with them in many local victories. Land disputes, for example, have been settled with the villagers winning compensation and also the right to stay in their homes thanks to this type of grass-roots leadership. Many areas have seen a rise in participation in politics. There have been an estimated 70,000 recorded protests in the last three years alone, and Chinese people have had success in achieving fairer pay and land ownership rights at a village level. Online 'netizens' are also managing to raise high-profile protests online (see Fact file below). However, there have been some backwards steps in terms of leadership at a national level.

Fact file

Successful online protests

In a country of 1.415 billion people, policing the internet can be quite a challenge. The Central Cyberspace Affairs Commission (CCAC) set up in 2018, headed up by President Xi Jinping, polices the internet in order to try to reduce online protests and manage internet security. However, despite this tough internet censorship, which means that the CCP controls what can be accessed online, there have been some successful online protests in recent years. In April 2018, microblogging site Weibo (with 154 million users) stated that it would have to delete all LGBT-related information from its service in order to comply

Figure 2.5 #iamgay protest

with CCP guidelines on the promotion of homosexuality. This resulted in a mass online protest with over 150,000 complaints and comments. Many Chinese citizens started to use the #iamgay in protest at the company's decision. Just three days later Weibo reversed the decision to delete LGBT-related content, which showed the Chinese people's success in protecting LGBT rights online.

The previous law restricting the term time of a president to two terms has been revoked by Xi Jinping and this means he could rule indefinitely. Recent protests in Hong Kong and the Xinjiang region suggest that, while the Chinese leadership will accept some criticism of its actions and party officials, it will not tolerate any attempt to challenge the totalitarian rule of the Communist Party.

Challenges facing the CCP

In recent years, the two biggest challenges facing the CCP have been corruption and international pressure to implement the 'rule of law'. In terms of the latter, the CCP sees the laws and the Constitution as flexible guidelines that can be stretched/overruled by the CCP/Government. It believes that the law is in place to give the power to the Government and not necessarily to protect the rights of citizens. However, the international community and many Chinese protestors have called upon the CCP to abide by the rule of law, meaning that citizens' rights are protected above those of the Government. The Supreme Court of China can only scrutinise members of the CCP for misconduct if they have first gained permission from the CCP, meaning it is not a fully democratic

Fact file

China's political parties

Although the CCP has ultimate political power in China, there are actually eight other minor political parties. The Chinese Government describes China as a 'multi-party state' but in practice it merely tolerates the other political parties, which have no real political power or influence. All political decisions are made by the CCP, which can get rid of any of the other political parties at any time. The other political parties must swear to work under the CCP, share its values and, as a result, cannot be described as opposition parties. The CCP puts limits on the size of membership of these parties and their combined membership is less than 1 million people, far less than the CCP's 90 million members. The eight parties may be called 'democratic parties', and the CCP would argue that they allow China to be a democracy, but this is a far cry from the democratic political systems that we are accustomed to. Therefore, in the Western world of multi-party politics, where elections often result in different parties winning in different years or even coalition governments, we still consider China to be a 'one-party state'.

On top of this, there have been a number of anti-democracy crackdowns on high-profile lawyers, journalists, politicians and actors in recent years:

- **Meng Hongwei, Chinese head of Interpol** – in October 2018, Meng Hongwei was arrested and detained by the Chinese authorities. He was arrested as part of Xi Jinping's anti-corruption drive, but many Western observers have speculated that he has been detained for not toeing the party line and speaking too freely with Western media outlets.
- **Sun Wenguang** – in his eighties, Sun Wenguang, a retired professor of economics, was detained in August 2018 for speaking out against the Chinese government in a live telephone interview broadcast on Chinese TV. He has since been held under house arrest and is unable to leave his home unaccompanied. Two journalists tried to visit him and they too were detained by the Chinese authorities. This is not the first time Sun has been arrested – he was also part of the Charter 08 movement around ten years ago. At that time, he was badly beaten by Chinese authorities for pro-democracy protests.

court – it does not work independently from the Government.

In a country like China where the Constitution of the land is not upheld, and your family connections or *guanxi* can guarantee you power, corruption is rife. In 2017, the Central Commission for Discipline Inspection reported that around 1.3 million CCP officials were punished for corruption between 2013 and 2017. Xi Jinping vowed to reduce corruption within the Chinese political system and in 2018 created the National Supervision Commission (NSC). It is this organisation's job to oversee party members and whittle out corruption at all levels.

In October 2014, the CCP published a document that would use the Constitution to establish the rule of law. The document declared that 4th December would henceforth be national Constitution Day and that all party officials would swear an oath of allegiance to the Constitution. Officials 'must regard the Constitution as the fundamental guidelines of their activities'. As stated earlier, the Constitution does not offer the rights that we take for granted in the West but exists only to promote the socialist values of the people and the CCP. This move was designed to help the CCP establish the rule of law. Mr Xi wishes to strengthen the enforcement of the Constitution to root out corrupt party officials. However, some argue that his campaign against corruption was also used to remove any possible opposition to his rule.

Evidence of improving political rights

In 2016, the Chinese Government published a paper called 'New Progress in the Judicial Protection of Human Rights in China' and there have been some promising human rights improvements. In 2015, the country relaxed its controversial one-child policy and now people in China are allowed to have two children (without state permission). Also, in 2014, China announced the closure of all Laogai camps (or 're-education through labour' camps). The Laogai were a series of hard-labour camps designed as punishment for those detained for political activism and standing up against the CCP. Dismantling the Laogai system and releasing the prisoners held in the camps sent a positive human rights message worldwide. However, Amnesty International has revealed that the Laogai system is still very much in operation in the Xinjiang region (see also page 62). In September 2018, it was believed that up to 120,000 Uighur Muslims were being held and persecuted by Chinese authorities in the region; at the time of writing that number is thought to be 1 million.

There have been several high-profile protests over land seizures, internet freedom and the environmental impact of China's rapid economic growth, many of which have been permitted by the CCP. Recent cases have seen a rise in compensation being awarded to citizens from the CCP for judicial mistreatment.

The Chinese Government permits freedom of expression, such as mass demonstrations, when it suits their goals. All over China, citizens have marched in protest against Japan's actions in disputed islands. However, China finds it difficult to control spontaneous workers' protests against poor working conditions and communities protesting against the seizure of their land and property. Between 2015 and 2017 the China Labour Bulletin recorded 6694 strikes and workers' protests in the country.

1 Briefly outline the roles of the National People's Congress, State Council and the Supreme Court.
2 Explain how Village Committees are elected and what their main role is.
3 Explain why the power of Village Committees is limited by the village party secretary.
4 Who has the main power within the Chinese Government? Explain your answer.
5 Describe China's crackdown on corruption.
6 What happens to people who start up opposition parties in China? Give examples.
7 What evidence is there of improving human rights in China?

20-mark question

To what extent does the Chinese political system provide an effective check on its government?

Human rights

From a Western perspective, China appears to have very limited human rights and the strict control of the CCP dominates every aspect of people's lives. However, in recent years there has been some relaxing of the strict control the CCP has and Chinese people have been able to enjoy more social and economic freedoms. People are now allowed greater property rights, economic freedoms to start their own businesses and, on the surface, control over the internet has been reduced to allow foreign businesses to operate more effectively. Improved internet access for citizens has meant it is more difficult for the CCP to monitor freedom of expression.

The Constitution does provide a range of political and social rights but these rights can only be exercised in the interests of the socialist policies of the CCP (see page 60). While the new Chinese leaders promise a fairer legal system, the reality is completely different (see 'Yu Wensheng, human rights lawyer'). In its 'Freedom in the World Report 2017', Freedom House, an organisation that supports the growth of democracy around the world, reported that China was one of the poorest countries in the world for freedom of expression and political rights. Where 0 is worst and 100 is best, China had a score of 15. The UK had a score of 95.

Yu Wensheng, human rights lawyer

Human rights lawyer Yu Wensheng was arrested in January 2018 on his way to drop off his son at school. A SWAT (special weapons and tactics) team of several police officers detained Mr Yu and he has been formally charged with 'inciting subversion of state power' and 'obstructing official duties'. Yu was one of several lawyers who tried to sue the Chinese Government in 2016 over pollution and environmental damage. He has also represented many Chinese citizens in high-profile human rights cases against the Government. His arrest came after he wrote an open letter to the Chinese Government asking them to consider political reforms (including legitimate elections at a national level and human rights updates to the Chinese Constitution). He has also had his licence to practise law revoked. Many human rights organisations have condemned the detention of Yu Wensheng and there are fears for his safety and mental health.

Political rights

According to Article 35 of the Chinese Constitution, citizens have the right to 'freedom of speech, of the press, of assembly, of association, of procession and of demonstration'. On top of this, people can do the following:

- Vote in the Local Peoples' Congress and village elections. Candidates must be approved by the CCP.
- Submit petitions to the Chinese Government. In 2013, China launched a new online website that accepts e-petitions. People can submit petitions, but they must also provide their full name, address and passport number and many people are worried that anyone submitting petitions will then be monitored by the Government. Although this was initially successful, the number of petitions brought before the government in 2017 had fallen by 25 per cent amid fear of repercussions from the CCP.
- Hold protests/demonstrations with the permission of the Government.
- Join the CCP. People have to apply and be recommended by members of the CCP. There are now around 98 million members of the CCP (7 per cent of the population) and 12 per cent of those who applied to join were accepted in 2017.

Internet freedom

China has the world's largest population of internet users, around 802 million in 2018, who are based mainly in urban areas. Many academics have noted that the rapid growth of the internet in China has led to groups of like-minded people forming blogs, online forums and social networking groups to share political opinions, facts and complaints about the Government and CCP officials. People can now freely post political viewpoints and protests about the CCP, sometimes anonymously, and the Government in China is extremely concerned about the increase of 'cyber-democracy' and the calls for more political opposition in China. As a result, the CCP has introduced extreme methods of censorship to prevent loss of government control. Although anyone in China can use the internet, with the idea being that the internet can stimulate economic growth and strengthen communication for businesses, individual citizens are subject to scrutiny and website restrictions. The 'Great Firewall of China' is used to block Chinese citizens from accessing Western news websites like the BBC, human rights organisations like Amnesty International and even information on sexually transmitted infections (STIs) and HIV/AIDS. The Government employs a large number of workers to monitor the internet and remove 'sensitive' political content; it also encourages self-censorship by issuing rules for internet users and even employs bloggers to blog favourably about the CCP on high-profile websites.

Internet censorship is a very complex issue. Although there are some signs of decreasing government control, with websites such as Facebook and Twitter being unblocked in the Free Trade Zone in Shanghai, overall the internet is still heavily monitored and vetted. Revisions to the 2017 Cybersecurity Law are expected to remove anonymity for internet users by the end of 2019. It outlines proposals for tougher censorship and higher fines for internet service providers who do not abide by CCP regulations.

#MeToo movement

The international #MeToo movement has been trending on Twitter since 2018. This hashtag has been used to highlight the issue of sexual assault and harassment in many industries. The #MeToo movement has been gaining speed in China, with many high-powered celebrities, politicians and academics being accused of sexually inappropriate behaviour. However, the Chinese authorities have been trying to prevent this protest from gaining political power online. The CCP censors the internet for any sexual-related content and this political movement, which highlights sexual violations and abuse of power, makes many government officials uncomfortable. The CCP sees this movement as an anti-establishment movement and therefore is keen to shut it down. It has taken steps to do this by monitoring what Chinese citizens can access in terms of Western news websites and social media platforms such as Weibo.

Freedom of religion

According to Amnesty International, many religious groups face huge discrimination in China, if not persecution. Although Article 36 of China's Constitution says that Chinese citizens should have freedom to practise whatever religion they choose, this is not the case. The Government has increasingly cracked down on religion in recent years and especially since 2018. New Regulations for Religious Affairs were implemented in February 2017 under the premise of protecting the freedom of religious belief. The regulations put in place strict rules for religious organisations and prevent minors from entering religious places in several provinces in the country.

Christians

Religions like Christianity are permitted by the Government, but they are confined by very strict monitoring and regulations. In Chairman Mao's era, religion was totally banned by the state, but since the 1980s it has once again been allowed. However, the official religious stance of the CCP is atheism and people who practise different religions are often persecuted by the state. This religious crackdown has worsened in recent years. CCP government officials are concerned about the rapid growth of Christianity within China and have shut down many churches as they are 'illegal buildings'. New places of worship must be registered with the Government, and people may not practise their religion in the streets in any form of demonstration. Since 2017, many Christian churches in the Henan Province have been raided, and their worshippers and praise leaders have been beaten and arrested. CCP officials have said that Christianity is spreading through the country too rapidly and must be controlled by the state (see Table 2.1). China's new 'Religious Affairs Regulations' (2017) are supposed to provide people with the right to practise whichever religion they want, however the raids in Henan province show that the CCP continues to see organised religion and assembly as a threat to the state.

Table 2.1 **Christians in China**

Year	Christians (millions)
1950	3
1980	4
1995	15
2018	67
2020 (estimated)	72

Source: Pew-Templeton Global Religious Futures Project, Pew Research Center

Tibet

Tibet is an autonomous region of China, although many believe it should be an independent state. The Chinese Government clearly sees Tibet as part of China and says that it is ruled by Beijing. However, many Tibetans believe that it should be a separate nation and seek independence for Tibet. This has led to several bloody uprisings between Tibetans and the Chinese authorities. In 2017, the Chinese Government began to attack the Larung Gar, Tibet's largest Buddhist academy, by evicting 20,000 monks from their homes. The number of Buddhist monks at the centre has fallen from 12,000 to 5000. It is estimated that, since 2009, 150 Tibetans have set themselves on fire (self-immolation) in protest against Chinese rule. While the Dalai Lama, Tibet's exiled leader, does not encourage these acts, he has openly praised the courage of those involved for making the ultimate sacrifice for their cause. Xi Jinping has called these acts of self-immolation 'terrorist actions'.

Security in Tibet's capital is intense – security personnel are everywhere and surveillance cameras monitor its citizens' every movement.

Figure 2.6 **Buddhist monks protesting against Chinese rule of Tibet**

The Tibetan people are denied their cultural identity and the Chinese occupiers control all stations of influence – the political leaders are all Chinese and Tibetans are not even allowed to display pictures of their religious leader, the Dalai Lama. Foreign journalists are not allowed to visit Tibet to report on the plight of the Tibetan people.

Xinjiang

Xinjiang is another autonomous region where there is strong opposition to Chinese rule. The Uighurs, who are Muslim and live in Xinjiang, feel that their culture is being slowly destroyed by the Chinese Government. Mass immigration of millions of Chinese citizens to the region has taken place and the Han Chinese now account for over 40 per cent of the population and dominate urban communities. Xinjiang has been under Chinese control since 1949 (similar to Tibet).

In 2017, the CCP argued that Muslims in the Xinjiang region were 'extremists' and therefore there needed to be a crackdown on people practising Islam. Criminal arrests in Xinjiang accounted for 21 per cent of China's total criminal arrests in 2017. As of 2018 an estimated 120,000 Uighurs are currently thought to be detained in Chinese Laogai labour camps. These camps have been condemned by the international community because of the reported torture and abuse of Muslims being detained there. However, the Chinese Government has described them as 'transformation camps' offering job opportunities and educational courses.

Figure 2.7 **The Xinjiang region of China**

Show your understanding

1 Briefly explain the political rights that people in China have.
2 Explain how internet use in China is restricted and how it is monitored and influenced by the Chinese Government.
3 Are people in China free to practise their religion? Explain with examples.
4 Why have there been violent uprisings in Tibet?

Women's rights

As part of the UN's Sustainable Development Goals, countries around the world are supposed to be committed to the promotion of equal gender rights. However, in 2017, the World Economic Forum ranked China 100th out of 144 countries for gender equality and the empowerment of women and girls. This is based on several key issues. Firstly, there is a severe lack of women at the top of the CCP and women are very poorly represented in politics. Secondly, China is still one of the worst countries in the world for protection of women's rights when it comes to sexual violence and domestic abuse; many women who have spoken out against their husbands for sexual abuse have been arrested.

Death penalty

The Supreme People's Court decides on death penalty cases in China. However, it is very difficult to know how widespread executions are in the country, as no official figures are ever

Case study: Wu Rongrong

Wu Rongrong is passionately committed to standing up for women's rights in China. Between 2013 and 2014, she walked nearly 2000 km to highlight sexual abuse on university campuses. In 2015, Wu was part of the 'feminist five' women's rights group who protested against sexual harassment in the workplace and on public transport. She set up an online crowdfunding campaign in order to secure funds for her campaign. She was handing out leaflets and stickers when she and the other four women were arrested and detained. They were charged with 'picking quarrels and provoking trouble'. Although Wu was released shortly afterwards, she has been banned from leaving the country for a decade. She has also been banned from attending university. Wu is currently creating a series of campaign videos highlighting sexual violence, which she intends to upload to a new Weibo account.

Figure 2.8 #MeToo protest held in Hong Kong

published by the Government. Many prisoners are sentenced to death with little or no legal representation and there is a minute chance of appeal. Although there were only 85 executions recorded by the state in 2014–17, Amnesty International has estimated that China executes more people than the rest of the death penalty states combined and that the real figure is in the thousands every year. A total of 46 crimes are punishable by the death penalty in China, including robbery, fraud and selling state secrets.

There have, however, been small improvements to China's death penalty usage. Death penalty sentences are now reviewed by the Supreme People's Court and 10 per cent of these have been overturned in favour of life sentences. Also, the number of crimes that carry the death penalty was reduced from 55 in 2013 to 46 in 2017, with most economic crimes being removed from the list. Pregnant women, those under the age of 18 and those over the age of 75 at the start of their trial are also not meant to face the death penalty.

Human rights defenders

Throughout China those who try to stand up to the Government, even in the smallest of ways, are often persecuted, tortured, imprisoned without trial or sent to Laojiao camps ('re-education' camps, where people can be held for four years without trial). In recent years, there have been a number of high-profile cases of human rights defenders in China

Case study: Human rights defenders

Workers' strikes

In July 2018, 14 workers were arrested for their part in a general strike at the Jasic Technology factory in Shenzhen. Many workers were beaten and sacked for demanding better pay and working conditions. The resulting protest was supported by many students, a number of whom were also detained and held under house arrest for standing up for those who had lost their jobs. The 14 workers have been detained indefinitely and their whereabouts have not been revealed.

Figure 2.9 Strike action in Hong Kong

Qin Yongmin

Qin Yongmin has been a human rights advocate in China for the last 30 years. In July 2018, Qin Yongmin was sentenced to 13 years in prison for 'subversion of state power'. However, this is not the first time the human rights defender has been arrested for standing up for increased political transparency and fairness. Qin's trial has been condemned by the international community as illegal; Qin was given no right to speak at his trial and he was given no legal representation. Although he fainted during the trial, it continued with him unconscious in the same room. His family were not even allowed to attend his trial and the charges against him were not allowed to be covered by the media.

who have come to the attention of international human rights organisations and the media.

China's one-child policy

During the 1970s, the Government was concerned about China's massive population growth rate and as a result introduced the one-child policy in 1979. This policy aimed to curb population growth, which was causing a strain on feeding and educating the country. In many areas of China, the policy limited married couples to having only one child, although there were some exceptions: for example, families in rural China were allowed to have a second child if their firstborn was a female. This policy is thought to have prevented the birth of around 400 million extra children since its implementation.

China was previously criticised for its harsh family planning laws and forced abortions and sterilisations. However, the Chinese Government has now relaxed its one-child policy. Since 2014, people in China are allowed to have two children providing they meet certain criteria. In order to be permitted to have two children, both potential parents must come from one-child families. The law has been relaxed in order to boost the number of younger people in China and to counteract the social and economic pressures put on the country by its large elderly population. In August 2018, the CCP announced that they were looking at relaxing the policy even further by removing any limit on the number of children people are allowed to have. However, there are a lot of families who still only wish to have one child; after a few generations of the one-child policy, having one child has become a cultural norm in some areas.

Figure 2.10 **A single-child Chinese family**

> ## Show your understanding
>
> 1 Explain the situation regarding women's rights in China.
> 2 What is likely to happen to someone who defends their human rights in China? Explain with examples.
> 3 Briefly outline the one-child policy. In what ways has this been relaxed in recent years?

China's economy

China's economic past

Economically, from 1949 to 1976, China was identified as a traditional communist country, where farmers worked under a commune system overseen by China's ruler, Chairman Mao. Under this system, farmers were told what they could grow and how much, and they were not allowed to sell any of the surplus food they grew to make profits. This system severely limited food production and both individual wealth and economic growth. In the 1980s, the system was overhauled when Chinese leader Deng Xiaoping introduced agricultural reforms that allowed farmers greater economic freedom. Deng stated that 'to get rich is glorious', which was an unfamiliar concept in a traditionally communist economy. People became wealthier, businesses were privatised and food production increased. Deng Xiaoping opened up China to trading with the West through the Open Door Policy, and an economically backward China began to take advantage of the world market. It also joined the World Trade Organization in 2001.

China's economy today

Today, China is one of the richest countries in the world with the second largest economy (behind the USA). In 2014, China overtook the USA to become the world's largest trading nation. Economically, China describes itself as a capitalist system with Chinese characteristics, with a modern market economy rather than its traditional state-planned economy. There are now thought to be around 2 million multi-millionaires in China, with around two billionaires being created every week. Many Chinese people have amassed huge wealth and purchase many luxury goods because of their high disposable incomes. China has become wealthy in recent years because of its massive economic growth.

Figure 2.12 clearly indicates the significant rise in individual wealth. (The purchasing power of a currency refers to the amount of one currency needed to buy a good or goods and services. Purchasing power depends on the relative cost of living and inflation rates in different countries. *Parity* means equalising the purchasing power of two currencies considering these differences in cost of living and inflation.)

Figure 2.11 **Deng Xiaoping**

Fact file

China's wealth

- The China Private Wealth Report (2018) shows that there are nine times more extremely rich people in China now than a decade ago.
- In 2016, 1.6 million people in China were earning more than 10 million yuan annually (around £1.2 million), a number that is expected to continue to rise.
- In 2018, the Hurun Global Rich List named Beijing as the 'billionaire capital of the world'. There are thought to be 131 billionaires living in Beijing alone (compared to the city with the second highest number, New York, with 92 billionaires).
- In total, there are 819 billionaires in China.
- The wealthiest man in China is Ma Huateng, with an estimated worth of $47 billion (£37 billion).

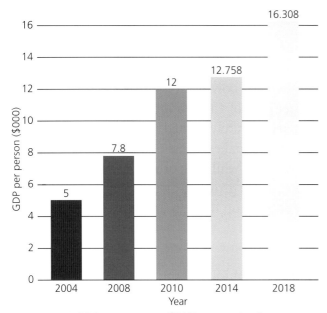

Figure 2.12 **GDP per person ($000) at purchasing power parity**

Source: https://tradingeconomics.com/china/gdp-per-capita-ppp?

China's Special Economic Zones (SEZs)

A Special Economic Zone is an area in which **foreign direct investment** is encouraged. Companies from all around the world were initially encouraged to set up businesses in SEZs because of their close proximity to the economically valuable Hong Kong, and because companies were offered low tax rates, cheap labour and reduced building costs. The first SEZs in China were set up in 1979 in Shenzhen, Shantou and Zhuhai (all in Guangdong Province) and Xiamen (in Fujian Province). Since their introduction in China, they have been seen as pockets of capitalism within an otherwise communist–socialist state. Trading regulations and government control within these areas have been relaxed to allow Westernised companies to function in a capitalist manner. Economic growth within these areas has been revolutionary; Shenzhen, a fishing village of 30,000 people 35 years ago, now has a population of 13 million people. It is the largest

Foreign direct investment

Foreign direct investment can be simply defined as a company investing money or setting up premises in a different country from where the company is based. In recent years, many British and US firms have set up in China's Special Economic Zones. Foreign direct investment in China for 2019 is 478.3 billion yuan or $70.4 billion.

Figure 2.13 **Shenzhen: China's first SEZ**

manufacturing base in the world and home of China's international stock market. Over the last five years, the GDP of Shenzhen has increased by nearly 80 per cent. In 2018, it overtook that of Hong Kong to reach $354 billion.

World leader in technology

China is now seen as the world leader in technology. Nearly all of Apple's iPhones are made in China. Areas of China such as the city of Shenzhen have been dubbed China's 'Silicon Valley' because of their role in global technological innovation. Shenzhen's technology sector, mainly dealing with the manufacturing of items like phones and tablets, has seen its GDP increase three times as fast as that of the real Silicon Valley (in San Jose, California).

Figure 2.14 **The location of Shenzhen in China**

Fact file

China's technology and innovation

- Much of China's wealth comes from its natural resources and mining. In 2017, China was the largest producer of steel (50 per cent of the world's steel) and it also has massive reserves of coal and iron.
- China produced 30 per cent of the world's cars in 2017 – around 25 million cars.
- China's new main industries are in telecommunications, coal, steel and ICT. It is fast becoming the technology centre of the world.

Agriculture

China is responsible for 22 per cent of the world's food production despite the fact it only has 7 per cent of the world's farmland. China's agricultural system faces many challenges; it has to feed the largest population in the world (1.415 billion people). Agricultural trade has increased since China joined the World Trade Organization in 2001. In 2018, China produced 39 per cent of the world's fruit and vegetables and 30 per cent of the world's rice.

Industry

In the past, businesses in China would have been predominantly state-owned enterprises (SOEs), but now most are privately run. Today, 33 per cent of China's industries are SOEs; the rest are privately owned. China's agricultural workforce makes up 28 per cent of the population, while the urban workforce is increasingly growing. In 2017, 57 per cent of the population lived in urban areas of China.

Income

As a result of joining the World Trade Organization, and through foreign direct investment, much of China's urban population has been able to gain well-paid jobs and average income in China has risen by 500 per cent since 2001 (Forbes.com). Disposable income rose 9 per cent from 2016 to 2017. China is not only producing technological and luxury goods for export; there is now an increasing internal market for these products and many Chinese people are purchasing top-of-the-range cars, appliances and designer clothing. The rise of capitalism in a previously communist country means that many Chinese people within urban areas have large disposable incomes and there is a growing trend for Western fashion, food and television. This has benefited the UK; China bought one-quarter of the UK's Bentley cars in 2017 as the demand for luxury items, and middle-class affluence, in China increased.

Challenges facing China's economy

China's rapid economic growth and huge manufacturing output has had a massive effect on both China's people and its environment. China is now facing a number of economic challenges.

Environmental damage

China is home to seven of the top 30 most polluted cities in the world. In these cities, smog and fumes from factories are often so bad that people wear face masks, and the Chinese Government has taken to broadcasting the sunrise and sunset on large television screens in areas like Tiananmen Square because the air quality is so poor the sun cannot be seen through polluted skies. In the cities, air pollution is killing an estimated 1 million citizens per year. In rural areas, the opening of new factories, as cities expand, has led to chemicals and toxic by-products being released into rivers, killing wildlife and poisoning farms and crops. This has resulted in over 50,000 protests about environmental issues in China, demonstrating how concerned Chinese people are becoming about environmental damage. In 2017, China was responsible for 26 per cent of the world's greenhouse gas emissions; an increase of 20 per cent since the 1990s.

Figure 2.15 **Smog is a problem in many Chinese cities**

Migration

Over the last 30 years, 300 million Chinese people have moved from rural areas of China to the cities in the south-east of the country. In 2018, 57 per cent of China's population lived in the cities. This is set to rise to 68 per cent by 2050. Unequal economic development has driven people from rural areas, which tend to be associated with poverty, fewer job opportunities and lower-quality education, to cities where many job opportunities exist. Chinese people are now keen to get their share of wealth, and the capitalist economy has encouraged many to move to the cities in the hope of a better life. Many parents from rural areas have moved to cities thousands of miles away, to earn a decent wage to send back to their children at home, who often live with their grandparents. This 'floating' workforce contributes hugely to the success of China's economy, but this mass migration is not without its issues. It is estimated that this 'floating population' will be made up of 310 million people by 2030. Many families are separated, with children only seeing their parents a few times a year. In addition, this large-scale migration to certain areas has caused pockets of unemployment where there are often more people in a city than jobs available and also a lack of affordable housing.

Show your understanding

1 Briefly explain China's movement from communism to 'capitalism with Chinese characteristics'.
2 What evidence is there to show that China's economy is growing rapidly? Why is China becoming so wealthy?
3 What is a Special Economic Zone? Outline its main features.
4 What has happened to make China's urban population richer?
5 Briefly outline the main challenges facing China's economy.

Social and economic inequality

Although China's average economic growth rate has been no less than 7 per cent per annum in the last 25 years, wealth distribution is extremely unequal, and economic and social progress throughout the country is varied. Indeed, the poorest 25 per cent of the population own just 4 per cent of the country's wealth. In urban areas, there is a large emerging middle class of consumers who aspire to buy the latest technological goods, luxury items and status symbols.

This rapid rise of affluence, however, has been very much an urban phenomenon; people in the countryside have a relatively low average income, which is only around a quarter of the average urban income. This is reportedly the largest gap in urban–rural incomes since 1978, meaning that, although China's economy is growing rapidly, this is not benefiting China's citizens equally. In 2018, China had the highest level of social and economic inequality in the world. Many believe that the Chinese Government must do more to tackle rising inequalities in China. However, the Chinese Government has been making some headway in reducing social inequalities; in 2016 the 'Report on Sustainable Financing for Poverty Alleviation in China' revealed that Chinese Government policies helped to lift 68 million people out of rural poverty over the previous five years.

Employment and income

The average income in China is now 74,318 yuan (£8162) a year. However, according to Chinese Government figures there are now over 100 million rural poor in China who earn on average 2300 yuan (£225) a year, although the actual number of rural poor is thought to be more. Many academics argue that this is due to the Government's over-development of China's east coast in places like Beijing and Shanghai, while largely neglecting to build and develop inner, rural China. However, the Chinese Government has pledged to lift all people out of rural poverty by 2020 and, as reported in *China Daily*, has 'allocated about $334 million of its

welfare lottery fund for most poverty-stricken provincial areas, accounting for 80 per cent of the total allocated amount in 2018'. The rural–urban difference is also due to different types of employment in the two areas of China: rural areas are associated with poorer paid jobs like farming and mining, while urban jobs are often well paid by comparison and in technologically advanced petrochemical or service industries such as finance, insurance and banking. Although the overall unemployment rate (according to the Chinese Government) is a very low 4 per cent, this is not the case in all areas. According to China's National Bureau of Statistics (NBS), urban unemployment in March 2019 was around 5.3 per cent. The CCP has been accused of covering up the true unemployment figures in rural areas, which are seen as tarnishing China's economic growth.

Rural to urban migration

Lack of job opportunities and the low pay that residents in rural China now face have pushed many people to migrate to urban areas, especially to Special Economic Zones (SEZs). Villagers can see that urban life offers them many luxuries compared with rural life and they now want to achieve the 'Chinese Dream'. Many of these people are seen as China's 'floating population' because they have migrated illegally without permission from the Government, ignoring the Hukou system (household registration required by law, identifying people as resident in a particular area). In 2018, there were an estimated 288 million rural migrant workers in China. This problem is expected to worsen over the next three decades, when it is estimated that another 310 million people will move to urban areas to live and work. Many migrant workers live in the cities, leaving their children behind to live with grandparents in the countryside and sending home money to better their lives. However, according to Li Ben, the current Head of the National Population and

Family Planning Commission, 60 per cent of those moving to the cities to work are now moving their children with them, exacerbating the lack of housing and schools in some urban areas.

China's middle class

China's rapid growth in GDP from just 1.1 trillion in 2001 to 12 trillion in 2018 has led to a marked increase in China's middle-class population. Relaxed government ties over business ownership and state intervention, and taxation incentives, have allowed Chinese people to start their own businesses, many of which have flourished in China's increasingly capitalist economy. Private businesses in China now contribute 60 per cent of China's GDP. The Chinese middle classes are characterised as having a high level of disposable income, professional careers and a university-level education, and they are mass consumers. In 2017, 70 per cent of urban residents in Shanghai were classified as middle class and their drive to have

the latest products has led to a rapidly expanding internal market for luxury goods. China's initial economic growth resulted from large levels of production of relatively cheap goods and technological goods for export. However, there is now a huge market within China itself for the latest goods: internal consumer spending now makes up around 40 per cent of China's economy.

Figure 2.16 **Enjoying the good life**

Case study: Identifying China's middle class

In 2018, the average middle-class family in China had around $6000 disposable income a year. The middle class can be identified as people who send their children to private schools, own their own homes (often fashionable apartments in the city), own cars and take up to two holidays a year. These people often have a very different lifestyle from their parents, who would have had very little income, basic food and shelter and no luxuries. Nowadays, China's middle classes can afford tablet computers, top-of-the-range mobile phones and designer clothes, and they are influenced by Western fashion trends and fast food. In China today, 4000 cars are sold every hour and there is a Starbucks coffeehouse opening on average every 15 hours.

Show your understanding

1 What are the main reasons given for differences in wealth between urban and rural areas of China?
2 Explain why many people from rural areas move to the cities.
3 What has happened in China to allow many people to own their own businesses?
4 Explain in your own words the main characteristics of China's middle class.

Health care

Organising the health-care system for a country with a population of 1.415 billion people brings many challenges. Health care in China is not universal in the way it is in the UK; it works through a combined insurance scheme of both individual and employer-based contributions. Although there is basic state health insurance, many Chinese people have to pay medical bills for things that are not covered and there are often out-of-pocket expenses. Structurally, the health-care system is run by the National Health and Family Planning Commission, which has a Bureau of Health in each province. Where health care has to be paid for through insurance, there are inherent inequalities, with those who are well off receiving better care than those living in poverty. Those who can afford to pay for private care often experience shorter waiting lists and better-quality treatment, leading to a two-tier system in terms of the quality of care received.

Patients in China still have to pay directly for around a third of their health care and this can lead to great inequalities between those who can afford to pay and those who cannot. Once a patient is admitted to hospital, their public insurance will pay for around half of all treatment they receive, but this is a far cry from a universal health-care system. As some doctors receive payments from drug companies, they sometimes over-prescribe medicines that patients do not need in order to increase their incomes. In 2019, however, the *British Medical Journal* reported that reforms to the health-care system mean there is now less of an incentive to do this.

China's health problems

Health concerns in China are now beginning to mirror problems in the West; as lifestyles change, so do the types of health problems that a country faces. China's improving access to health care since the 1980s has led to reduced infant and maternal mortality rates, and the country suffers less from curable diseases and conditions such as diarrhoea and pneumonia. However, China's increasingly Westernised lifestyles have created other health problems such as obesity, high smoking rates and alcohol addiction. Because families still have to pay large medical bills for treatment, despite having some of the costs covered by insurance, many mental health issues also go untreated and are often largely ignored.

Government health reforms

As part of China's health reforms, the Ministry of Health published the 'Healthy China 2020' strategy, which set out ten health targets that China was to achieve by 2020. These included raising life expectancy, reducing infant mortality rates and providing basic universal health care to all. It is thought that, by 2020, health spending will account for 7 per cent of the country's GDP – amounting to a total spending of $1 trillion. The strategy has had some success: in 2017, the National Health and Family Planning Commission announced that approximately 95 per cent of the Chinese population now have access to basic state-provided health care. There has been a massive reduction in infant mortality rates in China (from 12 deaths per 1000 live births in 2012, to 8 deaths per 1000 in 2015) and average life expectancy is currently at 76 years. China's health-care system went from being ranked 144th in the world in 2013, to 92nd in 2018. Environmental monitoring has reported a reduction in heavily polluted days from 58 in 2003 to 23 in 2017. However, there are still vast inequalities in health care. In the region of Hong Kong, health care is ranked 7th in the world – there are 11 private and 42 state-run hospitals for a population of around 7 million people. An increase in wealth and standards of living is now pushing the Government to do more about improving health care provision and so it recently launched

Fact file

China's health problems

Smoking

Smoking is a huge health issue in China, and it is very gender specific. According to the World Health Organization (WHO), in 2018, only 3 per cent of women in China smoked compared to a staggering 55 per cent of men. This huge difference is thought to be because of the culture within the country that it is socially unacceptable for women to smoke and also due to women's often lower socio-economic status. Today, China is home to around 38 per cent of the world's smoking population, with over 300 million smokers. To tackle this, the Chinese Government introduced a ban on smoking in government buildings, restaurants and hospitals in 2015. Those who break the law face fines of 200 yuan and repeat offenders have their names displayed on government websites. Shops within 100 metres of primary schools are now no longer allowed to sell cigarettes.

Obesity

The rise in disposable incomes for many Chinese people, combined with less exercise, has led to a huge increase in obesity levels which have doubled in the last 35 years. This is a staggering contrast in a country where, 50 years ago, 45 million people died of hunger in the Maoist famines. This rapid change in China reflects developments already seen in countries like the UK and the USA. More and more people are now buying cars when the previously favoured mode of transport was bicycles, and there are now thousands of Western and American fast-food chains in China. Increasingly fatty diets have led to a huge rise in health problems such as type 2 diabetes (affecting 92 million people), heart disease and high blood pressure. In 2018, the WHO reported that China now has the highest rates of type 2 diabetes in the world: almost 10 per cent of the adult population has the condition.

Figure 2.17 China has seen increasing levels of obesity in recent years

the 'Healthy China 2030' plan. This ambitious plan, which contains 169 targets, aims to raise life expectancy by another three years (from 76 to 79 years) by 2030. It also aims to reduce air pollution (and the associated public health risk) further and increase the number of doctors available. In 2018 there was one doctor per 6666 people in China – far behind provision in the UK where there is one doctor per 1500–2000 people.

Infant mortality rates are expected to reduce further, from 8 per 1000 live births in 2015 to 5 per 1000 in 2030, and the programme aims to reduce premature death rates, caused by poor lifestyle choices such as smoking and poor diet, by 30 per cent by 2030.

Show your understanding

1 Briefly describe how health care is paid for in China.
2 Explain some of China's main health problems and why they are occurring.
3 What evidence is there that the Healthy China 2020 programme has led to some health improvements?
4 Outline the main aims of the Healthy China 2030 programme.

Education

Figure 2.18 **Students in Shanghai Gezhi High School, Shanghai**

China's education system is often renowned as being the best in the world, with the Programme for International Student Assessment (PISA) ranking China as first in the world for maths and seventh for science teaching. China has the largest network of universities in the world and educational expectations are extremely high. However, it is a deeply unequal system that is based on location, wealth and postcode-lottery-style funding. In China, children are required to undergo nine years of mandatory education, but this does not always happen and children from rural areas often receive sub-standard education. For example, although 84 per cent of teenagers in Shanghai city go on to university, only 5 per cent of children from rural areas do. Overall, while 80 per cent of urban students graduate from high school, only 20 per cent of rural students do. This large disparity is caused by poorer funding in rural schools, fewer resources and poor standards of teaching. Also, China has highly competitive entrance exams for high school, and children from poorer rural areas tend to do less well in these tests, because of proven links between poverty and poor educational attainment. Many children from rural areas drop out of school to support their families financially or to work the land. Research by REAP (Rural Education Action Program) has shown that teachers in rural areas are given fewer training opportunities and fewer resources and it is estimated that around another 300,000 establishments would be needed in rural areas to meet the demand for high-quality pre-school education. In contrast, some of the most expensive private schools in the world are in Beijing; the most expensive school, the BISS International school, costs around 300,000 yuan ($48,330) a year per child. In 2018, the State Council recognised the need to improve rural education and released guidelines for improvement.

Challenges facing Chinese education

Although China's education system is ranked by the OECD (Organisation for Economic Co-operation and Development) as one of the best in the world, it is not without flaws. Many people are critical of the system because of the pressure it puts on students; admission to the best schools and universities means passing extremely difficult entrance exams or *Gaokao*. These *Gaokao* exams have been reported to last up to nine hours for some institutions and there have been a number of high-profile suicides in China in recent years due to the pressure of these exams.

Also, schools receive funding based on their performance, and teachers in rural schools are often paid half of what teachers in top performing urban schools receive. Educational experiences for students across China vary enormously and, although literacy rates for the country have dramatically improved, huge disparities in educational opportunity, quality of schools and teachers remain.

There are also stark inequalities for migrant children. The 2016 OECD report 'Education in China: a snapshot' revealed that 15 per cent of migrant children are no longer in schools by the time they are 13, leading to a major lack of opportunities for children of these families. A report into education for migrant children by REAP (Rural Education Action Program) found that, although urban schools are mostly rated 'good' and rural schools are rated 'improving', schools that are designed for migrant children in urban areas are rated as 'poor' in terms of teachers, curriculum and resources.

Concern has been raised about the growing wealth division of students in China's elite universities. In the 1970s, at Tsinghua University in Beijing, where President Xi studied, there were equal numbers of first-year students from poorer rural areas and wealthier urban areas. In 2018, only 16 per cent of the first-year intake was from poorer rural areas.

However, there have been some educational improvements, thanks to the Education 2020 programme; for example, illiteracy rates have dropped from 6.7 per cent in 2000 to 4 per cent in 2015. Also, better training programmes and pay for rural teachers are encouraging staff in rural areas to stay in their teaching positions and this is improving educational standards. In 2019, the Ministry of Education reported that 542.6 billion yuan ($81 billion) had been invested in school buildings and resources from 2013 to 2018.

Government educational reform

China's educational system is undergoing swift reform. As the economy rapidly advances, China needs a workforce with technological, economic and scientific expertise and the Government recognises this, stating it now needs a country that is 'rich in human resources'. In 2018, the national media in China started to talk about an 'AI (Artificial Intelligence) Arms Race', which involves China wanting to develop its technological skills to be the best in the world and beat the USA on its AI technology. The 2030 Education Plan wants to see Chinese children developing the skills to grow an Artificial Intelligence sector worth $150 billion by 2030.

The 2030 Education Plan has several aims to improve education; to improve access to early years education, to create more vocational education opportunities and increase educational access for students with disabilities. The plan aims to increase compulsory schooling from 9 to 12 years and ensure that there are 1 million new vocational apprenticeships every year. It also puts the focus on improving education in rural areas, with Xi Jinping stating that better access to quality education is the number one way for Chinese families to be lifted out of poverty.

Housing

Standards of housing across China vary enormously, with many of those in rural areas suffering from poorer housing and reduced access to water, electricity and sanitation. In contrast, those living in the city often live in nice apartments with many amenities and modern appliances. However, with China's rapid urbanisation, the boundaries between urban and rural areas have begun to blur and this has led to the creation of many urban villages (see Case study on page 76); (see Case study on page 76) these are areas that would have been considered to be countryside 20 years ago, but have now been engulfed by urban development from all sides, making them slums within the cities themselves. This has led to a reduction of farmland for farmers whose land has now been filled with skyscrapers and apartment blocks. Inhabitants of these slum areas often live in appalling conditions, with roadways so narrow they cause major fire hazards.

The types of housing in China have also changed. In the Maoist socialist era, most people lived in work units provided by the Government. However, nowadays in capitalist China there is a scramble over luxury, privately owned housing in cities like Beijing and Shanghai for the wealthiest and dilapidated shared housing for the less fortunate.

Show your understanding

1 Create a table with two columns showing the current positives and negatives of China's education system.
2 Describe the differences in the quality of education that students receive between rural and urban areas.
3 What evidence is there that the Education 2020 plan has led to some educational improvements?
4 Explain how the Chinese Government wants to improve the education system. Mention the aims of the 2030 Education Plan.

Case study: Urban villages – China's poor

Many people in China now live in what are defined as 'urban villages'; areas that used to be rural until cities were built around them and the rural village itself became a slum part of an otherwise modern city. People living in these areas often suffer from some of the worst housing in China, although it has slowly improved in recent years. Many academics have noted that the urban villages have become areas for local gangs and criminals to work from and that they are now becoming home to mass numbers of China's floating population, as housing can be acquired cheaply. However, these areas still house some of China's poorest workers. People living in these areas tend to have very low incomes or none at all, and they often rely solely on renting spare rooms of their properties to migrant workers. There are estimated to be 1044 urban villages in Shenzhen. In August 2018, thousands of residents of one urban village in Shenzhen were forcibly evicted to make room for new housing development projects. Around 133 informal shops were torn down and it is thought that renovating these areas will plunge tens of thousands of people into further poverty, as they will not be able to afford the rent in the resulting new housing developments.

Case study: China's wealthy

In comparison to those living in urban villages, China's wealthy live in unlimited opulence. Many luxurious apartments and penthouses have sprung up rapidly in desirable areas such as Shanghai to house the city's 'super-rich': 200,000 millionaires. Many of these apartments take up whole floors of skyscrapers, have fantastic views of the city and come with a multi-million pound price tag, not to mention the butlers, cleaners and chefs hired to cater for the needs of their owners. This capitalist phenomenon is a far cry from life in Mao's time in the 1950s, when communism meant that normal Chinese people could not accumulate this level of wealth for themselves. In 2017, the Hurun Research Institute found that China's housing prices are the fastest growing in the world.

Housing problems

China's urban revolution and mass migration has caused several problems in its housing market. Like many other developed countries in the world, house prices have soared and this makes it hard for some first-time buyers to afford property in the cities. China now has seven of the world's top ten most expensive cities for housing. In June 2017, 400 people were discovered to be living in the basement of a high-rise building in Beijing. One family had even occupied an old air raid shelter in order to find somewhere to live affordably in the city. A report by the Global Cities Business Alliance in 2016 found that monthly accommodation rates in the city were approximately 1.2 times the average monthly wage, which explains why many people working in Beijing cannot afford to live to an adequate standard in the city.

However, a study by HSBC in 2017 found that home ownership levels in China are still high, with 70 per cent of millennials owning their own homes in China compared to just 31 per cent of millennials in the UK.

There has also been a rise in people occupying 'micro-apartments', where people cook, eat, entertain and sleep in one room. There are often shared toilets on the landing.

Government housing reforms

The 12th Five-Year Plan (2011–15) outlined the Government's need to tackle the housing crisis by providing 36 million more affordable homes in urban areas where most property was privately owned. Projects were also trialled in areas of Beijing where more affordable housing was being introduced by capping the sale price of certain properties and ensuring the availability of more affordable rental properties for migrant workers. Around 41 million new affordable homes were built across the five-year period. The 13th Five-Year Plan that began in 2016 introduced new targets, which included building even more affordable housing in key cities, removing 20 million shanty town houses by 2020 and encouraging a policy of 'urbanisation with Chinese characteristics'. This policy involves attracting highly skilled workers to cities who can contribute to the urban economy and enables over 100 million urban

residents to obtain an urban Hukou (see page 70). This, the Chinese Government has argued, would lead to a reduction in urban villages but the evidence from Shenzhen (see Case study: Urban villages – China's poor) suggests this would not be the case.

Show your understanding

1 Describe what life is like for those living in urban villages.
2 What type of housing do China's wealthy live in?
3 What are China's main housing problems and what is the Chinese Government trying to do to tackle these problems?

Crime

The strict discipline of the CCP seems to have had a trickle-down effect on crime rates in China, with most citizens obeying the laws of the country. The fact that 46 crimes still carry the death penalty and criminals often face harsh punishment and lengthy detention seems to have deterred many Chinese citizens from committing crime. China is viewed as being a safe place to live, with a low crime rate. Violent crime rates, for example, are very low; the UN put China's murder rate at 0.74 per 100,000 of the population in 2017 compared with the UK's rate of 0.93 and the USA's rate of 4.88. However, studying crime rates in China must be treated with an element of caution; the official crime figures put forward by the Government are often seen as unrealistic and there is no uniform way of reporting and recording crimes in different provinces. The CCP has not prioritised reducing crime or reforming the criminal justice system in their 13th Five-Year Plan, instead focusing on issues it sees as more pressing such as the economy, health-care services and the environment.

Cybercrime

One of China's most recent socio-economic issues is cybercrime. In recent years, there has been a staggering rise in online fraud in the country. Statistics released by the Beijing Public Security Bureau recorded 20,623 cases of internet fraud in 2016 alone. Vast gangs of computer hackers operate on what has become known as the mobile underground by hacking into people's mobile phones, a problem that is only set to grow as 92 per cent of mobile phone users in China have access to the internet on their devices. In recent years, these hackers have used a huge variety of scams, such as signing up mobile phone users to text services and charging them premium rates without their permission, and sending spam emails asking people to log on to false websites to change their banking details. This has led to large profits being made by cyber gangs, something that the Government has been trying to crack down on. Cybercrime costs China greatly, with a loss of $66 billion reported in 2017.

Government responses to crime

The Chinese Government has faced a number of difficult internal criminal problems in recent years such as corruption, terrorism, cybercrime and violent riots. In 2017, Xi Jinping announced that it was the CCP's job to eradicate the 'three evil forces' facing China: 'terrorism, separatism and extremism'. In an attempt to crack down on these areas, Chinese authorities have taken a hard line in dealing with people they see as terrorists – particularly the Uighurs in Xinjiang, Tibetan separatists and anyone who protests online.

Case study: Crime in Shanghai

The large police presence within China and the significant conviction rate for crimes (thought to be as high as 98 per cent in some areas) seems to act as a deterrent to those who would otherwise seek to commit crimes. Certain types of crime in urban areas like Shanghai, however, still present some issues. The crimes committed are mostly petty crimes, for example, theft and pickpocketing, and many have argued this is a result of the huge social and economic disparities that people in China are facing. A number of tourists in recent years have come forward about robberies and sexual assaults they have faced when venturing into unregistered taxis, and tourists are often targeted by Chinese criminals because of their supposed affluence. There is also a high level of corruption and bribery, and a rise in white-collar crime.

In terms of tackling corruption, Xi Jinping introduced a crackdown on this activity, resulting in several thousands of arrests across China. And as cybercrime in China is largely monitored by the Chinese authorities, cyber gangs have been targeted and shut down to reduce economic crime. The 13th Five-Year Plan has also put emphasis on the need to implement stronger 'rule of law' in the financial sector by increasing the punishment for financial crimes. However, the Government may be condemning actions that it openly pursues itself, as the USA has accused China of cyber attacks on its government and companies. Rob Joyce of the US National Security Agency has said that Chinese cyber activities undermining US infrastructure are a considerable security threat to the USA.

Show your understanding

12-mark question

Analyse the policies introduced by a world power you have studied to solve socio-economic issues.

20-mark question

To what extent do individuals or groups in a world power you have studied experience social inequality?

International relations

Is China the new 'superpower'?

China has a huge influence in the international community both economically and politically. It has the largest population in the world at 1.415 billion people and the second largest economy. China has overtaken the USA economically (in terms of purchasing power parity). As mentioned on page 66, purchasing power parity is one way to compare two countries in terms of their currency and the amount of one currency needed to buy a set amount of a good or common amount of goods or services. It is dependent on the relative cost of living and inflation rates in different countries and the parity comes from equalising the purchasing power of two currencies (how much it costs to buy X item in the two different currencies) considering these differences in cost of living and inflation. With an economic growth rate of no less than 7 per cent annually over the last three decades, the Chinese economy could be set to double by 2030, dominating the USA's growth rate of a mere 3 per cent. However, superpower status is not based on economics alone; other factors such as military strength and decision-making influence on an international scale must also be taken into account. In terms of the military, China spent

only 1.9 per cent of its GDP on military assets compared with the USA's 3.9 per cent in 2017 (see Table 2.2).

Table 2.2 **Selected military assets, China and USA**

	China	USA
Defence budget 2019 ($ billion)	175	717
Active personnel in 2018 (million)	2.3	1.4
Intercontinental missiles	66	450
Bombers	118	178
Nuclear-powered submarines	3	71
Main battle tanks	9,000	9,500
Aircraft carriers	1	11

Source: adapted from various US military sources

In recent years, China has been trying to increase its military prowess. Speaking at a military parade in January 2018, Xi Jinping stated that there was a need to 'create an elite and powerful [armed] force that is always ready for the fight, capable of combat and sure to win in order to fulfil the tasks bestowed by the party and the people in the new era'. Chinese relations with neighbouring countries have also been heavily monitored for fear of conflict in east Asia. On the international stage, China is a member of many major organisations such as the World Trade Organization, the UN (in which it has a permanent seat on the Security Council) and the G20. It is not a member of NATO or the OECD, although it has strong trade links with the EU.

China and the UN

Founded after the Second World War, the United Nations (UN) plays a vital role in international co-operation, peace and security. The People's Republic of China, as it stands now, has been a member of the UN since 1971 (although parts were previously a member under the Republic of China since 1945). China holds one of the five permanent seats on the UN Security Council, along with the UK, Russia, USA and France, and plays a key role in international relations.

Figure 2.19 **China has a seat on the UN Security Council**

Recently, China has taken a large role in improving international relations around the world. In 2018, China was responsible for providing 8 per cent of the total UN budget, 10.3 per cent of the UN's peacekeeping budget and provided 8000 reserve troops for the UN. While China has increased its spending on the UN recently, the USA has reduced its UN spending under President Donald Trump.

Peacekeeping missions are becoming increasing staffed by Chinese personnel; in 2018, over 2500 peacekeeping forces from China were involved in operations in African countries such as Mali, the DRC (Democratic Republic of the Congo) and South Sudan. China has also been involved in imposing some financial sanctions on North Korea in an ongoing attempt to force North Korea into denuclearisation.

However, many political observers have criticised China for being too interested in pursuing its own interests in the international community. There is no doubt that investing

more time and money into UN missions increases China's international influence whatever its motives behind this. Conflict between the five permanent members of the UN Security Council (UK, USA, Russia, China and France) is commonplace. In September 2018, the USA and China disagreed on imposing further sanctions against North Korea. Russia and China stated they would accept a slow step-by-step denuclearisation of North Korea while the USA argued that strong sanctions must remain in North Korea until there is full, immediate denuclearisation. China is a close trading partner of North Korea, which may explain Beijing's reluctance to impose heavy penalties.

China's challenge to the US

In June 2018, US Defence Secretary James Mattis met with Chinese President Xi Jinping in Beijing to discuss economic developments in south-east Asia. Tensions ran high at the meeting when President Xi stated that he would not give over 'one inch' of south-east territories to US dominance. The comments came shortly after US and Chinese warships clashed in the South China Sea over freedom of navigation operations in the area. The Chinese Government has been trying to assert its authority and sovereignty in the South China Sea in recent years and is becoming increasingly aggressive towards US ships in the area.

Hostile relationships between the USA and China over the territory of Taiwan have always been a source of friction. The USA protects Taiwan from Chinese rule although the Chinese would like to make sure that Taiwan comes back under Chinese rule.

Relations between China and the USA have become increasingly frosty in recent months after the USA imposed additional taxes on around $200 billion worth of Chinese goods.

The Chinese Government was quick to retaliate with its own taxes and tariffs on US goods, sparking an aggressive trade war. These examples show that both the USA and China are trying to assert their superiority on a global stage – something that will probably continue for years to come.

China has also been seen to be flexing its military power recently over territorial disputes in areas of the South China Sea. China positioned an oil rig in an area of the South China Sea that Vietnam claimed was its territory. This led to a stand-off between Chinese and Vietnamese ships that became very hostile when China used water cannons to disperse the Vietnamese ships. This has led to knock-on tensions in Vietnam, and a number of bloody anti-Chinese protests within the country. China says the waters belong to them historically. China also has territorial claims against Japan and the Philippines.

China and the G20

Figure 2.20 **Trump and Xi Jinping**

China is a key member of the Group of Twenty countries or G20. This group includes representatives from some of the most important economies in the world – 19 different countries and a representative from the EU. This international organisation accounts for 90 per cent of the world's economic output and focuses on improving world economies (especially in the light of the global economic crisis), trade and employment. In 2017, the G20 summit was held in Hamburg and issues such as the Paris Climate Agreement and migration were high on the list of priorities. At the summit, there were obvious tensions between the USA and China's leaders, although they both described each other as 'great friends'. However, after the Buenos Aires 2018 G20 summit, the USA and China reached agreements to prevent introducing higher economic tariffs on each other and settle their trade war.

China's relationships with other countries

China and the European Union

China is obviously not part of the European Union (EU), but relations between the EU and China play a huge role in international diplomacy, foreign affairs and global economic prosperity. The year 2018 marks the fifteenth anniversary of the EU–China Strategic Partnership and the two powers have recently launched a new 'EU–China 2020 Strategic Agenda for Co-operation'. This 2020 agenda focuses on stronger peacekeeping agreements between the EU and China and also enhanced trade links. The EU and China trade over $1 billion of products and services every day. However, China does not invest heavily in the EU in terms of foreign direct investment (FDI); approximately 2.6 per cent of the EU's total FDI is from China.

There are signs of friction as well as co-operation between the two powers. The Chinese Government has been coming under fire from developed nations around the world for not doing enough to prevent the production of counterfeit goods; around 60 per cent of the counterfeit goods confiscated by authorities across the EU are thought to have been made in China.

Every year since 1997 a China–EU summit has been held and the summit in 2017 looked towards improving a mutual climate change agreement and increasing security ties over North Korea.

China and the UK

China and the UK are used to working together through international organisations like the UN and the G20. China is currently the UK's fifth biggest trading partner and the UK has turned to China for more economic deals in light of Brexit. In 2017, trade deals between China and the UK increased by 30 per cent on the previous year. In 2017, the UK agreed a deal which will see a Chinese and a French energy company together build a nuclear power plant at Hinkley Point in Somerset. In August 2018, the UK agreed a £240 million deal to supply dairy products to China.

Jeremy Hunt, the UK's former foreign secretary, stated in recent months that the UK will consider free-trade talks with China as part of Brexit negotiations.

At a press conference in Beijing in July 2018, Hunt said that 'China and Britain have very different systems but we do have a lot in common, and we in the UK think that the rise of China and China's economy and Chinese power can and must be a positive force in the world'.

Despite this, the two powers frequently clash with differing views on human rights and free elections, particularly in Hong Kong, which was a British colony until 1997.

Show your understanding

1 In what ways can China be described as a 'superpower'?
2 In what ways is China not yet considered to be a 'superpower'?
3 Briefly explain the role that China plays within the UN.
4 What evidence suggests that China wishes to challenge America's dominance in south-east Asia?
5 Briefly explain the role that China plays within the G20.

20-mark question

To what extent does a world power you have studied have influence in international relations?

3

The Republic of South Africa

Background

The 'rainbow nation'

South Africa is a nation reborn. In 1994, the country elected its first democratic government after the end of white rule under a system known as apartheid (see page 90). Nelson Mandela, the leader of the ANC (African National Congress), became the first democratically elected president. Before Mandela, white people had used apartheid to deny non-white people political, social and economic rights: this has left a legacy of vast inequalities between the races, which will be discussed later in this chapter. The new 'rainbow nation' has made great progress in the creation of a more prosperous country for all, and in 2010 the football World Cup finals were held in South Africa. It was fitting that South Africa was the first African country to hold such a prestigious event. However, the election of 2014, following the death of Nelson Mandela in December 2013, raised questions about the future path of the country. The corrupt leadership of President Jacob Zuma and his fellow ANC leaders threatened to steer the country towards a one-party dictatorship but the removal of Zuma in December 2017 and the promise made by new President Cyril Ramaphosa to curb and expose corruption offers hope for democracy and the declining economy.

The legacy of the 2010 football World Cup

The ten stadiums that were built for the 2010 World Cup symbolise the achievement of a nation reborn. Nobel Peace Prize Laureate and anti-apartheid hero Archbishop Desmond Tutu summed up the majority view by saying 'With all the negative things that are taking place in Africa, this is a superb moment for us. If we are going to have white elephants, so be it.'

Economists also say World Cup construction cushioned South Africa from the global recession and contributed close to R56 billion ($7.3 billion) to the economy. 'It has been a huge blessing for South Africa in view of the recession' said Gillian Saunders of business consultants Grant Thornton.

Nevertheless, the stadiums' spectacular style can perhaps be seen as going way beyond football – the affirmation of the capabilities of a young, democratic country in the face of doubts and cynicism both at home and abroad. 'For the many little boys kicking a ball in the streets of the world's townships and squatter camps, football is the stuff of dreams,' said commentator Tinyiko Sam Maluleke.

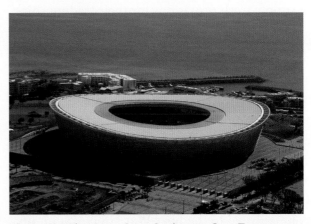

Figure 3.1 The Green Point Stadium in Cape Town was built for the 2010 football World Cup

One of the greatest benefits for South Africa was the upgrading of its infrastructure – improved national roads and airports and investment in public transport. The World Cup put South Africa and Africa on the map and this is reflected in the decision to invite South Africa to join the BRIC Group (see pages 127–8).

I can testify to the majestic appearance of the Green Point World Cup stadium in Cape Town. Sailing into Cape Town, the dominant landscape is the iconic Table Mountain but nestled below it on the waterfront is the impressive modern stadium.

The land and the people

South Africa is five times the size of the United Kingdom with a population of over 57 million. Owing to its size, it has different climates and landscapes in different parts of the country. Much of the west of the country is desert, while the south, around Cape Town, has a Mediterranean climate. South Africa is divided into nine provinces (see pages 87–8).

Its diverse population is made up of numerous ethnic groups and this is reflected in the recognition of 11 official languages. Black South Africans make up over 80 per cent of the population (see Table 3.1). The most recent census statistics reveal that 65 per cent of the population now live in urban areas.

Boers, British and Africans

In 1752, a settlement was established by the Dutch East India Company in the Cape Colony to supply fresh provisions for their trading ships.

By 1806, the British Government had decided to control Cape Colony and consequently took it over. The resultant increase in immigration from Britain established two distinct white communities: the Afrikaners (Boers) and the English-speaking white people (Anglos). With the discovery of diamonds and gold, Britain proceeded to annexe the Afrikaner republics of Transvaal and the Orange Free State. This eventually led to the Boer War (1899–1902), in which the Boers were defeated.

British dominance ended in 1948 when the Afrikaner National Party won the election and began its policy of apartheid and total white control of all aspects of life.

South Africa's economy

South Africa is a middle-income emerging economy with an abundant stock of natural resources. It is served by a modern infrastructure ensuring an efficient distribution of goods to major urban areas. The country has well-developed financial and legal sectors with a stock exchange that ranks among the top ten largest in the world.

Unemployment is a problem. Official figures show 27 per cent unemployed, but the real figure for those between 18 and 39 is close to 40 per cent, with about 50 per cent of the population living below the poverty line. Half of all South Africans aged 18–24 are not in education, training or employment. About 70 per cent have no qualifications or work skills. Yet there are many job vacancies, with employers desperate to employ young people with appropriate qualifications and skills.

Massive economic inequalities still exist between the white population and the new black middle class and the majority of black South Africans. South Africa is one of the most unequal societies in the world alongside the USA, China and Brazil, in terms of wealth distribution among its citizens (see Figure 3.22 on page 128).

South Africa is one of the wealthiest countries in sub-Saharan Africa in terms of natural resources and its manufacturing industry. However, the world financial crisis of 2007–08 and the subsequent economic recession has had a far greater impact on South Africa than its neighbours. In April 2014, under revised GDP (Gross Domestic Product) estimates, Nigeria overtook South Africa to become the biggest economy in sub-Saharan Africa (see pages 126–7). Zuma's nine years of misrule had a serious impact on the country's economy. Living standards are lower than they were when he came to power in 2009 and the ratio of debt to GDP rose from 26 per cent in 2008–09 to 56 per cent in 2018–19.

South Africa is one of the top five producers of gold. Large-scale commercial farming ensures an abundant supply of food. In the less fertile areas pastoral farming dominates, with sheep rearing and cattle ranching particularly strong. South Africa is the region's economic superpower. It accounts for 85 per cent of southern Africa's energy consumption and 90 per cent of its GDP.

Ethnic groupings

South Africa's official classifications of race list the four main ethnic groups as follows:

1 The predominant black indigenous population, who are subdivided by tribal group.

The two main tribal groups are Xhosa (former presidents Nelson Mandela and Thabo Mbeki) and Zulu (former president Jacob Zuma).

2 The white population is divided into English-speaking and Afrikaans-speaking.

3 The coloured population are of mixed race.

4 Asians, or Indians, are descended from workers who were brought from India to work, especially in Natal, in the nineteenth century.

Figure 3.2 **South Africa's population of 57 million is made up of numerous ethnic groups**

Table 3.1 shows that South Africa's population has now reached 57 million. In 2009, the coloured population overtook the white population – over 800,000 white people are thought to have left South Africa since 1994. With a higher birth rate than the other races, the black indigenous population has increased by about 15 million

Table 3.1 **South Africa's population**

	1996 population (millions)	Percentage	2018 population (millions)	Percentage
Black	31.3	76.8	46.68	80.9
White	4.7	11.4	4.52	7.8
Coloured	3.3	9.0	5.07	8.8
Asian	1.2	2.8	1.45	2.5
Total	**40.5**	**100**	**57.72**	**100**

Source: Statistics South Africa, Mid-Year Population Estimates, 2018

since 1996 and now makes up 80 per cent of the total population. The Rainbow nation came together in November 2019 to celebrate the victory of their rugby team winning the rugby world championship in Japan. The team was led by Siya Kolisa, the first black captain, with 11 of the 31-man squad being black or mixed race.

While there are significant inequalities in South Africa based on race, there are also significant inequalities between urban and rural areas, and between provinces.

Illegal immigrants

Official figures detailing South Africa's population fail to include the millions of Africans who have flocked to the country to escape poverty and persecution in their home nations. It has been estimated by the South African Institute of Race Relations that around 4 million immigrants are living illegally in South Africa. It is ironic that while highly skilled and educated white people leave the country for better jobs abroad and educated black South Africans flock to London to take up jobs in health and education, South Africa is being left with an unskilled and uneducated workforce, which the country, with its official unemployment rate of 27.5 per cent, does not need.

Most refugees originate from the Democratic Republic of Congo, Rwanda, Somalia and Zimbabwe. Around 2 million Zimbabweans are thought to be currently living in South Africa, although many may return home if peace and stability return to Zimbabwe. Many immigrants, especially from Zimbabwe, are well educated and contribute to the economy but illegal

immigrants can face great hostility from South Africans. Over the last five years numerous vicious attacks against foreign immigrants have taken place in townships around Johannesburg (Gauteng), Cape Town (Western Cape) and in the province of Mpumalanga (see Table 3.2). In February 2014, in the informal settlement of Refilwe, east of Pretoria (Gauteng), more than a dozen foreign-owned shops were looted. And in March 2019 a group of unemployed South Africans attacked migrants from Malawi in the city of Durban (KwaZulu-Natal). In September 2019, a disturbing number of xenophobic violent riots rocked South Africa. Shops owned by foreign nationals were looted and burnt and a mosque was attacked. In total ten deaths were reported.

Table 3.2 **Xenophobic violent incidents in selected provinces, 1994–2018**

Gauteng	212
Western Cape	111
KwaZulu-Natal	67
Limpopo	40
Eastern Cape	33
Mpumalanga	22

Source: 'Xenophobic Violence in South Africa: 1994–2018: An Overview', African Centre for Migration and Society, 2019, xenowatch.ac.za

During a stay in Cape Town, I was surprised by the number of foreigners working in the tourist sector and also learned that many South Africans who live in RDP homes (government low-cost homes) rent their rooms out to foreigners and sleep in their gardens.

Profile of the provinces of South Africa

Province/Capital	GAUTENG/Johannesburg
Population	14.7 million (24.8 per cent of total)
Area km²	18,810 (1.6 per cent of total)
GDP per person ($)	59,000
Agriculture and industry	Gauteng is South Africa's engine room, where about 40 per cent of the country's GDP is generated. Gauteng means 'place of gold' and this is a highly urbanised and industrialised area. It is a magnet area for a large inflow of migrant labourers.
Comment	Pretoria, the administrative capital of South Africa, is situated in the province.

Province/Capital	NORTHERN CAPE/Kimberley
Population	1.2 million (1.9 per cent of total)
Area km²	361,800 (29.7 per cent of total)
GDP per person ($)	38,700
Agriculture and industry	Extremely rich in mineral wealth – including copper, manganese and marble.
Comment	It covers the largest area in South Africa and has the smallest population. It is a semi-arid region with low summer rainfall and is the home of the San (bushmen) people.

Province/Capital	WESTERN CAPE/Cape Town
Principal language	Afrikaans (55 per cent), English (20 per cent), isiXhosa (23 per cent)
Population	6.6 million (11.5 per cent of total)
Area km²	129,379 (14.4 per cent of total)
GDP per person ($)	50,000
Agriculture and industry	It is the food basket of South Africa with a harvest of top-grade fruits, vegetables and meats. The head offices of many South African businesses are in Cape Town. Some 96 per cent of its population is urbanised.
Comment	Cape Town is the legislative capital of the country.

Province/Capital	FREE STATE/Bloemfontein
Population	2.9 million
Area km²	129,480 (10.6 per cent of total)
GDP per person ($)	38,200
Agriculture and industry	The Free State is 'the granary of the country' with 31 per cent of the potentially arable land of South Africa. Its main economic base is mining.
Comment	It lies in the heart of South Africa and is the third-largest province (size).

Province/Capital	NORTH WEST/Minabatha
Population	3.9 million
Area km²	116,190 (9.5 per cent of total)
GDP per person ($)	23,000
Agriculture and industry	Its main economic base is mining and its major agricultural products are maize and sunflowers. High unemployment levels in the province contribute to the poverty experienced by many of its citizens.
Comment	It is developing its tourist industry through national parks.

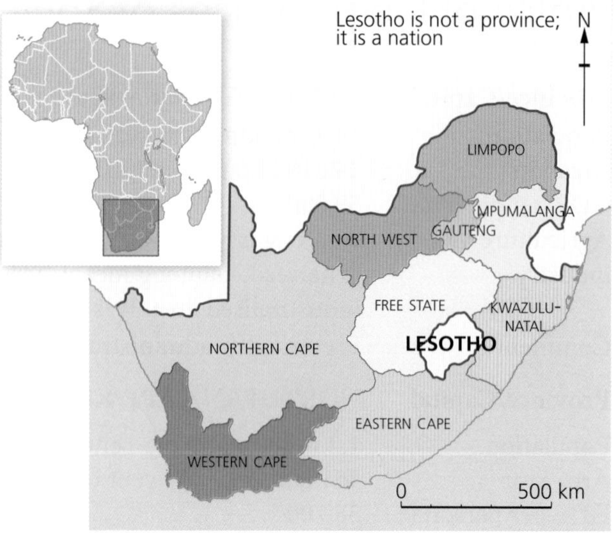

Province/Capital	**EASTERN CAPE/Bisho**
Population	6.6 million
Area km²	169,600 (13.9 per cent of total)
GDP per person ($)	21,600
Agriculture and industry	The province has both rich agricultural and forestry land. The urban areas of Port Elizabeth and East London are based primarily on manufacturing.
Comment	It includes the former homelands of Transkei and Ciskei.

Lesotho is not a province; it is a nation

N

Figure 3.3 **South Africa's nine provinces**

Province/Capital	**LIMPOPO/Pietersburg**
Population	5.7 million
Area km²	123,280 (10 per cent of total)
GDP per person ($)	21,000
Agriculture and industry	Although the province is extremely rich in minerals including coal, copper and platinum, unemployment is high. The per capita income is by far the lowest in the country.
Comment	The province is the country's gateway to the rest of Africa as it shares borders with Botswana, Zimbabwe and Mozambique.

Province/Capital	**MPUMALANGA/Nelspruit**
Population	4.5 million
Area km²	78,370 (7.3 per cent of total)
GDP per person ($)	26,000
Agriculture and industry	The province produces sub-tropical fruits and its tree plantations supply half of the country's total timber needs. It is rich in coal reserves and the country's three biggest power stations are based in the area.
Comment	Mpumalanga (formerly Eastern Transvaal) means 'place where the sun rises'. The province attracts migrant labour from neighbouring states. It suffers from extreme levels of poverty and low levels of literacy.

Province/Capital	**KWAZULU-NATAL/Pietermaritzburg/Ulundi**
Principal language	isiZulu (79 per cent), Afrikaans (2 per cent), English (16 per cent)
Population	11 million (21.4 per cent of total)
Area km²	92,180 (7.6 per cent of total)
GDP per person ($)	24,000
Agriculture and industry	Durban is one of the fastest growing urban areas in the world. There is a huge gap between the urban and rural per-capita income.
Comment	It is the only province with a monarchy specifically provided for in the 1993 Constitution. Ulundi is the traditional capital of the Zulu monarchy.

Source: SA Government Yearbook, 2018

Western Cape – goodbye to the ANC?

In January 2014, I visited South Africa and had the opportunity to take the social and political pulse of the citizens of the Western Cape four months prior to the 2014 elections. I have been writing about South Africa since 1985 and my visit was an opportunity to experience the new rainbow nation and to assess recent social and economic progress.

The Western Cape's political and population profile is unique to South Africa. It is the only province not controlled by the ANC and also the only province that does not have a black majority – the coloured population is the largest population group.

We stayed in a modern hotel overlooking the sea, with the iconic Table Mountain as a stunning background. Most of the staff were black and the majority of the guests were tourists. The hotel was based in a residential complex occupied by all shades of the rainbow nation and protected by CCTV and patrolling guards. Only the wealthy South Africans experience this racial togetherness in their neighbourhood, workplace and in the beautiful and opulent shopping malls in the centre of Cape Town. In our tours across the Western Cape, we passed the sprawling Khayelitsha township, which consists of planned new RDP homes (recognised by their red roofs) and the informal settlements with sub-standard dwellings that are plagued by violent crime.

Our driver, Robert, enjoyed our wide-ranging discussions. Robert is coloured and had originally supported the ANC, but in the 2009 election had voted Democratic Alliance (DA) and would do so again in 2014. The ANC was no longer the party of liberation and hope but had become the party of maladministration, greed and corruption. He was

Figure 3.4 Cape Town

confident that the DA would retain the Western Cape despite ANC propaganda.

One of the comments that I regarded at the time as being far-fetched and unfair was when Robert said that the ANC did not want a well-educated and mature electorate; they were content that the education system was failing the vast majority of the black population. He argued that in this way many black people would believe the propaganda of the ANC: that the DA was racist and would reintroduce apartheid if they won … that Nelson Mandela's spirit would haunt them if they did not vote ANC, and so on. Yet in May 2014 when I examined the voting patterns, one inverse conclusion was clear: the two provinces with the poorest matriculation (exam) results had the highest ANC support and the two worst results for the ANC were in the two best educated provinces of Western Cape and Gauteng. (See Table 3.8.)

And this is the problem the DA faces. The black community might not like the corruption within the ANC, but they are not ready to commit 'heresy' and endorse the DA. In my conversation with numerous black people, it was clear that their ANC loyalty was solid. When I mentioned Jacob Zuma, none challenged my corruption accusation and could only invoke the mantra of Nelson Mandela.

The apartheid years 1948–94

It is important to have an understanding of the vast inequalities between the races created during the apartheid years – its legacy still exists today in South Africa.

Apartheid

The Afrikaans word 'apartheid' means separate development, and describes the segregation that took place between the races in South Africa. Numerous laws such as the Group Areas Act and the Pass laws were passed to divide the people and land on racial grounds.

The apartheid system was set up by the white group known as Afrikaners whose ancestors came mostly from the Netherlands. In 1948, they gained control of the country from the English-speaking white people and set up a government that denied all non-white people their political, social and economic rights. South Africa was to be white only, with just 13 per cent of the land area being given to the 70 per cent of the population who were black and given self-governing tribal homelands to live in. For example, the largest tribe, the Zulu, were to live in the homeland of KwaZulu-Natal and run their own affairs there. The black population were treated as foreigners, had to have permission to live outside their homelands and were expected to live in segregated areas called townships, the most famous being Soweto on the outskirts of Johannesburg.

The escalation of black unrest and international action against the white government of South Africa persuaded President F.W. de Klerk, leader of the National Party, that he must negotiate with Nelson Mandela, the imprisoned leader of the ANC. In 1990, Nelson Mandela was set free from prison, and the ANC was declared legal. Prolonged negotiations took place and finally, in 1994, a new constitution was agreed and elections held. For the first time the black population could vote; Nelson Mandela and the ANC won and formed the new government. All the political parties agreed to the setting up of a **Truth and Reconciliation Commission** (TRC) to investigate illegal actions that had taken place during the apartheid years.

Truth and Reconciliation Commission

The TRC, chaired by retired Archbishop Desmond Tutu, was set up to establish as complete a picture as possible of the 'causes, nature and extent of the gross violations of human rights committed between 1960 and 1994'. The Commission had the power to grant an amnesty to anybody whose crime had a political purpose as long as they admitted their wrongdoing. Victims of apartheid had the opportunity to share their grief with the nation and to discover what had happened to their loved ones. The hearings, aired on television, shocked and horrified the nation. The revelations damaged the National Party and led to the resignation of de Klerk. In total 6000 people applied for amnesty and 22,000 victims testified to the Commission.

(In 2011, Desmond Tutu, still the nation's moral conscience, denounced the infighting and corruption within the ANC. In his speech he called the ANC 'worse than the apartheid government'. However, he also asked white people to pay a wealth tax as an act of atonement for their privileged positions.)

1994 election analysis

- It was a triumph for democracy with the election remaining free from intimidation, fraud and violence.
- As expected, the ANC dominated the election, winning over 12 million votes but just failing to receive two-thirds of the votes (which would have enabled it to create a new constitution without consulting the other political parties).

At the provincial level the ANC won seven of the nine provinces with narrow defeats in the Western Cape and KwaZulu-Natal.

- The New National Party, by winning the support of white, coloured and Asian South Africans, gained an impressive 20.4 per cent of the vote and thus the post of deputy president. Its best performance was in the Western Cape where it won the Provincial election. The Democratic Party, a white party that had always opposed apartheid, did badly.
- The Inkatha Freedom Party (IFP) gained a narrow victory over the ANC in KwaZulu-Natal and won control of the province. The results reinforced the status of the IFP (and the New National Party) as regional rather than national players. While the IFP gained 1.8 million votes in KwaZulu-Natal, its combined vote in the eight other provinces was only 214,000.

Nelson Mandela

Nelson Mandela was born on 18 July 1918, the son of a tribal chief of the Xhosa nation. He graduated from the University College of Fort Hare and later set up a legal practice with Oliver Tambo in Johannesburg. Both men were leaders of the ANC Youth League, which supported boycotts, strikes and acts of civil disobedience.

The introduction of apartheid in 1948 and the brutal use of force by the white regime made him question the ANC's policy of non-violence. In 1961, Mandela went underground to organise the military wing of the ANC. On 2 August 1962 he was sentenced to life imprisonment for attempting to overthrow the Government by violent revolution. It was not until 11 February 1990 that he gained his freedom, when he was released from prison by President de Klerk. He was reunited with his wife, Winnie, but their marriage ended and they were divorced in 1996. Nelson Mandela was elected president of

Figure 3.5 Nelson Mandela

the new democratic South Africa in 1994 and retained this post until 1999, when he retired from politics. Mandela preached reconciliation between the races and worked hard to create a new 'rainbow nation'.

An ailing Nelson Mandela died on 5 December 2013 and the 'rainbow nation' mourned. President Zuma stated 'our nation has lost its greatest son'.

Show your understanding

1 Outline the benefits to South Africa of holding the 2010 World Cup.
2 Describe the main racial groups in South Africa and discuss what conclusions can be reached about population change. Refer to Table 3.1 in your answer.
3 Create a brief profile of the nine provinces.
4 Describe the inequalities that non-white people experienced during the apartheid years.
5 What impact did the Truth and Reconciliation Commission have on the South African people?
6 Outline the main political parties that participated in the 1994 election and their performance.

Archbishop Desmond Tutu, 1994

'Apartheid has left a ghastly legacy. There is a horrendous housing shortage and high unemployment; health care is inaccessible and not easily affordable by the majority; Bantu education has left us with a massive educational crisis; there is gross maldistribution of wealth and an inequitable sharing of resources with which South Africa is so richly endowed. Some 20 per cent of the population owns 87 per cent of the land. Then there is the hurt and anguish of those who have been victims of this vicious system, those who were forcibly removed from their homes, nearly 4 million people. Those

Figure 3.6 Desmond Tutu, a former archbishop and a South African Nobel Peace Prize winner

whose loved ones were detained without trial or banned, or who died mysteriously in detention, such as Steve Biko, or at the hands of death squads.'

Social and economic issues

Legacy of apartheid

The provision of the vote to all citizens ensured that the black South African people would run their own country. The *political* legacy of apartheid was removed by this action. Much more difficult for the new ANC Government would be the removal of the social and economic inequalities between the races. In its 1994 election manifesto, the ANC promised 'a job, a decent home and a chicken in every pot'. Over 25 years on, many Africans are still waiting for this to be achieved. The legacy of apartheid, which created vast inequalities between the races, is outlined in the statistical survey and comments that follow.

Education

The population growth within the black South African community is one of the challenges facing governments. Of the 46 million black African population, 18 million are under the age of 16. The paradox that South Africa faces is that, although it has an unemployment rate

of 27.5 per cent, it is desperately short of skilled and educated black South Africans.

The culture of violence, with 'no education before liberation' being the slogan for a generation of young black South Africans, contributed to the decline of educational standards. This was reflected in the low matriculation results achieved by black South African students (see Figure 3.7). Overcrowded classrooms and few resources were also factors that help to explain poor educational performances and low African literacy rates.

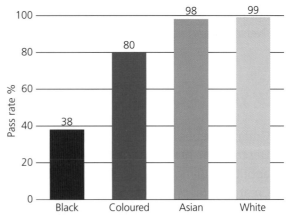

Figure 3.7 **Percentage pass rates for high school leaving exam by race, 1993**
Source: SA Department of Education, 1993

Health

Table 3.3 **Health inequalities, 1990**

	Infant mortality rate (per 1000 births)	Life expectancy (at birth)
Black	65	60
Coloured	35	62
Asian	14	67
White	8	72

Source: SA Department of Health, 1990

During the era of apartheid, while the white South Africans enjoyed an excellent health service, the non-white population was condemned to a second-rate service that struggled to cope. In 1994, there was a white doctor for every 400 white people and an African doctor for every 44,000 Africans. The situation was worse in the rural areas of the homelands. Poverty, hunger and disease, combined with the lack of doctors and nurses, explained the high level of malnutrition and undernourishment among rural children.

The existence of a strong private health-care sector also created inequalities between the races. In 1994, 90 per cent of the white community relied on private medical care, while the vast majority of black people could not afford it.

Land

As Archbishop Desmond Tutu highlighted, almost 4 million non-white people were forcibly removed from their homes by the apartheid regime. The homeland and township systems created squatter camps, shanty towns and sprawling townships such as Soweto, where the majority of dwellings lacked basic amenities such as electricity and proper sanitation. In the rural areas many black South Africans were forcibly settled in arid lands that could not sustain them. The outcome was malnutrition, disease and abject poverty.

Cyril Ramaphosa, then ANC general secretary, stated in 1993 that 'unless we settle the land question we tear South Africa to pieces'. As part of the 1994 peace agreement between de Klerk and Mandela, the white farmers were guaranteed that their land would not be taken from them through nationalisation or expropriation policies (see pages 108–9).

Show your understanding

1 Refer to the comments made by Archbishop Desmond Tutu in 1994. What evidence does he give to support his statement that 'apartheid has left a ghastly legacy'?
2 Outline the vast inequalities between the races that existed in 1994 in terms of: education, health and land.

Reducing social and economic inequalities

As indicated earlier, all ANC governments since 1994 have faced the apartheid legacy of vast social and economic inequalities and widespread poverty. President Mandela gave hope and raised expectations (1994–99), President Mbeki created disillusionment (1999–2007), President Zuma created economic stagnation and 'state capture' (the illegal control of the state for personal benefit by politicians, the military or companies through bribery of public officials) (2009–18) and President Ramaphosa offers hope and recovery.

RDP and GEAR

The Reconstruction and Development Programme (RDP) and Growth Employment and Redistribution (GEAR) were central policies in bringing wealth to the African population and reducing poverty. The Government was prepared to upset the trade unions and the South African Communist Party by selling state-owned enterprises, such as electricity and gas, to the private sector. This policy of privatisation provided income to enable the Government to improve services. The downside was that private firms raised prices and consumers had to pay higher charges for essential services. This placed a heavy financial burden on the poorer sections of society.

GEAR encouraged growth and employment by providing economic stability which in turn encouraged foreign investment. GEAR also promoted a black enterprise culture. 'Wealthy, black and proud of it' was the slogan of the Government.

President Mbeki was aware of the need to transform South African society. The shift of power that took place in the political field needed to cover all aspects of economic and social life (Black Transformation). To try to narrow the huge gap between black and white people, the Government embarked on a programme of Affirmative Action, which President Zuma and President Ramaphosa have continued.

Affirmative Action

Mandela did not wish to antagonise the white population and did not pass legislation to compel employers or institutions to discriminate in favour of non-white people. His successor, Thabo Mbeki, used Affirmative Action legislation to speed up the 'transformation of South Africa's economic life'.

There are two major pieces of Affirmative Action legislation: the Employment Equity Act and the Black Economic Empowerment Act.

The Employment Equity Act

The Employment Equity Act, 1998, set up a directorate called 'Equal Opportunities' to ensure that organisations 'democratically represented' the black people of South Africa. The Act decreed that the correct balance of a workforce should be 75 per cent black, 52 per cent female, 5 per cent people with disabilities. The Act promoted reverse discrimination, which meant that black South Africans were entitled to preferential treatment in hiring, promotion, university admission and the awarding of government contracts.

Any company that has more than 50 employees is covered by this Act and can be fined up to £100,000 if it does not meet its terms.

The Black Economic Empowerment (BEE) Act

The Department of Trade and Industry (DTI) states that 'Our BEE strategy is not affirmative action, although employment equity forms part of it. Nor does it aim to take wealth from white people and give it to black people. It is essentially a growth strategy, targeting the South African economy's weakest point: inequality. The purpose of BEE is to stimulate economic growth and create employment.'

President Zuma had dismissed calls from the Afrikaner Freedom Front Party to end the discrimination towards young white people as they were not responsible for the inequalities created by apartheid. He stated that 'it was unthinkable for the ANC to abandon it'.

Table 3.4 **Achievements and criticisms of the BEE Act**

Achievements	Criticisms
• The African middle class now numbers about 6 million and is growing. Their new wealth has led to a consumer explosion. Their spending power is now far greater than that of their white counterparts. The number of black middle-class families living in the former white suburbs has increased from 20 per cent in 2004 to 58 per cent in 2018. • State-owned industries such as Eskom now have black majorities on their boards. Around 55 per cent of senior managers are black compared with about 4 per cent in 1996. • To achieve government contracts, firms must now file a BEE scorecard to prove that they are promoting 'previously disadvantaged individuals' including black, coloured and Asian South Africans. The Government spends R13 billion a year on government contracts, much of which benefits black businesses and the black workforce.	• Many black-owned firms win government contracts despite submitting higher bids (the government rule is that bids from previously disadvantaged individuals, PDIs, can be up to 10 per cent higher than others). Having won the contracts they sub-contract the work to their losing competitors. In effect the PDI/10 per cent rule constitutes a special tax on all taxpayers with the proceeds going to the black businessmen who win the contract. • Several high-profile black empowerment businesses such as the African Bank and Community Bank have collapsed. Eskom, the state-owned power company, is regarded as inefficient and incompetent, and numerous power cuts took place in 2014. • Many BEE activities simply enrich a small number of individuals and do not offer any economic benefits to the black majority. White businessmen give directorships and shares to black business people to conform to BEE regulations (see `Tenderpreneur', page 123).

The controversial fabulous four

It is significant that former ANC leaders who fought against apartheid have crossed over from politics to the boardroom to become millionaires. The four who symbolise the new black elite are Cyril Ramaphosa, who re-entered politics to become deputy president in 2014 and president in 2017, Tokyo Sexwale, former ANC provincial premier, Saki Macozoma, former political prisoner, and Patrice Motsepe, who is married to an ANC minister. They are aware of the growing criticism coming from fellow black South Africans, but they argue that their goal is to create a million black capitalists. However, Moletsi Mbeki, an economic analyst, claims that BEE has struck 'a fatal blow against the

Figure 3.8 Cyril Ramaphosa, millionaire and now president of South Africa, has been criticised for his involvement in the Marikana massacre (see page 111–12)

emergence of black entrepreneurship by creating a small class of unproductive, but wealthy black crony capitalists'.

Cyril Ramaphosa, the new Mandela?

In February 2018, Cyril Ramaphosa finally became the president of South Africa. In the 1980s Ramaphosa was the leader of the National Union of Mineworkers and was a key negotiator in the peaceful handover of power from the white minority to black African majority. Ramaphosa was Mandela's preferred successor in 1999, but he was persuaded to accept Thabo Mbeki as the new leader. Ramaphosa gave up politics and prospered through 'black economic empowerment'. In 2012, he returned to the political arena and was elected the ANC's deputy president, becoming deputy president of the country. In December 2017, he became president of the ANC defeating Zuma's candidate by the narrow margin of 179 (out of 4701 votes). As such he must move carefully to end party corruption as there are powerful figures in the ANC who are eager to remove him.

The gap is closing

In a controversial speech in 2004 the then president Thabo Mbeki referred to South Africa as being a land of two nations – one white and rich, the other black and poor. While there are still significant inequalities between the races, progress has been made through the BEE project. There is now a rich African middle class, referred to by many as the 'Black Diamonds'.

The divide is now not so much based on race but on social class.

White poverty

It is true that rich, white South Africans have retained their wealth since apartheid ended, but many poorly educated white people have sunk into poverty and white beggars are a common sight in South African cities. In 2008, Jacob Zuma, then leader of the ANC, visited a poor white community in Bethlehem, Pretoria. Bethlehem has no electricity, running water or sewerage system and the people survive by selling vegetables they grow near the shacks. Solidarity, a union whose base is among white workers, claims that white poverty has increased from 3 per cent in 1994 to 13 per cent today and that their plight had been ignored by the Government. One Bethlehem resident stated 'When we tried to apply for food aid and social security payments, we were told by black social workers that you whites can suffer now. When we applied for jobs, we were turned away because of our colour. We are now the victims of the new apartheid.'

The broadcaster Trevor McDonald returned to South Africa in 2018 and visited a white informal settlement similar to Bethlehem.

Go to **www.youtube.com** to watch Trevor McDonald's 2018 documentary on his visit to South Africa. The documentary reflects on the broadcaster's previous visits to the country and considers the progress and problems faced by South Africans today.

However, there is a dispute over the number of white citizens living in poverty after (see Table 3.5). There are three categories of poverty in South Africa and this partly explains the conflicting figures.

The accepted view is that around 6 per cent of white people live in poverty. The majority are unskilled Afrikaners who, unlike the wealthy white people, do not have the financial means to leave South Africa.

Table 3.5 Number of people living in poverty in South Africa by population group, 2018

	Number of people living in poverty	Percentage of population group
Black	28,267,530	64.2
Coloured	1,989,304	41.3
Asian	79,460	5.9
White	47,494	1.0

Source: africacheck.org and Stats SA's poverty trends in SA

Emerging middle class

Evidence of the emergence of a black elite can be found in the number of black people now living in the wealthiest suburbs of South Africa's cities, once the exclusive domain of white citizens. Houghton, the grandest suburb in Johannesburg, has witnessed the growing number of black inhabitants. The new black elite now live in their walled estates and in luxury homes with a BMW in the driveway. Their children go to the middle-class mixed-race state schools or to the best private schools. Previously called 'Black Diamonds', these members of the emerging middle class are categorised as educated, professional African workers who earn at least R7500 a month. They now number over 4 million and make up nearly a third of the country's buying power. Black middle-class women now represent over 45 per cent of all female consumer spending power.

Statistics from the World Bank clearly highlight the increasing numbers and wealth of the black middle class (see Tables 3.6 and 3.7).

Table 3.6 Percentage of middle classes by population group between 2008 and 2016

Group	2008	2016
Black	42%	51%
White	36%	28%
Coloured	16%	14%
Asian	6%	7%

Source: World Bank 2018

Table 3.7 Percentage of wealthiest by population group between 2008 and 2016

Group	2008	2016
Black	18%	25%
White	63%	56%
Coloured	12%	12%
Asian	7%	7%

Source: World Bank 2018

Figure 3.9 A member of South Africa's new black elite – the emerging middle class

The coloured and Asian community

As stated previously, the coloured community is now the second largest racial group in South Africa (see Table 3.1). Eighty-five per cent of the almost 5 million coloured people live in the Western Cape, especially around Cape Town, and in the Northern Cape. The majority speak Afrikaans and many feel that they are being ignored by successive ANC governments and that their lives have not improved since 1994.

Many of the 1.4 million South African Asians have established themselves as successful business people, traders and professionals. Their economic and educational success over the last 45 years and their strong cultural beliefs have at times brought them into conflict with the African majority. In 2002, an African playwright wrote a song called 'Amandiya', which urged Africans to rise against the Asian community. The Asian and coloured communities feel that the policy of Affirmative Action discriminates against them: 'Under apartheid we were not white enough, now we are not black enough.'

What progress has been made with Transformation since 1994?

Distribution of income

Despite declining poverty levels, national income inequalities have not reduced. The Gini international index, which measures wealth inequalities (scale 0–1, where 0 means everyone is equal), has increased from 0.63 in 1995 to 0.64 in 2018. The gap between the rich and poor in all race groups has grown since 1994. The richest 4 per cent of South Africans, a quarter of whom are black, now earn a hundred times more than the average person.

The growth in inequality is linked to the emergent black middle class and growing unemployment among the lower deciles of the black population.

A growing black middle class

- The emergent black middle class is the largest component in an increasingly multiracial national middle class.
- The public services have made substantial progress in achieving employment equity goals.
- Black representation in the public services increased from 76 per cent in 1995 to over 90 per cent in 2012.
- In the private sector, white South Africans still hold just under 60 per cent of senior posts.
- Among the 295 companies listed on the Johannesburg Stock Exchange (JSE), black people comprise 50 per cent of directors.

Show your understanding

1 What is GEAR? Outline its achievements and criticisms.
2 What is Affirmative Action and why was it introduced?
3 Describe the main features of the Employment Equity Act.
4 Outline the achievements and criticisms of BEE.
5 What evidence suggests that social class rather than race is the main cause of wealth and poverty in South Africa?

Tackling poverty

Income poverty has declined in South Africa over the last 20 years and there has been a significant decline in child poverty. The proportion of households living below the poverty line stands at 37 per cent compared with 53 per cent in 1996. Between 2006 and 2016 around 2.6 million South Africans escaped from poverty. However, while many poor South Africans have been lifted from abject poverty, the rich in South Africa, especially the new black middle classes, are getting richer.

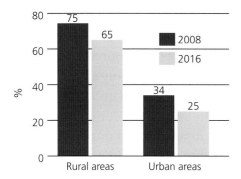

Figure 3.10 Living below the poverty line: urban and rural areas in selected years
Source: World Bank 2018

Social grants have played a critical role in this regard. In 1999, 2.5 million people benefited from grants. By 2018, this figure had risen to over 17 million. The social grants system is the largest form of government support for the poor. The two provinces with the highest number of social grant recipients are Eastern Cape (42.0%) and Limpopo (40.1%). These two provinces have significant rural areas and the situation has improved as outlined in Figure 3.10. The dependence on the ANC Government is astounding – almost 44 per cent of households rely on welfare payments to make ends meet. South Africa is proportionally one of the world's biggest spenders on social grants and uses about 12 per cent of total government spending on social protection.

Education

Under Mbeki and Zuma much was done to improve the horrendous legacy of African education from the time of apartheid. The Government is aware that education and training are crucial for the creation of economic prosperity. There is a shortage of skilled and highly educated black South African workers, yet an abundance of poorly educated, unskilled black South Africans who face a lifetime of formal unemployment.

In 2018, the Government invested over 20 per cent of the entire budget in education. At over

6 per cent of the country's GDP, this is one of the highest rates in the world. Yet while much has been achieved, such as the introduction of the 'Mandela sandwich' (free school lunch), there are still major shortfalls. Fighting the culture of non-attendance and resistance to learning, the pressures caused by population growth, and the legacy of apartheid in terms of provision of resources between the races is a long uphill struggle, but one that is essential to enable South Africa to end poverty, unemployment and illiteracy among its people.

One major problem is the incompetence of many of the officials employed in provincial education departments. Another major issue is the quality of teaching, especially in mathematics and the sciences. Recent reports claim that over 75 per cent of maths teachers would fail the international tests for 12- or 13-year-old students. The ANC teachers' union is so powerful that it is difficult for officials to fire teachers. Even when a teacher is suspected of sexual harassment of students, they are more likely to be transferred to another school than prosecuted. Headteachers do not face accountability for academic failure or blatant mismanagement. According to Corruption Watch, 750 schools have been accused of acts of corruption.

South Africa's education system

South Africa has a single national Education Department and system providing learning for 14 million pupils. There is also a sizeable and growing private education sector. Provincial legislatures and local governments have substantial powers to run educational affairs (excluding universities and technikons – further education colleges) subject to a national policy framework.

Figure 3.11 **Inequality is still a problem in South Africa's school system**

The South African Schools Act, 1996, ensures that no state schools are racially segregated. While former white schools now take in students of all races, many former black South African and disadvantaged schools have no white students and have the highest number of matriculation failures. The Act also provides compulsory education for learners between the ages of 7 (Grade 1) and 15 (Grade 9). The first year of education, Grade R, and the last three years are not compulsory. From Grade 10 to Grade 12, students either attend school or engage in Further Education and Training (FET).

National norms and standards for school funding have been set to address the inequalities between the races. Schools are divided into five categories based on needs: the poorest 20 per cent receive 35 per cent of the resources and the richest 20 per cent receive 5 per cent of the resources. Education is not free in South Africa for many students, and school fees are paid by parents. This explains why many students from the poorest communities – and those who are disadvantaged most in their quality of life – do not attend school. The Department of Education now exempts the poorest 60 per cent of schools (all black South Africans) from fees. However, provincial education departments do not always provide the poorest schools with the money to cover the non-payment of fees.

Corruption in South African schools

Below are examples of corruption and poor management in schools and the impact on students:

- One school operated with eight illegal bank accounts and had a R6.2 million surplus. The school management claimed that the school was in deficit to further raise school fees.
- A total of 750 schools have been accused of acts of mismanagement and corruption.
- A school in Port Elizabeth with 1700 students had only 41 actual teachers. The school charged the authorities for having double that number, and management pocketed the money.
- In Eastern Cape, one school has 165 Grade 1 learners in one 'classroom', with one teacher and very few desks and chairs. In the whole school there are 14 toilets for 1175 learners.
- In Mthatha, in the Eastern Cape, one school has 935 learners and 23 teachers, who all share eight filthy pit toilets.
- In a primary school, in Libode district of the Eastern Cape, 235 learners are being taught in two mud huts and a nearby mud church. The nearest running water is 5 km away.

Matriculation results

The pattern of matriculation results (see Table 3.8), while highlighting significant progress since 2009, still reflects large inequalities in performance in spite of a more equitable allocation of resources across schools and provinces – clear evidence of massive regional inequalities that also cover wealth and health. The number presented for the exams in 2018 was 796,543, the highest ever figure. However, many argue that standards have been lowered and so pass rates are now meaningless. Johnathan Jansen of the University of the Free State stated 'these pass rates are calculated at a base of 30 per cent in some subjects and 40 per cent in others'.

Table 3.8 **Percentage pass rate for Grade 12 Matriculation Senior Certificate**

Province	Pass rate	
	2009	2018
Western Cape	75.7	81.5
Eastern Cape	51.0	70.6
Gauteng	71.8	87.9
Limpopo	48.9	69.4

Source: SA Department of Education, 2019

However, these figures only apply to those who sat the exam. Gauteng may have the highest pass rates but only 55 per cent of Grade 10 students in 2016 sat the matriculation exams in 2018. In contrast, 60 per cent of Grade 10 students in 2016 sat the matriculation exams in 2018 in the Western Cape. Moreover, the pass rate in the poorest schools in the Western Cape has increased from 57 per cent to 70 per cent over the last five years.

The missing students

Of the 1,171,323 students who started school in Grade 1 in 2007, only 796,543 sat their exams in 2018 – so over a third did not complete their schooling.

Modernisation of schools

Successive governments have made the upgrading of schools a priority and progress has been made in providing basic infrastructure within schools, such as electricity, water and sanitation. The 2017–18 report of the National Education Infrastructure Management System (NEIMS) provided the following statistics on the infrastructure of schools:

No electricity   269 schools

Use of pit toilets   8702 schools

No piped water   7816 schools

Source: www.education.gov.za

However, it did highlight that the situation was slowly improving as outlined in Table 3.9.

The tragic death of Lumka Mketwa, a five-year-old primary pupil who drowned in a pit toilet in March 2018, horrified the nation and led to a national debate about the inadequate sanitation provisions in many South African schools. Four years earlier, another child had met the same horrific fate. President Ramaphosa immediately ordered an audit of the country's 25,000 schools.

Table 3.9 **The infrastructure of schools (percentage)**

Year	Pit toilet	No sanitation	No water	No electricity	No library
2014	31.3	2.0	22.3	16.4	77.1
2015	28.8	0.5	22.2	16.0	76.8
2016	21.1	0.3	21.1	14.5	76.7

Source: www.education.gov.za

He promised that within two years no school would use these pit toilets. He stated 'This is an initiative that will save lives and restore the dignity of tens of thousands of our nation's children.'

The Sanitation Appropriate for Education (SAFE) initiative 2018

The SAFE initiative is being funded in partnership with private groups including the Nelson Mandela Foundation and the UN children's agency (UNICEF). The cost of the programme is estimated at R6.8 billion. President Ramaphosa said, 'The SAFE initiative reaches beyond the bricks and mortar of water and sanitation. It seeks to contribute to building a cohesive society in which schools are the heartbeat of wholesome communities.'

Crisis in education

The findings of the Institute for Justice and Reconciliation (IJR) report of 2006 are unfortunately still relevant today. The report states that nearly 80 per cent of high schools are failing their children and that the overwhelming majority of children in the failing schools are black African. The IJR also states 'the best schools are those that were reserved exclusively for white children prior to 1994 and these schools today should enrol the poorest children'. It was also widely reported that, of the top 200 schools in South Africa, 180 took only white students under apartheid. These 200 schools produced more distinctions in maths and science exams than the other 6476 secondary schools put together. The standard of teaching is low. South Africa needs 25,000 teachers a year but only around 10,000 qualify. Maths and science teachers are in especially short supply. The IJR also argued that the 500 Dinaledi schools should be

The tragic death of Lumka Mketwa

Her name is Lumka Mketwa and she was five years old. On Monday, Lumka fell into a pit latrine at her school, Luna Primary School in Bizana, in the Eastern Cape, and drowned. At first, nobody knew what had happened to the little girl. Her family and residents gathered and began searching until her body was found on Tuesday, a day after she had died. Monday had begun like any other day, with Lumka being driven to school along with her schoolmates in the scholar transport. But at the end of the school day, shortly after noon, as the children were making their way back to the vehicle, the five-year-old was not among them.

The family started a manhunt for Lumka. 'The whole village was looking until the morning. Some people slept at the school, hoping the child might come back during the night, but it didn't happen,' said Nomveliso [a local resident]. The police arrived in the morning with search dogs. The dogs would eventually latch on to Lumka's scent, close to where much of the search had been focused the previous night. Her little body was found at the bottom of one of the school's pit latrines.

Extracted from the *Mail & Guardian*, 16 March 2018

expanded as these schools were on the way to excellence. The Dinaledi project is a partnership between state schools and the business sector with the emphasis on maths and science.

Literacy and numeracy rates are low and these figures were confirmed in a 2018 report by the World Economic Forum. It ranked South Africa 128 out of 137 countries for its primary education and 128 for the poor quality of its science and maths. Violence (including rape of schoolgirls), pregnancy and poverty were factors in the high dropout rate in secondary schools. It is reported that teachers in black schools teach an average of 3.5 hours a day compared with 6.5 hours a day in former white schools.

Case study: Forte High, Soweto

In the township of Soweto in South Africa, Forte High School used to be known as a poorly performing school with few resources. In 2007, it had no running water, no computers and no area to play sports. Though designed to cater for 800 students, it had approximately 1300 students. Only half of those who reached the final year ended up with the most basic certificate for finishing school.

But a transformation took place when rich sponsors stepped in to help the school. An international charity, Art of Living Foundation, also provided free food for the students and additional lessons in maths and science outside of school hours and during the holidays.

By 2012, the school jumped up to achieve an 80 per cent pass rate. This had a dramatic impact on the students' prospects after school, with half of its matriculation students qualifying for university. Flourishing with the support the school could now give them, students spoke of their aspirations, though the cost of university was still often a worry, and how they no longer needed to turn to crime to buy food or to alcohol and drugs to help with mental strain of the constant hunger.

University and technikon students

Despite the shortcomings in attainment, a significant change has taken place in higher education. There is clear evidence of progress. Black South Africans now make up around 70 per cent of university and technikon students. Under BEE legislation all higher education institutions must have equity targets to ensure that black students are not under-represented. White students argue that they are being discriminated against but can take no action as the Constitution supports 'Black Transformation'. In 2018, over a million students enrolled in higher education, up from around half a million in 1994.

However, there is a growing crisis over the number of young people who do not find work, training or go into higher education. This NEET generation (not in employment, education or training) now stands at 3 million, with most facing a lifetime of unemployment and poverty.

At the other end of the educational spectrum, the Government's Adult Basic Education and Training (ABET) programme has led to a steady increase in the literacy rate of adults, which now stands at

95 per cent. The Kha Ri Guide (Let us Learn) mass literacy campaign was launched in 2008. The Government pledged to spend R6 billion over five years to enable 4.7 million South Africans to achieve literacy by 2013. However, significant provincial inequalities remain. Provinces with the largest number of illiterate people are KwaZulu-Natal, Limpopo and the Eastern Cape. The lowest numbers occur in the Western Cape and the Free State.

In his 2018 state of the nation address, President Ramaphosa confirmed that fully subsidised higher education and training will be phased in over a five-year period to provide for the poorest families.

Show your understanding

1 Outline the impact of social grants.
2 Describe the South African education system and new exam reforms.
3 To what extent has progress been made in exam results, modernisation of schools and African entry to further and higher education?
4 What evidence suggests that South African education is in a poor state?

Health

Under successive governments significant progress has been made in improving primary health care (PHC) in both urban and rural areas. South Africa spends 8.8 per cent of its GDP on health. For those not covered by medical aid schemes, free health care is provided at public PHC facilities such as clinics and community health-care centres. Some 42 per cent of all South Africans live in poverty and more than half of these live in rural areas where health services are least developed. Regional inequalities reflect the urban–rural divide. Gauteng and Western Cape are highly urbanised and have the best health provision. This health inequality is reflected in the lower life expectancy in the poorest provinces (see Table 3.11). Malnutrition is a major problem in rural areas alongside recent outbreaks of cholera in KwaZulu-Natal and tuberculosis in the Eastern Cape. Since 1996, 11 state-of-the-art hospitals have been built to tackle the poor hospital facilities available in provinces such as the Eastern Cape.

A key weapon against ill health and disease has been the availability of clean water. Over the last 20 years, 13 million South Africans have been provided with a clean water supply. As with other things, regional inequalities still exist in the percentage of households with no toilet facility. Child mortality rates double when there is no access to clean water.

There is a very strong private health service, which inevitably reflects a racial imbalance in favour of white people and ensures that they have access to better health provision. The private sector spends over R38 billion and serves around 12 million people, while the public sector spends R38 billion and serves over 40 million people. At present, hospital patients who do not have private health insurance pay for examinations and treatment on a sliding scale in accordance with their income and number of dependants. Those who meet the 'poverty criteria' have their fees paid by the provincial government.

State health provision faces severe problems. Under the former president, Jacob Zuma, state hospitals were under-funded despite the burgeoning AIDS epidemic (see page 105). This was reflected in the low pay of state health-care workers including doctors. Many health-care workers have moved to the private sector or have gone abroad to countries such as the UK. Health unions claim staff morale is low and that there is a shortage of vital medical equipment. However, the present crisis is also linked to the corruption and maladministration at the provincial level, whereby health funds have been misappropriated, leading to a shortfall in funding. The Democratic Alliance conducted a health survey in 2018, which highlighted that the Tenbisa hospital in Gauteng only had 40 per cent of the nurses that are required. Many wards that were supposed to have ten nurses had only one. The *Sunday Times, South Africa* (6 June 2018) highlighted the shortage of doctors, nurses and equipment and stated that some health authorities were not replacing staff because of a budget crisis. One doctor stated: 'I estimate … Gauteng will be 40–50% down in absolute number of qualified doctors employed in the state. That's going to collapse an already terrible system further.'

Table 3.10 Doctors per 100,000 of the population, by province (selected), 2016

Province	Doctors
Western Cape	41.0
Gauteng	39.0
Eastern Cape	15.2
North West	14.6
Limpopo	12.5

Source: SA Health Statistics, 2017

Primary health care

The primary health care programme offers a comprehensive range of services delivered by health professionals and associated organisations, such as school and nutritional services. Water and sanitation services, both of which have an obvious connection to health, are also included.

The strategy embraces health education, nutrition, family planning, immunisation, screening for common diseases, HIV/AIDS education and counselling, maternal and child health, oral health and the provision of essential drugs.

Projects such as the National Primary School Nutrition Project for needy primary school children have improved educational achievement as well as health standards. Every day about 6 million children in over 18,000 schools munch on a 'Mandela sandwich'. This has increased attendance at school and improved concentration and alertness levels.

Immunisation against tuberculosis, whooping cough, diphtheria, polio and measles is available free of charge to all children under the age of six. Such has been the success of this programme that South Africa has been declared polio-free by the Global Certification Commission.

Alongside the free health-care programme for children under six and pregnant women, an impressive clinic building and upgrading programme has been implemented. Around 3500 primary health-care clinics have been built and more than 700 mobile clinics set up, providing basic health care in the most remote and isolated areas.

HIV/AIDS

The one regret Nelson Mandela had from his period in office was his failure to tackle the outbreak of HIV/AIDS in South Africa (in 1994 2 per cent of those aged between 20 and 64 were HIV-positive). Unfortunately his successor, Thabo Mbeki, was very slow to react to the crisis. HIV/AIDS is the biggest health and social issue facing South Africa today and Mbeki was criticised, even by Nelson Mandela, for his failure to accept that AIDS is caused by HIV. For this reason Mbeki initially refused to give free anti-AIDS drugs to all HIV-positive pregnant women and their children.

In November 2001, a small group of AIDS activists, the Treatment Action Campaign (TAC), took the Government to the highest court of the land, the Constitutional Court, to force it to provide the anti-AIDS drug, Nevirapine, free to mother and child at birth. The Court ruled in favour of TAC and, in October 2002, the Government announced that it would investigate ways of providing the anti-retroviral drugs that keep people alive – a dramatic reversal of policy.

Fact file

AIDS pandemic: the present and the future?

- Life expectancy had dropped from 62 to 50 but has risen again to 63.
- South Africa has the largest HIV epidemic in the world with 6.8 million people infected with the virus.
- 35 per cent of deaths among pregnant women are caused by AIDS.
- Over 1 million children under the age of 18 have lost their mothers to AIDS.
- Around 400 South Africans die every day from AIDS.
- Almost 40 per cent of women aged between 25 and 29 are infected by HIV/AIDS.
- 500,000 people are infected each year.
- Racial divide – 13 per cent of black South Africans suffer AIDS, compared with 3 per cent of coloured and Asian citizens and 1 per cent of white citizens.

Table 3.11 **Life expectancy, 2018, selected provinces**

Province	Life expectancy
Western Cape	72.1
Gauteng	69.8
Eastern Cape	65.8
Limpopo	65.4
Free State	61.5

Source: SA Health Statistics, 2018

Figure 3.12 Nkosi Johnson

'I want people to understand AIDS – to be careful and respect AIDS. You can't get AIDS if you touch, hug or hold hands with someone who is infected. Care for us, and accept us, we are all human beings, we are normal. We have needs just like everyone else. Don't be afraid of us. I just wish the Government would give anti-AIDS drugs to all HIV-positive pregnant women and their children.'

These are the words spoken by 11-year-old Nkosi Johnson at an International AIDS Conference held in Durban, South Africa, in July 2000. Nkosi had been born HIV-positive and abandoned by his mother. He was sent to a hospice to die. There he was adopted by a white woman,

Gail Johnson, and he outlived both his parents (who died of AIDS). Within a year of speaking at the conference he was dead. Such was the impact he had made on the international community that his death was mourned around the world.

The South African National HIV, Behaviour and Health Survey 2012 indicated that KwaZulu-Natal, Mpumalanga and the Free State have the highest HIV prevalence and that, among the races, Africans had the highest HIV prevalence. According to government figures, over 6 million South Africans suffer from HIV/AIDS and it is women in their late twenties who are the hardest hit.

The resignation of President Mbeki in December 2007 led to greater urgency in tackling the AIDS crisis through treatment and prevention. In December 2009, on World AIDS Day, President Zuma announced ambitious plans to expand the free treatment for HIV-positive babies and pregnant women by April 2010. Zuma had already appointed Dr Aaron Motsoaledi as his health minister, described by AIDS activists such as TAC as 'a man who trusts science and is willing to learn from past mistakes'. Zuma's Government had earlier set a target of getting AIDS drugs to 80 per cent of those who need them by 2011. At the time of writing, 4.4 million people receive anti-retroviral treatment, approximately 61 per cent of infected adults.

Table 3.12 **AIDS deaths in South Africa, selected years**

Year	Number of AIDS-related deaths
2002	215,568
2006	293,166
2010	175,375
2014	122,139
2017	115,167

Source: SA Health Statistics 2018

1 Outline the progress that has been made in the provision of primary health care and other health improvements.
2 What evidence supports the view that health inequalities are a major problem? (Refer to regional inequalities and the role of the private sector.)
3 Why was President Mbeki criticised over his handling of the HIV/AIDS crisis and what action did President Zuma take?
4 What evidence suggests that HIV/AIDS is the biggest health crisis in South Africa and that the situation is improving?

Land and housing

There is a distinct racial and urban–rural divide in terms of housing. The situation is not helped by an influx of people into the cities from the rural areas. There are now 15 million people living in RDP starter homes. The creation of a black middle class has led to a growth in the number of homes provided by the private sector. Between 2002 and 2012 the number of black property owners increased by just under 60 per cent, and over 50 per cent now own their own homes. Townships such as Soweto now have a middle-class area and a shopping mall. In the Diepkloof neighbourhood of Soweto, new cars are parked next to elegant houses protected by security gates.

Progress has been made in providing basic amenities such as electricity and running water. The electrification programme has seen a further 3.6 million homes provided with electricity. The Community Water Supply Programme has brought clean water to over 10 million mainly rural homes. Unfortunately, a culture of non-payment of rents and amenities charges persists. The situation has not been helped by the privatisation of services, which led to an increase in charges.

A significant number of the new black middle class have moved into the former exclusively white areas. They live in mansions with spacious grounds or luxury apartments with controlled entry and security guards. In contrast, those black South Africans who live in informal settlements (squatter camps) have witnessed little progress since 1994. Their makeshift homes lack electricity and sanitation provision, crime is high and health is poor. Schooling is basic; many of the children do not complete secondary school and do not have the skills to contribute to or benefit from the BEE programmes. Gauteng and North West have the largest number of informal settlements. There has been a shift from rural to urban areas. In the main urban areas, 20 per cent of people are new migrants.

Spatial apartheid

In Cape Town there is a continuation of geographical or spatial apartheid. The majority of black and coloured citizens live in their own townships on the edge of the city or alongside dual carriageways, while most whites live in the wealthy suburbs. Government success in providing electricity, water and housing to the poor areas has had the unintended consequence of strengthening spatial apartheid by encouraging people to remain in their segregated communities.

In Johannesburg local officials ended this spatial apartheid by narrowing the great distances between the black majority homes and the industrial centre. A stylish pedestrian bridge has been built that now links Alexandra township, where Nelson Mandela once lived, with Sandton, the city's wealthiest suburb, and also where massive shopping malls are located. The two areas are close to each other as the crow flies, but were cut off from each other by a busy motorway. At least 10,000 people make their way between Alexandra and Sandton every day.

Figure 3.13 The bridge won the 2019 Fulton Award

However, clear progress has been made since 2004. Then one household in eight had no toilet; now only 5 per cent are without a flushing toilet. The percentage of households without sanitation decreased from 12.6 per cent in 2014 to 3.1 per cent in 2017. The number of homes with electricity has increased from 77 per cent to 88 per cent. Two-thirds of homes now have their rubbish collected. Living standards have improved and this is reflected in over 80 per cent of homes having a television, mobile phone and an electric stove.

Table 3.13 **Access to basic services, 1996–2017**

Households using electricity	1996 (%)	2002 (%)	2017 (%)
For lighting	58	70	88
For cooking	47	58	77
For heating	45	49	65

Source: South Africa General Household Survey, 2018

Land reform

Land reform, especially in the countryside, is a major issue. A new Department of Land Affairs was created in 1994 with responsibility for developing and implementing a policy of land reform. The plan involves:

- compensating those who lost their land because of apartheid laws
- redistributing the productive land to those who were disadvantaged
- creating an independent Commission on Restitution of Land Rights as well as a Land Claims Court; any claimant will have to prove that he or she was dispossessed after 1913 without financial compensation or alternative land being provided
- setting up the Land Reform Pilot Programme to 'establish mechanisms for state-assisted entry into the land market for the most disadvantaged sectors of rural society'
- giving tenants the right to buy the land on which they farm and protection from eviction.

The original Reconstruction and Development Plan (RDP) promise of redistribution of 30 per cent of agricultural land within five years was totally unrealistic. The revised target date of 2014 was also not achieved. Black ownership of land increased from 13 per cent in 1994 to 20 per cent in 2014. Most people in urban areas prefer cash compensation to land redistribution. This, therefore, partly explains the limited increase in black land ownership. By 2014, all of the 80,000 land claims made by 1998 had been settled at a cost of R29 billion, including the transfer of 1.6 million acres benefiting 370,000 households. It was announced in May 2014 that there would be a reopening of land claims to run until 2019. This did not satisfy the radical wing of the ANC, who demanded a review of the 'willing buyer–willing seller' principle.

The 'willing buyer–willing seller' principle has been at the core of South Africa's land settlement, guaranteeing that land will be acquired by the state at fair prices and given to the landless black population. The Government has the power to force a compulsory sale if the white farmer rejects the original offer. This policy, despite its good intentions, has had an adverse effect on agricultural production. White farmers are reluctant to invest in improvements, while others have abandoned their farms.

Many white farmers are concerned about the brutal attacks on their farms and the lack of police action.

At the ANC conference in December 2017, the party voted to change the Constitution to let the state seize land without compensation. This controversial decision was endorsed in Parliament in March 2018. Pressure from the radical Economic Freedom Fighters (EFF) and the left wing of the ANC has forced President Ramaphosa to implement a policy that could damage the economy and could frighten foreign investors. White farmers are afraid that this policy will encourage racial attacks against them.

Crime

The fear and impact of crime is one issue that unites all races. While many white people and rich Africans seek safety in their walled estates, ordinary black and coloured South Africans protect their families as best they can. The availability of guns is a major problem. You can buy an AK47 rifle in any taxi queue for £30. On average, 57 murders take place every day. Of these, around half are caused by guns. The 2018/2019 State of Urban Safety in South Africa Report produced by SaferSpaces highlights that many of the illegal guns obtained by rival gangs are provided by corrupt police officers.

Official government figures clearly indicate that South Africa is a less violent country than previously. The number of murders has declined by 30 per cent since 1994 – the 2018 figure was 20,336. However, this still represents 57 murders a day, making South Africa one of the most dangerous places to live. This figure equates to 36 murders per 100,000 South Africans. The Democratic Alliance argues that many crimes are not reported as the public have little faith in the culprits being caught. Furthermore, the murder and sexual assault rates are beginning to rise again, as outlined in Table 3.14. Many citizens do not trust the police and in fact the police officer initially in charge of investigations against Pistorius (see box on page 110) was himself being investigated on a charge of murder; he resigned from the police force and no further action was taken (see 'Police brutality and corruption' box, pages 110–11). A study by the Human Sciences Research Council in 2016 found that 66 per cent of adults thought corruption was widespread in the police. Less than half (41 per cent) of the population had any trust in the police at all and 35 per cent of South Africans interviewed admitted to being scared of the police. For wealthier citizens, protection comes from private security firms and life in gated communities. For the majority of black people, the threat of violence is constant and many vigilante groups dispense their own punishment to criminals, ranging from beatings to killings. In 2012, Andile Mtsholo was beaten, stabbed and 'necklaced' by Khayelitsha residents in a vigilante attack. No arrests have ever been made.

Table 3.14 Violent crime in South Africa, 2017–18

	Murder	Sexual offences
2017	19,016	49,660
2018	20,336	50,108
Percentage increase	6.9	0.9

Source: africacheck.org

Case study: Why was there a crime explosion in South Africa after 1994?

- The dismantling of the rigid controls imposed by the security forces in the apartheid years brought crime into the former white suburbs.
- The apartheid years created a culture of violence.
- The association of law enforcement and the rule of law with the apartheid regime created a lack of respect for the police within the black community.
- The vast inequalities in terms of wealth in South Africa created a 'war' between the 'haves' and the 'have nots'.
- Massive influxes of poor people from the countryside to the towns and the arrival of illegal immigrants (estimated at 4 million) from other African countries created a group in society who ignore its laws.

South Africa's culture of violence and Oscar Pistorius

In September 2014, Oscar Pistorius was found guilty of culpable homicide (manslaughter) for the death of his girlfriend Reeva Steenkamp. He was given a five-year prison sentence. In February 2013, the world-famous paralympic athlete had shot dead his girlfriend. He blamed South Africa's culture of violence for his actions. He said he was afraid that there was an intruder in the bathroom who might murder the couple.

Figure 3.14 Oscar Pistorius

Pistorius and Reeva Steenkamp were staying in a gated community in Cape Town, surrounded by an electric fence and high walls, yet he still did not feel safe. The former wife of the last white president of South Africa, F.W. de Klerk, was shot dead in a similar well-protected gated community.

Initially, Pistorius was given a suspended jail sentence. However, there was a public demand for a harsher sentence and he was given a 13-year jail sentence. Pistorius took the case to the highest court of the land. In April 2018, the court rejected his request to appeal against the sentence and Pistorius is now serving his sentence.

Police brutality and corruption

The Nondo Commission is examining evidence of police corruption, extortion and brutality over the past ten years. The shooting of striking miners at Marikana and the recorded killing of a Mozambican taxi driver dragged behind a police

van have already tarnished the reputation of the police. The following disclosures from the Nondo Commission and statistics from the Independent Police Investigative Directorate (IPID) highlight the crisis facing the police:

- Senior officers such as Robert McBride, the former director of IPID, investigating the corrupt activities of criminals and politicians were suspended after allegations of corruption (later proved to be false) were made against them.

- Whistle-blower Aris Danikas had to flee the country in 2009 after collecting incriminating evidence against Durban's Organised Police Crime Unit, which was running a death squad. Finally, in 2019, charges were brought against 27 members of the unit.
- Between 2015 and 2018, more than 5500 cases of police criminal offences were reported every year. Of these numbers, according to Annual Report Statistics, more

than 3500 cases of torture and assault (police brutality) were reported. Yet only 1.9 per cent of police officers have been convicted and shockingly, there was a zero conviction rate for torture.

- The report found there were 207 deaths as a result of police action in 2017–18: 'deaths in police custody contributed to 43% while deaths as a result of police brutality contributed 57% of the total deaths'. Members of the South African Police Service were involved in 51 rape incidents, 61 torture incidents, 66 corruption cases and 159 other criminal cases.

Case study: The Marikana massacre

On 16 August 2012, the police shot dead 34 striking miners at Lonmin Mine, a platinum mine near Marikana in North West province. Archbishop Tutu, Nobel Peace Prize Laureate, summed up the shock of the nation when he said, 'Marikana felt like a nightmare, but that is what our democracy is in 2012.' Further disbelief grew after the National Prosecutor charged 259 miners with the murder of their colleagues, citing a 'Common purpose' law used by the white apartheid government. Under public pressure this charge was dropped, but it highlighted the political interference of President Zuma in the judicial process.

President Zuma commissioned an inquiry into the shooting to be headed by former Supreme Court of Appeals Judge Ian Gordon Farlam to 'investigate matters of public, national and international concern arising out of the tragic incidents at the Lonmin Mine in Marikana'.

What is clear is that the video and photographic evidence presented contradict the police version that they only opened fire after the striking miners had fired on police units. Photographs clearly show some of the dead miners on the ground without weapons at their sides; in the police photographs they are holding weapons.

The Marikana Support Campaign firmly places the responsibility for these murders on political interference and collusion between the state and Lonmin. It stated, 'The most central figure in this collusion is none other than the Deputy President of our country, and Lonmin shareholder and previous non-Executive board member, Cyril Ramaphosa.' The deputy president wrote in a string of emails:

Figure 3.15 Striking miners in Marikana

Case study (continued)

'The terrible events that have unfolded cannot be described as a labour dispute. They are plainly dastardly criminal and must be characterized as such. In line with this characterization there needs to be concomitant action to address the situation.'

The inquiry completed its evidence in December 2014. The final report was presented to the president in April 2015.

No prosecutions have been brought against any police officers. The families are still fighting for an apology and compensation. The authorities have offered compensation without apology and as of June 2019 no payments have been made or agreements reached with the families.

Added Value idea

The investigation into the deaths of miners in the Marikana massacre is hugely topical. This would be a good opportunity for your Added Value unit assignment. You will need to research and develop your own sources and present your findings in the form of a report. Discuss this with your teacher.

Show your understanding

1 Describe the progress made in the provision of adequate housing and basic services in South Africa.
2 Outline the South African Government's policy on land reform.
3 Why has there been a crime explosion in South Africa?
4 What evidence suggests that serious crime is still a significant problem in South Africa?
5 What evidence suggests that the police in South Africa abuse their powers?

12-mark question

Evaluate the effectiveness of government policies to reduce social and economic inequalities.

The political system

The 1994 elections and the creation of a liberal, progressive Constitution transformed South Africa into a stable, multi-party democracy with all the features of a pluralist society including a free press and an independent judiciary. Six successive elections have been held and Nelson Mandela's dream of a rainbow nation has been achieved. The Truth and Reconciliation Commission (see page 90) has brought closure to the horrors of apartheid. Yet some fear that the dominance of the ANC and the corrupt activities of some of its members are turning the country into a one-party state where criticism of the government, especially when Mbeki was president, is seen as white racism or, if by black citizens, as a betrayal of fellow Africans. Jacob Zuma's comment in 2008 that 'the ANC will rule South Africa until Jesus returns' horrified many South Africans for its arrogance.

While South Africa has on paper a federal system of government, the reality is that the central government totally dominates the provinces. Only in Western Cape is there an alternative to ANC rule; in 2009 the Democratic Alliance (DA) gained overall control of the province and retained control in the 2014 and 2019 elections. However, there is concern that the ANC will attempt to further reduce the powers of the provinces to weaken the power of the Western Cape provincial government.

The Constitution of South Africa

The Constitution includes a Bill of Rights, which guarantees an extensive range of human rights. This includes equality before the law, the right to life, including the abolition of the death penalty, and freedom of speech and religion.

The Constitution provides for an independent judiciary. The Constitutional Court is the highest court in the land. It deals with the interpretation, protection and enforcement of the Constitution and exclusively with constitutional matters. The Constitutional Court plays a crucial role in upholding the rights of the citizens of South Africa. There are 11 judges including the Chief Justice. One of its most recent decisions was to uphold the right of South African citizens living abroad to vote in national elections.

The Constitution makes clear reference to the need to address the inequalities created by apartheid. Article 9.2 states 'To promote achievement of equality, legislative and other measures designed to protect or advance persons or categories of persons disadvantaged by unfair treatment may be taken.'

Central government

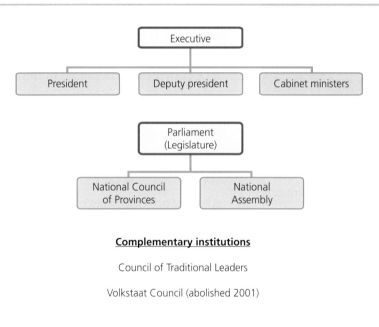

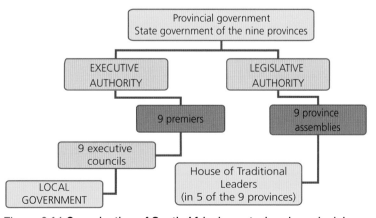

Figure 3.16 **Organisation of South Africa's central and provincial governments**

Parliament

South Africa has a bicameral (two-chamber) parliament consisting of a National Assembly (400 members) and the National Council of Provinces (NCOP). The council has two roles, both as an upper house and also as a body with special responsibilities to protect provincial interests. The NCOP consists of 90 delegates (ten from each province) and ten delegates representing local government. Elections for both houses are held every five years based on a system of proportional representation (PR).

Figure 3.17 **The South African Parliament in Pretoria**

The president and the Cabinet

The president is elected by the National Assembly from among its members. He or she is the executive head of state and leads the Cabinet. The president may not serve more than two five-year terms in office.

The present Cabinet consists of the president, the deputy president and 36 ministers (with 37 deputies). The significant increase in the Executive was part of Zuma's strategy to keep his supporters happy and loyal. The president appoints the deputy president and ministers, and may also dismiss them. Thabo Mbeki sacked Jacob Zuma as deputy president in 2005. However, Zuma's supporters forced Mbeki to resign in 2008.

Table 3.15 **Presidents of South Africa, 1994–2018**

President	Terms of office
Nelson Mandela	1994–99
Thabo Mbeki	2000–08 (forced to resign)
Kgalema Motlanthe	2008–09
Jacob Zuma	2009–18 (forced to resign)
Cyril Ramaphosa	2018–present

Law making

Legislation may be introduced in the National Assembly only by Cabinet members, deputy ministers or a member of a National Assembly committee. Bills amending the Constitution require a two-thirds majority vote in favour in the National Assembly as well as a supporting vote of six of the nine provinces represented in the NCOP. Any bill amending Section 1 of the Constitution, which sets out the state's founding values, requires a 75 per cent majority vote in the National Assembly.

Provincial government

All nine provinces have their own legislature and government led by a premier. In 2019, eight of the nine premiers were appointed by President Cyril Ramaphosa. This ensures that the ANC leadership controls the provincial parties and weakens the powers of the provincial governments. Provincial constitutions and laws must correspond with the National Constitution as confirmed by the Constitutional Court. Provinces have legislative powers over agriculture, cultural affairs, education (except higher education), environment, health services, housing, local government, police, welfare services, and urban and rural development.

Local government

There are 283 local councils, which are referred to as municipalities, and large cities such as Cape Town and Johannesburg have their own

The South African Constitution:

Maintains unitary government. The Constitution of South Africa shall provide for the establishment of one sovereign state, a common South African citizenship and a democratic system of government committed to achieving equality between men and women and people of all races.

Supports cultural identity. The diversity of language and culture shall be acknowledged and protected, and conditions for their promotion shall be encouraged.

Offers limited powers to the provinces. The powers granted to the provinces are to be used to improve the well-being of their inhabitants in accordance with the policies and priorities of the national government.

metropolitan municipalities. Under the corruption of Jacob Zuma, much of the funds devolved to local government to improve local services ended up in the pocket of unscrupulous businesses and politicians. This led to an increase in civil unrest.

Participation opportunities

Apart from voting and being a member of a political party, South Africans can join pressure groups including trade unions and community groups. An educational pressure group Equal Education has taken the Government to court over its failure to install proper sanitation in all schools (see page 101). In 2018 the courts ordered the Government to end the practice of 'pit latrines'. President Ramaphosa has promised that all schools will be provided with basic sanitation.

Unfortunately, many local groups have lost confidence in their politicians and resort to illegal protests that in many cases become violent. Virtually every day in South Africa a violent protest occurs, especially in the townships denied the amenities promised by the Government. Large-scale riots in townships linked to public grievances reached a record

high in 2018 with 198 'service delivery protests' taking place (previous highest was 191 in 2014). Rioters typically block roads with burning tyres. In February 2014, the Dangerous Weapons Act came into effect, which prohibits the carrying of firearms, and other weapons such as spears and axes.

Many South Africans do not trust the police, and events such as the Marikana massacre of 2012 reinforce the view that official trade unions are there to serve the ANC and not the people. Workers are becoming disillusioned with the ANC-dominated unions. The leaders of the National Union of Mineworkers (NUM) receive a salary from mining companies. It was the breakaway union AMCU that organised the mining strikes across South Africa, including Marikana.

Elections

National elections are held every five years under the National List proportional representation system, which closely matches votes to seats won by a political party. It encourages the formation of new parties. In the 2019 general election Patricia de Lille, a disaffected member of the Democratic Alliance, formed a new party, GOOD, and won two seats. However, as parties divide to form new parties this weakens the formation of a strong opposition to the ANC. The use of a party list means that the loyalty of ANC MPs is to the party and not to the people as there are no constituency links to the electorate. Many Africans do not choose to vote for the ANC based on their policies or their record, but base their support on their loyalty to the party of liberation and to the memory of Nelson Mandela.

Voting turnout has witnessed a steady decline. In 2014, 74 per cent registered to vote, compared to only 65 per cent in 2019, the lowest ever turnout. But this figure excludes the millions who failed to register. As such, just 46 per cent of South Africans adults actually voted in the 2019 election, and just

Political parties

African National Congress (ANC)

The ANC dominates South African politics and is the party of Nelson Mandela and black liberation. It has won all six of the national elections and in 2019, despite the cloud of corruption hanging over former President Zuma, it won 58 per cent of votes and 230 seats. Africans, especially the poor and poorly educated, remain loyal to the ANC.

Democratic Alliance (DA)

The DA is the second largest party, with 84 seats, and in the 2019 election it retained control of the Western Cape. It did, however, for the first time fail to increase its support, with its MPs falling from 89 to 84. Its main supporters are white and Asian people and people of mixed race. It now has the support of a growing number of middle-class African voters.

Economic Freedom Fighters (EFF)

Julius Malema, the former ANC Youth leader, formed EFF in October 2013 and gained an impressive 6.4 per cent of the votes in the 2014 election. In the 2019 election EFF increased its votes to 11 per cent. EFF won the support of the far left and young disillusioned and poor Africans. It advocates nationalisation of the mining sector, the doubling of public expenditure and land redistribution without compensations.

Inkatha Freedom Party (IFP)

The IFP, led by Chief Buthelezi, draws its support largely from Zulu-speaking South Africans and wants greater powers to be given to the provinces. It is a party in decline and it lost heavily to the ANC in the 2009 and 2014 elections in KwaZulu-Natal. However, with the demise of Zulu-born Jacob Zuma, it increased its seats from 10 to 14.

Freedom Front Plus (FF+)

This Afrikaans-speaking party more than doubled its votes in the 2019 election, with many white conservative voters switching from the DA. The party is against Affirmative Action and the expropriation without compensation of land.

over a third of those aged 18–25 – the 'born-free' generation – voted.

The 2014 national election

As expected, the ANC won the 2014 national election with a clear majority – 62 per cent of the votes. Despite widespread ANC corruption, an economy with slow growth and massive unemployment, most Africans voted with their hearts and not their heads. At the time, about 44 per cent of households were dependent on welfare payments to make ends meet and the ANC was criticised for using political rallies to give out state-funded food parcels to those who turned up. Turnout from the 'born frees' – who had never experienced apartheid – was disappointing: just under 30 per cent voted.

Figure 3.18 Mmusi Maimane, first black African leader of the DA, who resigned as leader in October 2019

The DA, with 22 per cent of the votes, achieved its best ever result and, more importantly, it retained control of the Western Cape and significantly increased its support in Gauteng – gaining 30 per cent of the vote. In total the DA won over 4 million votes compared to its previous high of just under 3 million in 2009. It was clear that the DA was widening its support to include educated and middle-class black Africans. The DA's control of the Western Cape since 2010 has made it the least corrupt and most effective province. In May 2015, Helen Zille stepped down as leader of the DA and

was replaced by Mmusi Maimane, the first black African leader of the party.

The newly formed EFF became the third largest party with 25 MPs in the national parliament. Significantly, it came second in two of the poorer provinces, Limpopo and North West. With 1 million votes, EFF hope to win the further support of the unemployed and poverty-stricken citizens.

The 2019 national election

As expected, the ANC won the 2019 election and retained control of eight of the nine provinces. However, it received its lowest ever percentage of votes, winning around 58 per cent. It just managed to gain an overall majority in Gauteng, winning 50.2 per cent of the votes. Overall, the party lost over a million votes and just managed to reach 10 million.

Nevertheless the result was a solid mandate for President Ramaphosa to continue his campaign against corruption in the ANC. A party official admitted that if Zuma had stayed, support would have significantly fallen.

The election witnessed the two largest parties losing ground to some smaller parties. The ANC lost votes to the radical left-wing EFF and the DA to the right-wing FF Plus.

Although the DA finished second with 20.77 per cent of the votes and also retained the Western Cape, it was a disappointing outcome. The DA is the opposition once again in the Northern Cape, Eastern Cape, Free State and Gauteng. For the first time in five elections, it failed to increase its support. Division within the party in the Western Cape and the ANC policy to seize white land encouraged many conservative Afrikaners to vote for the FF Plus. The poor election result, with the drop in white support and a failure to significantly gain more votes from the black middle class, led to a demand for the party to change its policy direction. The party had endorsed policies such as BEE to readdress the inequalities of apartheid and it was clear that the election of Helen Zille as chairperson of the federal council would lead to the DA opposing affirmative action policies. In response Maimane resigned as party leader, leaving the DA in turmoil.

The EFF increased its seats from 25 to 44 and won 1.8 million votes. Its leader, Julius Malema, had expected the ANC to fail to win an overall majority in Gauteng and had hoped to form a coalition government in the province. The EFF is yet again the opposition in Limpopo and North West, while taking that role from the DA in Mpumalanga.

The Afrikaner party FF Plus fought on a platform of *Slaan Terug* – Fight Back. They doubled their votes and increased their seats from four to ten. It is estimated that the DA lost 250,000 conservative voters to FF Plus. In many ways this was inevitable with the DA trying to attract moderate black voters. The DA's support for Affirmative Action convinced many Afrikaners to vote for a race-based party.

The IFP made a modest comeback and increased its seats from ten to fourteen and became once again the opposition in KwaZulu-Natal. In total, 14 parties gained some representation in the National Assembly. A record number of parties – 48 in all – participated in the election and a record number of registered voters failed to vote.

Julius Malema

The young leader of the EFF is a charismatic figure who preaches hatred towards white people and scorn towards the ANC's Black Diamonds. He was the leader of the ANC Youth League but was sacked by Zuma for his outspoken criticism of the ANC leadership. He taps into the anger and frustration of black youths who are experiencing an unemployment rate of over 50 per cent and who are trapped in a cycle of poverty and crime (they are ineligible for state welfare). His singing of 'kill the Boers' (Afrikaners) has been condemned as a hate crime by the courts and his demands that land should be taken from white people has encouraged further brutal attacks on white farmers (see page 120). Helen Zille, the former leader of the DA, described him as a 'dictator in waiting'.

Figure 3.19 Julius Malema, leader of the EFF

Table 3.16 National Assembly election results for the African National Congress (ANC) and Democratic Alliance (DA), 2009–19

Party	Seats			Votes		
	2009	2014	2019	2009 (%)	2014 (%)	2019 (%)
African National Congress	264	249	230	65.9	62.1	57.6
Democratic Alliance	67	89	84	16.7	22.2	20.8

Table 3.17 Election results for the province of Western Cape, selected parties, 2014–19

Party	2014		2019	
	Votes	Seats	Votes	Seats
African National Congress	697,664	14	589,055	12
Democratic Alliance	1,259,645	26	1,140,647	24
Economic Freedom Fighters	44,762	1	83,075	2
Freedom Front Plus	22,502	–	54,762	1

Table 3.18 Election results of parties elected to National Assembly, 2019

Party	Votes	Per cent	+/–	Seats	+/–
African National Congress	10,026,475	57.5	−4.65	230	−19
Democratic Alliance	3,621,188	20.77	−1.46	84	−5
Economic Freedom Fighters	1,881,521	10.79	+4.44	44	+19
Inkatha Freedom Party	588,839	3.38	+0.98	14	+4
Freedom Front Plus	288,742	2.38	+1.48	10	+6

Show your understanding

1 Describe the main features of the South African Constitution. Refer to the Bill of Rights, an independent judiciary, a unitary government, limited power to the provinces and Article 9.2.
2 Describe the political structure set up by the 1996 Constitution. Refer to parliament, the president, the Cabinet and provincial governments.
3 Assess the impact of the 2019 elections on the four major parties.

The dominance of the ANC

In 2013, the ANC celebrated its centenary and 2014 marked 20 years of ANC rule. The ANC dominates South African politics and the South African people display intense loyalty to the party. The 'Triple Alliance' between the ANC, SACP (South African Communist Party) and COSATU (Congress of South African Trade Unions) remains solid despite criticisms of Mbeki and Zuma's free-market economic policies. The Triple Alliance supported Zuma in his power struggle against former president Mbeki. The latter was forced to resign as president in 2008, despite clear evidence of Zuma's corruption. Zuma used his powers to appoint his ANC supporters to key posts in local and central government, including the eight premiers of the ANC-controlled provinces. The removal of Zuma as president in 2018 and the appointment of Ramaphosa as president on an anti-corruption platform offers hope for the future of the ANC and nation (see pages 121–2).

Jacob Zuma

The former president of South Africa is a controversial figure. For some he represents the unacceptable face of democracy, a man accused of massive corruption and of a lavish lifestyle, supporting his six wives and his 20 children. On the other hand, his humble rural background and his lack of formal education make him highly popular among the majority of black South Africans who are poor. He is a '100 per cent Zulu Boy' who seemed to offer hope to those who live in poverty. However, while Nelson Mandela brought out the best in the ANC, Jacob Zuma brought out the worst. He has almost bankrupted the nation and now faces accusations of massive corruption referred to as 'state capture'.

Figure 3.20 Jacob Zuma

The Afrikaner community

There is deep anger and frustration among the Afrikaner community over the erosion of its culture, especially the Afrikaans language. Only 1 per cent of all schools in South Africa are now single-medium Afrikaans schools. Stellenbosch University and other Afrikaans universities have lost their status as Afrikaans-medium institutions. Dan Roodt, an Afrikaner journalist, stated, 'What nation-building really means in South Africa is the complete destruction of Afrikaans culture and the Afrikaner identity.' This frustration and anger led to the re-emergence of white, right-wing terrorist attacks. In 2012, five Afrikaners were each sentenced to 35 years in prison for setting off bombs and plotting to kill Nelson Mandela.

BEE legislation discriminates against poorly educated white people (in the Afrikaner community) who cannot get jobs and about 10 per cent of white people live below the poverty line. White beggars are a common sight in South Africa's towns and white squatter camps dot the cities.

Over 3000 white farmers have been murdered since 1994. The South African police have not made investigation and prosecution of these farm murders a priority, dismissing them as crimes by common criminals. The Government has disbanded the commando units of white farmers that once protected their farms, and has passed laws to confiscate the farmers' weapons.

In April 2010, Eugene Terreblanche, the leader of the paramilitary extreme Afrikaner group the AWB (Afrikaner-Weerstandsbeweging), was savagely murdered on his farm by two black farm workers. Terreblanche had consistently demanded the creation of an Afrikaner Volkstaat (homeland). After his murder, Pieter Steyn, one of the AWB leaders, stated 'All we want is a piece of land in South Africa where we can settle ourselves and call it our own and govern ourselves with our religion … and our own laws.'

A recent outbreak of violent farm invasions has led to casualties among white South Africans. The farm invasions are also direct results of calls by EFF leader Julius Malema and his former deputy, Ronald Lamola, for white farmers to give up their land without compensation, or face violence by angry black youths 'flooding their farms'.

To what extent is South Africa a successful democracy?

Table 3.19 Arguments for and against democracy in South Africa

Arguments for	Arguments against
South Africa is a stable model of democracy for Africa. There have been six peaceful elections based on PR. A total of 48 political parties participated in the 2019 elections with 13 parties sitting in the National Assembly. The PR system encourages the formation of new political parties.	There is a fear that South Africa is becoming a one-party state. The ANC controls eight of the nine provinces. Only in Western Cape is it in opposition. The ANC has 230 of the assembly seats. In contrast, the official opposition, the DA, has 84 seats.
A peaceful transition from Mandela to Mbeki occurred. The power struggle between Zuma and Ramaphosa was resolved peacefully with the resignation of Zuma as president in February 2018.	There is an issue of corruption with an investigation now taking place into the extent of state capture by Zuma and his associates.
South Africa has a federal system of government with powers divided between central and provincial governments. Local government structures provide local services. The Western Cape is controlled by the Democratic Alliance and this has prevented the ANC from totally dominating politics. Helen Zille, former leader of the DA, called her victory 'a triumph for democracy'.	The federal system exists only on paper. Minority rights, such as Afrikaner and Zulu culture, are under threat. Ramaphosa appoints all eight premiers of the provinces under ANC rule and there is a lack of democracy within them. The people do not directly choose the president or premiers of the provinces.
South Africa has a liberal Constitution guaranteeing freedom to its citizens. It provides for an independent judiciary. The Constitutional Court ordered Mbeki to provide drugs to combat AIDS. There is a free press and civil society able to criticise and monitor the actions of the Government. The success of the Truth and Reconciliation Commission highlights the openness of South African society.	Mbeki was intolerant of criticism. He accused critics of being racists and even attacked Archbishop Tutu. The policy of Transformation Politics could threaten the independence of judges and the rights of non-black South Africans. The South African Broadcasting Corporation (SABC) is regarded as being the mouthpiece of the ANC. Zuma threatened the independence of the judiciary through new appointments to the Constitutional Court.

Corruption and state capture

In 2017, a report by academics entitled 'Betrayal of the promise: How South Africa is being stolen' accused Zuma and his key supporters of state capture and of turning South Africa into a 'mafia-style fiefdom'. Under Zuma, corruption not only thrived but took place in plain sight. In his nine-year rule, Zuma and his associates ransacked state-owned enterprises (SOEs), looted provincial and local government and silenced the law-enforcement institutions set up to prevent such corruption. Zuma's mansion was not a symbol of presidency power but a monument to the president's invincibility.

However, all began to change when Cyril Ramaphosa won the December 2017 ANC leadership contest. Zuma and his allies had hoped that the other candidate, the former wife of President Zuma, would win. In a tense and vicious campaign Ramaphosa won by a narrow majority. He stated that he would challenge corruption and provide moral renewal and leadership. However, he had to move cautiously as three of the top six ANC leadership were key participants in Zuma's state capture. Ramaphosa would use the law-enforcement institutions to investigate Zuma and his associates. This would be a slow process and as such, ANC allies of Zuma, now accused of state capture, stood as candidates in the May 2019 general election (see 'Investigation into state capture'). In February 2018, Zuma was forced to resign as president and was replaced by Ramaphosa. The new leader announced a reopening of 783 counts of corruption against Jacob Zuma after a court ruled that the decision to drop the charges a decade ago was 'irrational'.

Transparency International

Under President Zuma, corruption intensified. In 2009, South Africa was ranked 54 out of 183 countries on Transparency International's Corruption Perception Index (1 is the cleanest and 183 the most corrupt). In 2019, South Africa is assessed as being more corrupt than poorer states such as Rwanda and Senegal. In the 2013 rankings, South Africa had fallen to 72.

Investigation into state capture

In 2018 a judicial inquiry, presided over by the deputy chief justice, Raymond Zondo, was set up to investigate state capture (the wholesale takeover of public institutions by associates of the former president). Among those accused of being the worst offenders were the Gupta brothers, three Asian businessmen. Such were the close ties with Zuma that both parties were referred to as the 'Zuptas'.

Below are some of the accusations made against this group:

- At the centre of state capture were the activities of the Gupta family. They are accused of influencing Cabinet appointments and looting state-owned enterprises (SOEs) and other public funds. It is estimated that they stole R20 billion, which could have improved schools, hospital and housing. Former ANC MP Vytjie Mentor claimed that she had been offered a government post by the Gupta brothers.
- Key SOEs were captured and their assets plundered. The worst example was Eskom, which provides 95 per cent of the country's electricity. It is alleged that senior ANC figures 'persuaded' Glencore, a commodities firm, to sell a coal mine to an investment company owned by one of Zuma's sons and the Gupta brothers. Eskom Management signed a contract with the new owners to buy poor-quality coal from the new owners at an inflated price. Not only that, the cash-strapped Eskom then proceeded to pay the full amount of the contract upfront. Eskom is now in a precarious state with debts of R420 billion.
- The head of the South African Revenue Service (SARS) is accused of preventing staff from investigating the non-payment of tax by wealthy politicians and criminals.
- The intelligence services were corrupted under Zuma, with investigations and intimidation carried out against those who challenged his corrupt activities.
- So far, the Zondo Inquiry has unearthed considerable evidence of illegal activities. The former chief of Bosasa, a logistics company, stated that to win tenders, firms had to pay bribes to key ANC personnel. Zuma's son received R2 million for 'advisory work'.
- Between 2001 and 2014, R1.2 billion was embezzled from the Gauteng health budget. The chief whip in the Gauteng Parliament is accused of purchasing a R7.2 million house with his share of the proceeds.

Action taken by Ramaphosa

- A Judicial Commission of Inquiry into allegations of state capture, referred to as the Zondo Commission, after its presiding judge, Raymond Zondo has been set up.
- A new board has been set up to run Eskom, and in February 2019, the Government gave the new management of Eskom R420 billion.
- There has been reform of the law enforcement agencies set up to curb wrong-doing, with Shamila Batohi, a respected lawyer, appointed head of the National Prosecuting Authority (NPA). The head of the South African Revenue Service (SARS) was replaced and a new transparent policy is now operating.
- There has been reform of the intelligence services with a new director installed.

'What was done (under Zuma) was quite deep. There was a network that was put in place to break down the institutions, to debilitate the process of making people accountable. The police have been compromised, the prosecutors have been compromised. The Internal Revenue Service was compromised.'

Cyril Ramaphosa, May 2019

Tenderpreneur

This term is applied to those ANC members and supporters who get rich from government contracts or from accepting payments for awarding contracts. The Auditor General states that about 40 per cent of all government contracts have been awarded to companies owned by officials or their families. An investigation in Eastern Cape in 2013 discovered that 80 per cent of government contracts had been allocated to officials or their families. Those who were investigated for suspected corruption include two ministers, the head of the police and the now leader of EFF, Julius Malema.

ANC corruption

- A popular saying in South Africa is that there are two types of ANC politicians: those who were in jail and those who should be in jail. Some argue that ANC now stands for African/Nepotism/Corruption.
- Many leading ANC leaders have been found guilty of corruption, including Tony Yengeni, chief whip of the ANC, and Winnie Madikizela-Mandela.
- Despite attempts to ban the reports, the media disclosed that President Zuma's state-of-the-art ranch mansion was costing the taxpayer R328 million (see 'Zuma's private home in Nkandla', page 124).
- Julius Malema owed the South African Revenue Services (SARS) more than R16 million by the time he was expelled from the ANC. By the age of 30, Malema, who has never worked, had become a very wealthy individual.
- Tshwane ANC regional secretary Paul Mojapelo's consulting company has received R75 million in contracts from the municipality between 2012 and 2014.
- President Zuma's daughter Thuthukile, at the age of 25, is the youngest head of a minister's office on a salary of almost R1 million a year. She was appointed in May 2014 without the post being advertised and her previous position was as a lowly public liaison officer.

Zuma's private home in Nkandla

In an official report leaked to the *Mail & Guardian* in December 2013, the full cost of Zuma's new private home was exposed. In total R328 million (about £20 million) of public money was used to build a house that includes a swimming pool, amphitheatre and cattle enclosure. In 2012, Zuma had told parliament that his family had paid for all of the building work except for the security features. In November 2012, a government edict forbade the publication of details of the Nkandla compound. Newspapers responded with defiance and splashed the house on their front pages.

The judiciary and the media

Critics of those who argue that South Africa is now moving towards a one-party state highlight not only the democratic electoral system and the numerous political parties, but also the existence of an independent judiciary, a free press and active pressure groups such as TAC (see page 105) and COSATU. They rightly claim that South Africa is not Zimbabwe (where all white farms were appropriated by the state with dire consequence for the country's agriculture).

Administration of justice

As highlighted on page 112, the Constitution grants judicial authority to its courts, which are independent and subject only to the Constitution and the law. The Public Protector, a body created by the Constitution, published a report in March 2014 that criticised Zuma's extravagance (see above). The Constitutional Court has already played an important part in monitoring the activities of the Government when it comes to availability of anti-AIDS drugs (see page 105).

An issue of concern to many commentators is the future independence of the judiciary. The dominance of white judges in the higher levels of the judiciary, especially the Constitutional Court, has led to demands from the ANC that the judiciary must reflect 'the racial and gender composition of South Africa'. This campaign of white judge-bashing was witnessed in the trial of Schabir Shaik and during the investigations into corruption charges against Jacob Zuma when the judges were called 'white racists' by members of the Communist Party, which is affiliated to the ANC.

The decision in 2009 to drop all charges against Jacob Zuma again raised concern over the future independence of the judiciary. Helen Zille, former leader of the DA, accused the Zuma Government of using the transformation of the judiciary (60 per cent were non-white; today the figure is around 70 per cent) to the advantage of the ANC. She stated 'It [the Zuma Government] wants a bench that is subservient to the racial ideology, policies and political control of the party-state.' Further concern was raised when Zuma stated, in a pre-election address, that judges were not gods, and he was accused of trying to undermine the independence of the judiciary. Desmond Tutu also criticised the appointment of a discredited Zuma loyalist, Menzi Simelane, to the post of national director of public prosecution. In contrast, the respected advocate Jeremy Gauntlett was not appointed to be a high court judge in 2014. The reason given was that 'he lacked humility and judicial temperament', which some have interpreted as another way of saying it is because he is white and independent of the ANC. President Ramaphosa is using the courts to investigate the wrong-doings of Zuma and his cronies and there is new hope in South Africa for the continuance of an independent judiciary as the last line of defence for democracy. At the time of writing, there are two vacancies to be filled in the Constitutional Court – only one of the present nine judges is white.

The media

South Africa has a thriving free and independent press with liberal newspapers such as the *Mail & Guardian* keeping a close and critical watch on the actions of the Government. (The newspaper was a fierce critic of the apartheid government in the 1980s.) However, an ANC spokesperson stated that 'the media can be a serious obstacle to advancement'. In a democracy dominated by one party a free press is essential to highlight abuse of power by the Government.

Television plays an important role in maintaining the culture and languages of South Africa. The impartiality and independence of the South African Broadcasting Corporation (SABC) is an issue of major debate in South Africa. Tony Leon, a prominent South African politician, has accused the SABC of 'becoming a virtual propaganda arm' of the ANC. COPE (Congress of the People, a new political party formed in 2008 by former Xhosa members of the ANC) also complained that the SABC failed to provide live coverage of its final rally before the 2009 elections, and refused to accept that it had been a technical fault. Again in the 2014 general election, the television political broadcast by the DA was pulled off the air. The SABC claimed it violated the electoral code.

Show your understanding

1 Why is Jacob Zuma a controversial politician?
2 What is the Triple Alliance and why is there tension within it?
3 Explain why the Afrikaner community feels threatened by the ANC.
4 With reference to Table 3.19, outline the arguments for and against South Africa being a successful democracy.
5 What is 'state capture'? Outline its impact on South Africa.
6 Outline the role of the judiciary in South Africa.
7 To what extent is there a 'free' media in South Africa without government interference?

20-mark question

To what extent does the South African political system provide an effective check on its government?

International relations

Under the apartheid era (1948–94) South Africa experienced international isolation. It was suspended from the United Nations and from the Commonwealth. International sanctions were also applied by the world community. The international stature of Nelson Mandela ensured that the new South Africa that emerged in 1994 would play a leading role among the

countries of the developing world and in international organisations such as the United Nations and the African Union. South Africa is the dominant regional power in Southern Africa and is the only country in sub-Saharan Africa to be a member of the G20 group of countries, which includes the European Union. Further evidence of South Africa's global influence is its membership of the BRICS bloc (see pages 127–8).

South Africa – the regional superpower?

A regional superpower is a country that completely dominates its neighbours in terms of population, military and economic strength and international influence. With one-third of the GDP of sub-Saharan Africa and two-thirds of that of the Southern African Development Community (SADC), the South African economy is the powerhouse of African development in this region. It accounts for 85 per cent of Southern Africa's energy consumption.

The Southern African Development Community

South Africa is the dominant nation within the SADC, which consists of 14 African countries (see Figure 3.21). The SADC is working towards regional integration in order to accelerate economic growth, reduce poverty and establish peace and security in a region with a population of over 250 million. The SADC's headquarters are in Gaborone, Botswana.

ICT task

Read more about the SADC at:

www.sadc.int/

However, Nigeria is now challenging South Africa's economic dominance of sub-Saharan Africa. In April 2014, under revised GDP (gross domestic product) estimates, Nigeria surged past South Africa to become the biggest economy in Africa, although based on population size South Africa's per capita is way above Nigeria's (see Table 3.21). Nigeria's internal problems and political instability, illustrated by the activities of the Islamist militant group Boko Haram, have exposed the weakness of the Nigerian Government and division in society.

Figure 3.21 **Map of the countries within the SADC**

Table 3.20 **Selected countries within the SADC**

Country	Population (m)	GDP per capita ($)	Life expectancy
Angola	28.6	4,883	61.8
Democratic Republic of the Congo	88.8	423	59.1
Malawi	17.3	365	58.4
Mozambique	28.8	439	54.4
Namibia	2.3	5,596	60.0
South Africa	56.5	15,483	64.0
Zimbabwe	4.3	1,246	59.7

Source: www.sadc.int

Table 3.21 **Nigeria and South Africa: annual GDP and GDP per capita**

	Nigeria	South Africa
Annual GDP	$397,270	$349,433
GDP per capita	$2,081	$6,182

Source: www.sadc.int

South Africa, with its stable democracy and progressive Constitution and Bill of Rights, is rightly regarded as a beacon of democracy for its fellow African neighbours. The world image of many African states is one of corrupt government, tribal conflict and denial of human rights to its citizens. The recent tragic civil war in the world's newest state, South Sudan, unfortunately reinforces this perception. South Africa's reputation as a successful democracy with a sophisticated economy attracts millions of immigrants from neighbouring states such as Zimbabwe.

South Africa is an active member of the African Union (AU). The AU consists of 54 African states and its role is to provide 'African solutions to African problems, to support economic growth and to achieve conflict resolutions between states'. Nkosazana Dlamini-Zuma, a leading member of the ANC, was elected chair of the AU Commission, highlighting South Africa's influence in the organisation.

South Africa has played a central role in seeking to end various African conflicts in Burundi, Democratic Republic of the Congo (DRC), Comoros and, more controversially, in Zimbabwe. Here, South Africa was criticised for its failure to force President Mugabe to end his brutal persecution of political opponents. President Zuma's support for Colonel Gaddafi and his belated attempt to resolve the Libyan crisis was an embarrassing flop. South Africa's peace-keeping activities in the Central African Republic were also a disaster with the death of 14 South African soldiers.

South Africa is also increasingly playing a role in post-conflict reconstruction and development and humanitarian affairs in the African continent and beyond. DRC, Sierra Leone, South Sudan, Somalia, Zimbabwe and Haiti have all benefited from technical expertise and financial support from the country.

The BRICS

The BRICS, which South Africa joined in 2010, consists of Brazil, Russia, India, China and South Africa, and plays an important role in the shifting distribution of power internationally. The BRICS bloc represents 43 per cent of the world's population and approximately one-fifth of global gross domestic product (GDP). South Africa also sees its role in BRICS to promote the African Agenda. As a government minister stated 'Our belief is that the membership of South Africa to BRICS represents the 1 billion people on the continent of Africa.'

Obviously South Africa is hardly in the same league as its fellow members – it has a smaller economy and population – but its inclusion brings to the group representation from all the developing-world continents (Latin America, Asia and Africa). The tenth BRICS summit was held in Durban in 2018.

South Africa's strong ties with China have, however, been criticised within South Africa (see bottom right of this page).

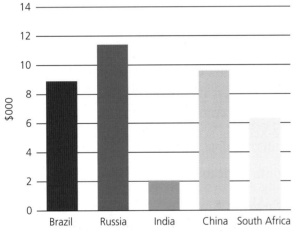

Figure 3.22 **BRICS countries GDP per capita ($000)**
Source: South African Government, 2019

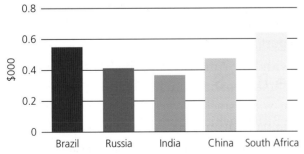

Figure 3.23 **Gini coefficient (wealth inequality:
0 = everyone equal), 2018**
Source: South African Government, 2018

United Nations

South Africa was one of the original members of the United Nations (UN) when it was set up after the Second World War with its headquarters in New York. However, as stated earlier, it was forced to leave the UN because of the apartheid policies of the white South African Government. South Africa rejoined the UN after the end of apartheid and its new leader, Nelson Mandela, had significant international influence. Today, South Africa is an active member of the United Nations and was elected in 2006, 2010 and again in 2019 by the UN General Assembly to serve on the Security Council as a non-permanent member. However, South Africa has been criticised by the West for placing its loyalties to the countries of the developing world ahead of human rights issues. In particular, a 'no' security vote on a resolution criticising the Burmese Government, and South Africa's original intentions to vote against economic sanctions to be imposed on Iran, attracted widespread criticism.

However, South Africa argues that the USA and Europe have too much influence in the Security Council of the UN. President Zuma argued that 'the Security Council should be opened up. In other words, regions of the world should be represented in the same way. You have one region that dominates, the European Union.'

South Africa's close ties with China have been criticised by many South Africans. In October 2014, Archbishop Desmond Tutu attacked the Government for refusing a visa to the Tibetan spiritual leader, the Dalai Lama. In a statement, Tutu said that he was 'ashamed to call this lickspittle bunch my government'. The event was the 14th World Summit of Nobel

Peace Laureates, which was to be held in Cape Town to celebrate the memory of Nelson Mandela, a former Nobel Peace Laureate. The meeting was cancelled as the other Nobel Peace Laureates refused to attend in protest and the summit was moved elsewhere. Economic interest and the desire not to upset the Chinese came before support for human rights and respect for Nelson Mandela.

Yet President Zuma welcomed Omar al-Bashir, when he was the president of Sudan, to South Africa. Bashir had been accused by the International Criminal Court (ICC) of being responsible for genocide in the Darfur region of Sudan. Zuma failed to hand Bashir to the ICC and allowed him to leave the country. South Africa's human rights record was further tarnished when Zuma announced that South Africa was leaving the ICC.

The early signs are hopeful that South Africa will place human rights and development issues at the centre of their foreign policy and restore the moral authority the country had under Nelson Mandela. Already South Africa has indicated that it will rejoin the ICC.

Below is an extract from an article published by the Center for Strategic & International Issues highlighting the opportunity for South Africa to repair its tarnished international reputation.

Can South Africa return to the global stage?

'In January, South Africa will fill a seat on the UN Security Council for the first time since the presidency of Jacob Zuma, whose support for "state capture" enabled cronies to exercise outsized influence over public entities and coffers, denting South Africa's image abroad while decimating the economy at home.

The timing for joining the UN's most influential body could hardly be better: UN Security Council membership can accelerate efforts by President Cyril Ramaphosa … to resuscitate South Africa's global brand and return the country to its previous position, established by former president Nelson Mandela, as a defender of democratic governance and human rights. Ramaphosa, who has a strong grounding in foreign policy, has an opportunity to be a leader with influence beyond South Africa and a counterweight to growing global authoritarianism.

Mandela's legacy, Zuma's retreat

During Mandela's presidency (1994–1999), South Africa had the world's attention and sought to advance a foreign policy that emphasized human rights. Mandela premised South Africa's engagement with the world "on the belief in the compatibility of human rights, democracy, solidarity politics and [South Africa's] own development needs."

…

Mandela's successor, Thabo Mbeki, largely continued this approach, while placing greater emphasis on pan-African solidarity and African economic integration, under the brand of an "African Renaissance."

Zuma undermined much of this, and under his leadership, South Africa's global standing declined rapidly. By the end of his near-decade in power (2009–2018), Zuma was not taken seriously by other leading heads of state, especially in the West, and was regarded with suspicion because of his strong personal relationship with Russian president Vladimir Putin, emphasis on the BRICS construct (the coalition of Brazil, Russia, India, China, and South Africa) at the expense of broader engagement, and close relations with China. At the G20 meetings in Hamburg in 2017, while all other heads of state conducted numerous bilateral meetings, Zuma had just one, with the Chinese president.

➜

...

On issues of democratic governance and human rights, South Africa under Zuma retreated from its earlier strong positions. At the UN General Assembly and in the UN Human Rights Council, South Africa's voting record was disappointing, to say the least, its diplomats consistently voting against or abstaining on resolutions seeking to defend human rights in Syria, Iran, North Korea and elsewhere. After refusing to arrest Sudanese president Omar al-Bashir when he traveled to South Africa in 2015, despite a warrant from the International Criminal Court (ICC), South Africa sought to leave the ICC. As part of its effort to curry favor with China, South Africa repeatedly refused to issue a visa to the Dalai Lama.

Change afoot?

Ramaphosa's ascension to the presidency in February – defeating Zuma's preferred successor, his ex-wife Nkosazana Dlamini-Zuma – was greeted with a mix of relief and enthusiasm. Canadian prime minister Justin Trudeau went out of his way to extend an invitation to Ramaphosa to attend the G7 meeting hosted by Canada in June, and other world leaders have sought to engage Ramaphosa after shunning Zuma.

...

Much of the task of restoring South Africa's international reputation falls to Lindiwe Sisulu, whom Ramaphosa appointed as minister of international relations and cooperation. She has significant political influence as a former minister of defense and minister of intelligence; ally of the president; and daughter of Walter Sisulu, one of the most revered anti-apartheid leaders. She has been clear in her commitment to restoring South Africa's image and commitment to defending human rights. In a high-profile speech in May [2018], Sisulu said, "We want South Africa to be once again a moral compass and a voice of reason in a world increasingly overcome with selfish, narrow

interests. We want to be the hope for all in times of despair." She affirmed that "the fundamentals of our foreign policy are based on human rights, peace, equality, freedom from oppression and racism, freedom from poverty."

To support her efforts, Sisulu has appointed a review panel of experienced foreign policy hands charged with learning from South African foreign policy since 1994 and advising her on reforms. Part of their task is to look at how to revitalize the beleaguered Department of International Relations and Cooperation – South Africa's foreign ministry – which suffered under Zuma as career diplomats were often sidelined in favor of politically-connected appointees, many of them ill-suited to their positions.

There are signs that policy is changing. South Africa recently announced that it is reversing its position on an upcoming vote in the UN General Assembly to condemn human rights abuses in Myanmar and will now support the resolution. Sisulu also announced changes that will lead to greater scrutiny of all votes in international fora, with her approving each vote.

Backlash and challenges ahead

Ramaphosa and Sisulu will face resistance to their reform efforts, including from within the ANC ... There is evidence of a disconnect between Ramaphosa and Sisulu's new rhetoric and the reality of policy execution. For example, in July [2018], South Africa joined China and Russia in voting against a proposal at the Organization for the Prohibition of Chemical Weapons to strengthen monitoring mechanisms; and in the September session of the UN Human Rights Council, South Africa abstained on a resolution to extend an international investigation into human rights violations in Yemen by the Saudi-led coalition and the Houthi rebels.

The "economic diplomacy" priorities of the Ramaphosa presidency may come into sharp conflict with a more rights-orientated approach.

➔

Already, in the early months of the new Ramaphosa administration there was debate within government and the ANC leadership about carrying out the ANC's resolution to close South Africa's embassy in Israel. Opponents argued that such a move could undermine possible foreign investment.

…

The case for global engagement

Will South Africa be prepared to offer global leadership? The primary argument in favor should be that South Africa has a responsibility to help progressive forces and institutions overcome attacks from those who oppose a rules-based international order and multilateralism. This provides an opportunity to re-brand South Africa while lending support to the defense of multilateralism, a principle that has traditionally been close to the ANC's heart. As South Africa prepares to join the UN Security Council, Ramaphosa's ANC supporters and civil society should push for South Africa to assert itself in defense of multilateralism, fundamental rights, and democratic governance …

Source: Center for Strategic & International Studies, 17 December 2018

Show your understanding

1 To what extent is South Africa the regional superpower in Southern Africa?
2 Describe South Africa's involvement in the United Nations and in the BRICS bloc.
3 In what ways did South Africa tarnish its international image under Zuma?
4 What opposition does Ramaphosa face within South Africa to his foreign policy reforms?

12-mark question

Analyse the international influence of a world power you have studied.

Development issues in Africa

Understanding 'development'

Throughout this chapter you will learn about the causes and consequences of a lack of development in Africa. Firstly, it is important to understand how we identify countries that are developed and less developed. It is not a simple process; a complex set of factors are analysed to determine a country's development status. There is no universal, agreed-upon criterion for what makes a country developed versus developing. There are general reference points such as a nation's gross domestic product (GDP) per capita compared to that of other nations. For the World Bank, a 'developed' country is one with a high gross national income (GNI) per capita. It then classifies countries according to their income level. But this doesn't tell the whole story – it doesn't give the distribution of wealth across a population like the Gini index attempts to do. The Gini index, or coefficient, is a number between 0 and 1, where 0 corresponds to perfect equality and 1 corresponds to perfect inequality (where one person has all the income and everyone else has zero income); the Gini index therefore measures the gap between the rich and the poor. The Human Development Index (HDI), reported on in the United Nations' annual Human Development Report, attempts to draw on a wider vision of development, including measures of education, health and standard of living in countries across the globe. From our point of view as Modern Studies experts, the HDI is a better way to learn about a country's social, economic and political issues.

Overview

Africa is a continent of over 1 billion people. The population has grown rapidly from 220 million in 1950. In many African countries, particularly those south of the Sahara, more than 40 per cent of the population are under 15 years of age. Africa is made up of 54 independent countries; among these are 34 of the least developed nations in the world. Seventy per cent of Africa's population subsist on less than $2 a day, yet Africa is full of natural resources such as minerals, oil, land and sea ports. How can this be?

There is no simple answer. A complex combination of social, economic and political factors interact to impede development. Some of these factors operate outside Africa while others operate within. No one factor explains the situation. Natural disasters hit the headlines and

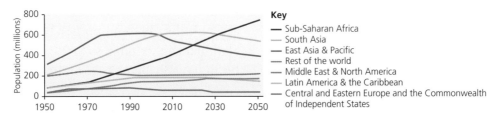

Figure 4.1 **Number of children under 18 by UNICEF region**
Source: UNICEF, 2012. Generation 2025 and Beyond

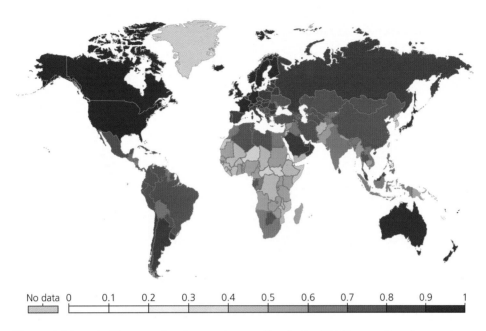

Figure 4.2 **Level of human development according to the UN Human Development Index by country**
Source: Our World in Data

lead us to believe that nature alone is the cause of the bleak situation facing many African people. Undoubtedly drought, flooding, crop failures and climate change play a major part in creating wide-scale food shortages, but unfortunately there are a plethora of other factors that blight the continent. A lack of democracy, widespread political corruption, a lack of basic infrastructure and a history of colonisation all combine to cause the desperate situation in many African countries today. The inability of social, economic and political structures within a country to respond to the variety of problems is the key issue.

A comparison between the profiles of the African country Chad and the United Kingdom reveals stark contrasts and provides a vivid insight into the gulf that separates the industrialised developed world from the developing world (see page 136).

From Table 4.1 you can see that Ethiopia, a developing country, has around the same level of

inequality as the UK. This does not mean Ethiopia is as wealthy as the UK, it means the gap between the richest and poorest in society is roughly the same. Relatively speaking, the difference between the poor in the UK and the poor in Ethiopia is quite simply the ability to afford food and shelter and access readily available health and education provision.

Table 4.1 **Gini coefficient by country, various dates**

Country	Gini coefficient
Iceland	0.25
Norway	0.26
Germany	0.31
Ethiopia	0.33
United Kingdom	0.34
USA	0.41
Zimbabwe	0.43
Brazil	0.51
Namibia	0.61
South Africa	0.63

ICT task

Visit **www.hdr.undp.org/en** to access and investigate the latest UN Human Development Report.

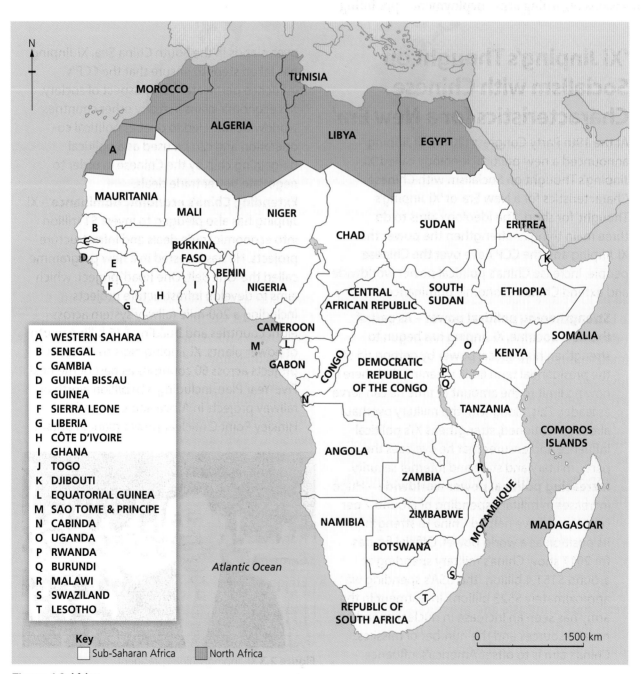

A   WESTERN SAHARA
B   SENEGAL
C   GAMBIA
D   GUINEA BISSAU
E   GUINEA
F   SIERRA LEONE
G   LIBERIA
H   CÔTE D'IVOIRE
I   GHANA
J   TOGO
K   DJIBOUTI
L   EQUATORIAL GUINEA
M   SAO TOME & PRINCIPE
N   CABINDA
O   UGANDA
P   RWANDA
Q   BURUNDI
R   MALAWI
S   SWAZILAND
T   LESOTHO

Key
Sub-Saharan Africa   North Africa

Figure 4.3 **Africa**

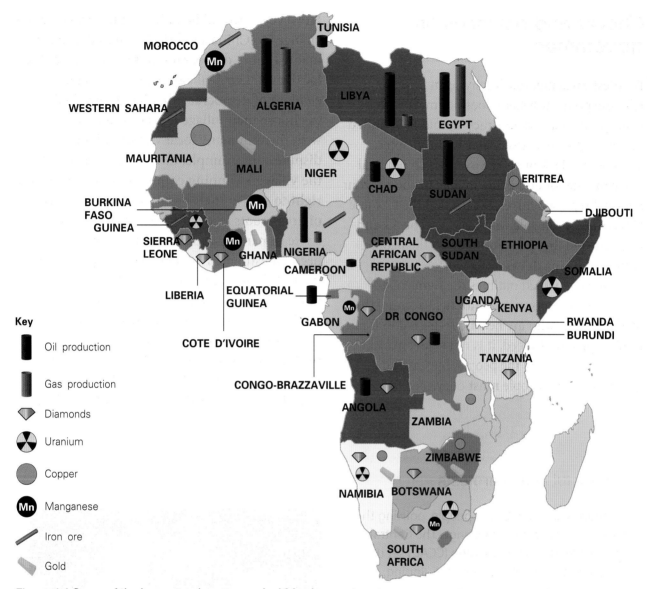

Figure 4.4 **Some of the key natural resources in Africa by country**

Profile of Chad

Population
12 million

Health
Life expectancy: 49 years
People with HIV/AIDS: 4.8%
Immunisation levels:
- TB 68% • Polio 56% • Measles 64%

Percentage of GDP* spent on health: 4.3%
Access to a clean water source: 50.7%

Education
Male literacy: 52%
Female literacy: 34%
Primary school enrolment: 52%
Secondary school enrolment: 16%
Percentage of GDP spent on education: 2.3%

Economy
**GDP per capita: $1035
Unemployment rate: 34%
Percentage below poverty line: 80%

Women
Risk of death in childbirth: 540 in 100,000
Infant mortality rate: 77 in 1000
Child labour rate: 48%

Profile of United Kingdom (UK)

Population
63 million

Health
Life expectancy: 79 years
People with HIV/AIDS: 0.2%
Immunisation levels:
- TB 100% • Polio 91% • Measles 81%

Percentage of GDP spent on health: 9.3%
Access to a clean water source: 100%

Education
Male literacy: 100%
Female literacy: 100%
Primary school enrolment: 99%
Secondary school enrolment: 98%
Percentage of GDP spent on education: 6.2%

Economy
GDP per capita: $36,500
Unemployment rate: 7.2%
Percentage below poverty line: 16.2%

Women
Risk of death in childbirth: 12 in 100,000
Infant mortality rate: 5 in 1000
Child labour rate: 0%

*GDP is the total monetary value of all final goods and services produced in a country in a year.
**GDP per capita is an approximate total value of goods and services produced per person in the country, dividing the gross domestic product (GDP) by the country's population.
Source: United Nations

Show your understanding

1 What are the various ways we can determine a country's development status?
2 Describe the demographics of Africa.
3 Study the comparison between Chad and the UK. Outline some of the key differences.

Social, economic and political factors affecting development

In this section you will learn about the causes and consequences of a lack of development in Africa. Such causes, and indeed the consequences, are many and it is therefore better to understand them under social, economic and political sub-sections.

Social factors affecting development

Health issues

The causes of health-related issues in Africa range from debt and poor governance to a lack of education and infrastructure. No country in Africa has universal health care, never mind having health care that would rival the standard of our National Health Service. The UK spent £195 billion (roughly 10 per cent of GDP) on health care in 2018, with African countries such as Ethiopia, Kenya and Nigeria each spending between 4 per cent and 6 per cent of GDP. Health care in Africa differs widely, depending on the country and also the region – those living in urban areas are more likely to receive better health care services than those in rural or remote regions. Many communities lack clean water and proper sanitation facilities, particularly in rural areas. This means that illnesses caused by poor hygiene, such as cholera and diarrhoea, are common in some countries and can be life threatening without decent health care.

HIV/AIDS

There is an HIV/AIDS epidemic in Africa; HIV/AIDS is one of the three major killers in Africa. An estimated 25 million adults and children were living with HIV in sub-Saharan Africa at the beginning of 2019. In 2018, 770,000 people died of AIDS. HIV/AIDS is one of the biggest challenges confronting many African countries but some progress has been made. Global new HIV infections have declined by 18 per cent in the past nine years, from 2.2 million in 2010 to 1.8 million in 2019. Many more people (59 per cent of those infected) are also accessing treatment for HIV. However, life expectancy in many countries remains very low. Swaziland, which has the highest HIV prevalence in the world, has a life expectancy

of just 50 years. Lesotho's situation is worse still at 48.7 years. Table 4.2 shows current life expectancy of people in the countries in sub-Saharan Africa worst affected by the HIV/AIDS epidemic.

Table 4.2 **HIV prevalence and life expectancy, 2019**

Country	HIV prevalence (%)	Life expectancy
Botswana	21.9	50
Lesotho	25	48.7
Malawi	9.2	54.8
Mozambique	12.3	50.7
Namibia	13.8	62.6
South Africa	18.9	53.4
Swaziland	27.2	50
Zambia	12.4	49.4
Zimbabwe	13.5	52.7

Fact file

HIV/AIDS in Africa

- At the height of the HIV epidemic in sub-Saharan Africa between 1990 and 2000, average life expectancy stagnated at 49.5 years.
- AIDS could slash the wealth of some African countries by as much as 20 per cent.
- 75 per cent of all people in the world infected by AIDS live in Africa.
- Half of all people with HIV become infected before they are aged 25.
- In some African countries, AIDS is the major cause of children being orphaned.
- Food is often the main need of poor families living with HIV/AIDS. Malnutrition increases as HIV progresses.
- Without good food, the anti-retroviral drugs used to treat the condition are not as effective as they could be.
- Education is the most cost-effective means of preventing HIV transmission.

Case study: Swaziland

In Swaziland, one in four adults are living with HIV. AIDS has spread through Swaziland at an alarmingly fast rate in the last 35 years and in 2019 Swaziland had the highest HIV prevalence in the world. As elsewhere in sub-Saharan Africa, the impact of so many AIDS-related deaths in Swaziland exacerbates existing poverty for families, and has resulted in a very youthful population. More than a third of the population are under 14 years old and only 5.2 per cent are over 65.

However, the problem is being tackled head on. Swaziland is one of just five sub-Saharan African countries to achieve the target of getting more than 80 per cent of eligible people on anti-retroviral treatment. Among pregnant women, treatment access is also high at 83 per cent. Consequently, the number of AIDS-related deaths in Swaziland is declining. More people are also coming forward to be tested for HIV, showing that people are less fearful of the stigma attached to the disease. The stigma of HIV has been a major issue in tackling the epidemic across the whole of Africa in the last few decades.

The consequences of HIV/AIDS

HIV/AIDS places huge burdens on societies in Africa. The vast majority of Africans living with HIV/AIDS are between the ages of 15 and 49, which is the prime of their working lives. The effects on the labour supply and the economy are dramatic, with employers, schools, factories and hospitals having to constantly find and train staff to replace those who have become too ill to work. For example, in some countries more teachers die of HIV/AIDS-related illnesses than are being trained. The HIV epidemic has had a severe and wide-ranging impact upon households in sub-Saharan Africa. Many families have lost their chief income earners, who have died or are too sick to work. This puts a heavy financial burden on families who have to pay ever-increasing medical costs, forcing many into poverty. In many cases, households simply dissolve because parents die and children are sent to relatives for care and upbringing.

Furthermore, the already limited medical services in African countries struggle to cope with demand as around 50 per cent of hospital beds in some countries have been given over to AIDS sufferers. Overall, the true impact and cost of HIV/AIDS on the economies of sub-Saharan Africa is difficult to measure. A country needs a healthy population to fuel the economy with their labour and HIV/AIDS certainly hinders this. However, clearly the social problems caused by the disease are immense.

Anti-retroviral treatment is not a cure for HIV, but it can stop people from becoming ill for many years. The treatment consists of drugs that have to be taken every day for the rest of the patient's life.

Malaria

In June 2019, the World Health Organization reported that a child dies from malaria every two minutes. Over 90 per cent of cases of the disease occur in sub-Saharan Africa. In 2017, 266,000 children under five years of age died from the disease. That is more than 700 children every day.

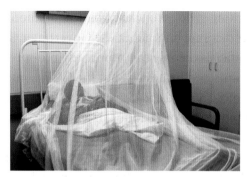

Figure 4.5 **An insecticide-treated malaria net will help to save lives**

Figure 4.6 **Children in an African classroom**

Malaria is an entirely preventable and treatable mosquito-borne illness. It thrives in hot temperatures that enable the parasite that causes the disease to mature more quickly in the bodies of the mosquitoes that carry it. Malaria is Africa's biggest killer and the consequences of malaria for African development are similar to those of HIV/AIDS. It is estimated that malaria accounts for economic losses totalling £10 billion per year among African countries.

However, malaria is preventable. When insecticide-treated malaria nets are used properly, malaria transmission is cut by 50 per cent, child deaths are cut by 20 per cent and the mosquito population drops by as much as 90 per cent. It is estimated, however, that fewer than 5 per cent of children in sub-Saharan Africa currently sleep under any type of insecticide-treated net. International targets for reducing malaria cases and deaths will not be attained unless considerable progress is made in the 18 most affected countries, which account for an estimated 80 per cent of malaria cases. About 40 per cent of malaria deaths occur in just two countries: Nigeria and the Democratic Republic of the Congo.

Education

Education transforms lives. Whether in Scotland or in Malawi, education is a route out of poverty and into prosperity. In the same way, education is vital to a thriving society. A society without education will become a breeding ground for violence and intolerance. An educated society will promote tolerance and peace, justice and understanding, innovation and advancement, and positive self-fulfilment. Mass literacy across a population allows people not only to take part in society but to actively contribute to it. A fully educated population leads to development in other areas as well, such as improved health, economic growth, political participation and greater equality.

Unfortunately, the provision of education in many African countries is lacking. In a similar way to health care, education is a privilege. Public spending by African nations on education averages around 5 per cent of GDP but there is a lack of finance targeted at providing universal access to primary school for every child. This has resulted in 35 million children in the sub-Saharan region missing out on school completely.

Nevertheless, it must be remembered that tight budgets and poor financial management have not been helped by a population boom that continues today. The children who do manage to make it through primary and secondary school will experience sub-standard facilities and resources. Schools find it difficult to employ qualified professional teachers, especially in rural areas. Class sizes are often upwards of 50 students and resources such as teaching aids and textbooks are limited.

Brain drain

Those who attain a high level of education in Africa often choose to emigrate to more prosperous countries such as Britain. This is often referred to as a '**brain drain**' of the country concerned. Brain drains cause countries to lose valuable professionals such as doctors, scientists and engineers. When these people leave, their country is harmed in two ways. First, expertise is lost with each emigrant, diminishing the supply of that profession. Second, the country's economy is harmed. Professionals often earn larger salaries, so their departure removes significant consumer spending from the country.

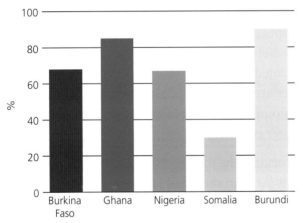

Figure 4.7 **Primary school enrolment in selected African countries**
Source: UNESCO.org

Women's rights

As with other regions around the world, gender inequality is a problematic and thorny issue in Africa. Traditional gender roles are more entrenched than in the UK. For example, in Sudan there are clearly defined gender roles. Men make the decisions but also bear the responsibility of providing financially for their mothers, sisters and aunts. Women take care of children, the sick and elderly, as well as running the household. Women frequently have a considerable amount of work to do, such as gathering firewood and water or tending family fields.

Girls are less likely to attend school and more likely to drop out than boys. In sub-Saharan Africa, 81 per cent of boys were enrolled at primary school during 2018, compared with only 77 per cent of girls. The tradition of early marriages in some cultures is also hindering social development. UNICEF UK estimates that two-fifths of girls in West and Central Africa are married before the age of 18. In some countries the proportion is much higher. For example, in Chad and Niger, a third of young women (aged 20–24) said they were married by the age of 15.

Figure 4.8 **Collecting water is a role allocated to women in some African countries**

Farming, food, famine and malnutrition

Famine is caused by the shortage of food or the inability of people to obtain food. This might be caused by low food production resulting from drought or other factors such as armed conflict or bad governance. Poor farming practices such as deforestation, overcropping and overgrazing are exhausting the land in many African countries. Increasingly, fertile farmland is under threat from erosion, salination or desertification. Added to these problems is poor irrigation and water management. These combined factors result in limited agricultural yields, which can cause mass food shortages.

Around one-third of all people who live in sub-Saharan Africa are undernourished and there are an estimated 275 million people in Africa who, each day, go hungry. Children are the most visible victims of malnutrition. Children who are poorly nourished suffer up to 160 days of illness each year. Poor nutrition plays a role in around half of all child deaths in Africa. Malnutrition magnifies the effect of every disease, including measles and malaria.

'Every morning our newspapers could read, "More than 20,000 people perished yesterday of starvation."' *(Professor Jeffrey Sachs, leading expert on development)*

Show your understanding

1 Why do many Africans lack access to health care?
2 a) Outline the HIV/AIDS situation in Africa with reference to Table 4.2, the fact file and the case study on Swaziland.
  b) What are the consequences of the HIV/AIDS epidemic?
3 What are the problems surrounding malaria in Africa?
4 a) What are the benefits of an educated population to a country?
  b) To what extent is educational provision experienced by African people?
5 Describe some of the issues surrounding women's rights in Africa.
6 What are the consequences of poor farming and famine?

Economic factors affecting development

Debt

The causes of Africa's debt crisis are neither few nor simple; they are the result of the complex interaction of numerous factors. When many African countries gained their independence from colonisation in the 1950s and 1960s they had the task of self-governance and social and economic development. This led to developing nations accepting loans that they struggled to pay back (unfortunately much of this money was misspent or embezzled – see page 145). In turn, further loans have followed from institutions such as the World Bank and the International Monetary Fund (IMF). China has also become increasingly economically involved in Africa in recent years. From Figure 4.9 you can see an increasing trend in financial support from the world's second largest economy.

Today, Africa has a $317 billion debt burden, which creates a major obstacle to the continent's development. African countries spend almost $14 billion annually on repaying debt, resulting in vital resources being diverted away from essential social programmes.

The money African governments have borrowed from the IMF or World Bank comes with high interest rates and strict conditions. Such conditions when lending money can lead to extreme hardship for the countries involved. For example, the IMF can insist that education programmes and health programmes are cut to reduce government spending. If such conditions are not followed, then finance can be stopped.

The inability of African governments to invest in social services and promote economic development is the enduring consequence of the debt burden. This can be understood by looking at Angola, which is a nation rich in natural resources. It is Africa's second largest oil

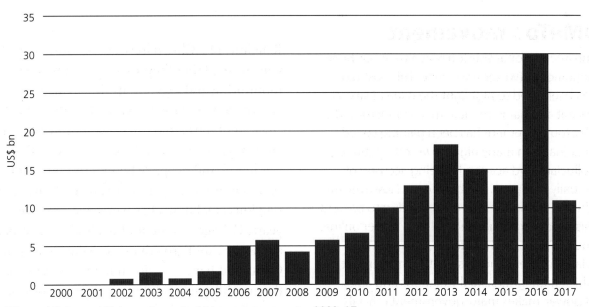

Figure 4.9 Annual Chinese loans to African governments, 2000–17
Source: www.sais-cari.org

producer and also has a wealth of diamonds, iron ore and coffee. These natural resources should mean that Angola is economically rich, yet this is not the case due to its troubled history of civil war and huge accumulation of foreign debts that have resulted from this. During the civil war that lasted from 1975 to 2002, the Angolan Government borrowed money from rich nations to fund its military. Angola has a wide proportional discrepancy between spending on external debt payments and spending on public healthcare. While 44% of government revenue is spent on repaying external debt, only 6% is spent on public health. At the end of 2017, Angola's debt to China amounted to $21.5 billion – this is about half of Angola's total external debt – and

this year Angola's debt to China is likely to grow significantly. Oil is used as collateral for Chinese credit and Chinese loans are often actually repaid in oil.

In 2005, some African countries had some of their debt cancelled. The resulting benefits have been considerable. After receiving partial debt cancellation, Zambia introduced free health care for people living in rural areas, scrapping fees that for years had made health care inaccessible for millions. In Ghana, debt cancellation has been used with success to fund free early education, and in Mali funds were invested in improving the water supply and roads. These examples indicate the progress that could be possible if debts owed by African countries were cancelled completely.

Case study: BRICS Bank – a new lender in global development

In 2014, the leaders of the BRICS (Brazil, Russia, India, China and South Africa) emerging market countries launched a $100 billion (£58.3 billion) development bank and an emergency reserve fund. Their first significant achievement since joining forces in 2009, the long-anticipated bank was an initial step in working for a greater say in the global financial order that has been traditionally dominated by the Western powers since the Second World War, centring on the IMF and World Bank.

However, the 2005 debt cancellation saw only around 60 per cent of Africa's debt cancelled and many countries are still indebted to the IMF, the World Bank or the developed world. Recently economists have warned of a potential new debt crisis with China, now the largest creditor nation, owed approximately £100 billion.

Trade

Being rich in natural resources, Africa should be a prosperous continent with many products available to trade and sell to the rest of the world. If Africa could earn more through trade, African countries would be able to rely less on foreign aid and loans. In 1980, Africa had a 6 per cent share of world trade. By 2019, this had dropped to just 3 per cent. If Africa could regain just an additional 1 per cent share of global trade, it would earn $70 billion more in exports each year – several times more than the amount the region currently receives in foreign aid.

Cash crops and terms of trade

Trade varies greatly from country to country. Sudan and Nigeria are blessed with large oil reserves and can export millions of barrels per day, whereas countries such as Malawi and Ethiopia depend heavily on growing and exporting cash crops such as fruit, tea and coffee, cocoa and cotton. These crops are called 'cash crops' as they are grown for money rather than as food. Around 60 per cent of workers employed in Africa work in agriculture, with 40 per cent of farmers working in the cash crop industry. Cash crops are highly controversial in many ways.

Buyers from developed nations can force down the price of cash crops and therefore reduce the finance flowing into developing countries. As the price of coffee has increased in the coffee shops of Scotland, the likelihood is that the price of the coffee beans acquired from Africa has decreased. Companies prioritise profits often at the expense of the African farmer. Moreover, the desire of African farmers to grow cash crops and export produce to large companies means that food is not grown for the purpose of feeding the African population. Indeed, the situation remains that Africa sends food all over the globe while thousands of Africans die every day of starvation.

Case study: The controversial role of multinational corporations in Africa

Part of the reason why African countries are not wealthy, despite their plentiful natural resources, lies in the role and conduct of multinational companies in Africa. Post-colonial Africa was encouraged to be a free market economy, similar to that of European countries where private businesses are free to provide services to citizens in return for profit. As African nations required financial support from the IMF or the World Bank, the loans they received often contained conditions that they must sell off their natural resources to big companies; this is called privatisation. This is not necessarily a bad thing; many UK enterprises have been privatised over the years. However, problems have occurred in Africa because many sub-Saharan countries have suffered civil war, corruption and dictatorships among other economic and political troubles. Multinationals have been accused of 'exploiting' such countries and 'plundering' their natural

Figure 4.10 Iron ore mining in Africa

Case study (continued)

resources. Large oil companies such as Shell and Elf have been implicated in corruption and bribery scandals, with companies somehow managing to operate in countries that lack democratic governance and transparency.

Furthermore, multinationals are accused of failing to pay their correct share of tax from the profits received through extracting African resources. This is for two reasons. Firstly, multinationals are not properly taxed because African authorities lack the capacity to put in place tax systems and secondly, multinationals have advanced and complex ways of avoiding tax. Tax avoidance and siphoning off profit is called 'capital flight' and costs Africa at least $160 billion per year, according to Christian Aid.

Susan Hawley, of Corruption Watch UK, states that 'Multinational corporations' corrupt practices affect [Africa] in many ways. They undermine development and exacerbate inequality and poverty. They disadvantage smaller domestic firms [and] transfer money that could be put towards poverty eradication into the hands of the rich.'

An interesting insight into the role of multinationals in Africa is discussed in the documentary *Stealing Africa – Why Poverty?*

Another consequence of cash crops is the increasing proportion of African land being leased to foreign companies (e.g. Monsanto) to grow their own cash crops. For example, Mozambique has leased 20 per cent of its agricultural land, while Ethiopia has leased 8 per cent. If this continues, communities will be left without access to resources and unable to make a living to feed themselves and their families. With 60 per cent of Africa's farmers being subsistence farmers, this is a serious ongoing issue. Many development experts have called this increase in agribusiness the 'new scramble for Africa'.

Lack of infrastructure is also a huge problem for many African nations, and the transportation of goods is not always easy. This severely hinders trade between African countries but also provides hope for future trade – if infrastructure can be improved, profit can be made through the consequential trade increase.

Show your understanding

1 a) What is the extent of debt faced by African countries?
   b) What problems does debt cause for African countries?
2 What is BRICS Bank and why might it be beneficial to poorer countries?
3 Why is trade important to African countries?
4 What are the various controversies surrounding cash crops?
5 Outline the controversial role of multinational corporations in Africa.

Political factors affecting development

Poor governance, corruption and kleptocracy

Bad (or poor) governance means the government cannot be trusted to deliver key services, taxes are not efficiently collected, there is corruption, the police are dishonest, human rights are abused and the legal system is not independent. Bad governance also means that there are no democratic elections and there is a lack of transparency that allows those in power to rule unchallenged.

Kleptocracy can go hand in hand with bad governance. Kleptocracy describes a situation where an elite group, and/or a dictator, exercises power to the benefit of themselves at the expense of the population at large. Funds or aid are diverted to equip the military which will ensure the government remains in power.

Corruption has also been a huge problem in African politics. It has been stated that the day corruption ends in Africa is the very day we

shall see the development of the continent. The lack of democracy has allowed many dictators to remain in power for decades enjoying lavish lifestyles while the population starves. Money and aid that should flow to the population and be spent on health centres or primary schools is siphoned off into the bank accounts of government officials. Former DR Congo dictator Mobutu Sese Seko amassed a personal fortune estimated by various sources (including Transparency International) at somewhere between $1 billion and $5 billion. Experts believe virtually all of it was illicitly acquired from the nation's funds and stashed away in Swiss banks.

Case study: Corruption in Africa

Contained within the diverse area of Sub-Saharan Africa, there is a mix of governments with democratic principles and those who are still governed by authoritarian and semi-authoritarian leaders. Yet, large areas of the region are rift with corruption and most democratic values face real and frequent risk.

Countries such as Seychelles and Botswana are the some of the rare exceptions, with both scoring high on the Corruption Perceptions Index (CPI) compared to other countries in the region. This is helped by the fact that both have relatively well-functioning democratic and governance systems.

Figure 4.11 Corruption

Recently a number of countries has seen a sharp decline in their CPI scores, such as Burundi, Congo, Ghana and Liberia. Mozambique, for example, moved from 31/100 in 2012 to 23/100 in 2018, dropping 8 points. Somalia currently has the lowest CPI score of 10/100.

There are similarities between many of the low-performing countries, including limited political rights, restricted press freedoms and a weak rule of law. Internal conflict and unstable governing institutions create breeding grounds for corruption, with bribes being made and taken and laws going unenforced. Despite the mix of political and socio-economic environments, anti-corruption efforts are often thwarted by the same persisting challenges, including autocratic regimes, civil trouble, weak institutions and unresponsive political systems. With poor resourcing, institutions are ill-equipped to handle the corruption complaints they receive.

He owned a range of Mercedes cars and divided his time between plush palatial residences in Paris and Lausanne, Switzerland. He also developed a special taste for pink champagne and flew in fresh cakes from Paris for his consumption. All this while the population of DR Congo barely survived on $1 a day.

It is estimated that corruption today costs the continent around $150 billion a year with Somalia perceived to be the most corrupt nation on Earth in 2019 (according to Transparency International). In December 2013, the then World Bank President Jim Yong Kim stated 'in the developing world, corruption is public enemy number one'.

Civil war and armed conflict

'I dream of an Africa which is in peace with itself.' (Nelson Mandela)

Figure 4.12 Soldier/rebel with rifle

Since the end of colonialism in Africa, there has been constant conflict, with the region being dubbed 'the Kalashnikov continent'. At any one point over the last 50 years, numerous countries have suffered from civil wars, which have plagued social, economic and political development. Civil war is both a cause and a consequence of poverty and underdevelopment. But further causes of conflict in Africa include ethnic, religious and

tribal differences that are complex in nature and can be traced back over thousands of years. Current examples of tribal conflict include the world's newest country, South Sudan, where various tribes are fighting over power and land. This conflict has caused nearly 2 million people to be displaced from their homes in the country and more than 2 million refugees to flee to neighbouring countries, and charities are warning that the conflict could cause critical food shortages due to farmers being forced off their land. Along with HIV/AIDS and malaria, armed conflicts are now a leading cause of world hunger. Armed conflict leads to food shortages on a large scale and for long periods of time, destroying any prospect of economic and social development. In 2019, the Democratic Republic of the Congo, Somalia, Sudan and Chad were all involved in armed conflicts. The effects of armed conflict are catastrophic for the countries involved and it can take decades to reconstruct after the conflict has ceased.

In 2007, an Oxfam report into 'Africa's missing billions' made clear the enormous impact of armed conflicts in many African countries. At that time, civil wars were costing Africa on average $18 billion per year. The charity demonstrated that the cost to the continent's development over a 17-year period was nearly $300 billion. In addition, African countries

'**Scorched earth policy**' is a common military strategy used in Africa during civil wars that involves destroying anything that might be useful to the enemy while advancing through or withdrawing from an area. This includes burning down homes and villages, burning food stocks, bombing fields and destroying transport and communication facilities.

'Peace is the greatest weapon for development that any people can have.' (Nelson Mandela)

Case study: The economic consequences of armed conflict

In 2011, when fighting in Côte d'Ivoire made access to the key Ivorian seaport of Abidjan virtually impossible, foreign trade was disrupted in Mali, Burkina Faso and Niger. Mali's cattle exports halted almost completely and Burkina Faso's total exports of cattle and animal products fell by 65 per cent. The economic disturbances caused by the Ivorian conflict weakened the financial position of the affected countries. Burkina Faso and Mali each lost nearly $30 million in government revenues in the first three months of the war in taxes, customs duties and other sources of revenue.

Tourism is also important to Africa. It is an essential source of foreign exchange to many countries, and for Kenya the largest source. However, armed violence deters millions of potential visitors. Oxfam's research of international opinion showed that more than half of people from the world's top tourism spenders (France, Germany, Japan, UK and the USA) said they would be less likely to go on holiday to a country with a reputation for armed violence or gun crime than to a country without such a reputation.

Case study: Conflict – the rise of terrorism in Africa

Terrorism is now a major deep-rooted issue for many countries in North Africa. Groups linked to Isis have grown in countries such as Somalia and Nigeria where they are able to take advantage of the lack of infrastructure and policing. They are able to recruit and train in the desert and move freely without restrictions from the law or the army. In Somalia, militant group al-Shabaab has wreaked havoc over the last few years taking control of towns and villages across the country. They have carried out suicide attacks in neighbouring

Figure 4.13 Terrorist training in North Africa

countries that have attempted to assist the Somali Government in fighting the group. The biggest attack was in Somalia's capital, Mogadishu, where 655 people were killed by a suicide truck bombing carried out by al-Shabaab.

Fact file

The results of armed conflicts

- Children suffer seriously from armed conflict. Children often become orphans or can be dragged into conflict to fight.
- Millions of people can be uprooted from their homes and land, destroying any prospect of being self-sufficient.
- Vast numbers of refugees are created who are without food, water, shelter and medical support.
- Emergency aid can be severely disrupted or temporarily stopped because of the dangers

caused by shooting, fighting, attacks and hijacking of aid trucks.
- Food becomes a weapon, with soldiers destroying food and livestock, adopting a scorched earth policy (see page 146). Wells are often contaminated or mined, which forces farmers off the land.
- Food production is seriously harmed by armed conflict with areas affected suffering annual losses of more than 12 per cent of production. In the extreme case of Angola, food production was reduced by 44 per cent during the civil war (1975–2002).

involved in conflict had, on average, '50 per cent more infant deaths, 15 per cent more undernourished people, life expectancy reduced by 5 years, 20 per cent more adult illiteracy … and 12.4 per cent less food per person'. Additionally, in non-conflict African countries, there were approximately two or three more doctors per patient compared with those involved in conflict. The report went on to say that the cost of conflict was equal to the amount of money received in aid during the same period.

Show your understanding

1 What is kleptocracy?
2 To what extent is corruption an issue in some African countries?
3 Read the case study on corruption in Africa. What evidence is there that corruption is rife?
4 Describe the extensive consequences of civil war and armed conflict. Make reference to the case study on Côte d'Ivoire and the fact file.
5 Outline the issue of terrorism in North Africa.

12-mark question

Analyse the causes of a world issue you have studied.

20-mark question

To what extent has a world issue you have studied had an impact in different countries?

Responses to development issues in Africa

The starvation of children, the widespread contagion of disease, corruption and the plague of conflict mean the general state of Africa is an international issue of huge significance to the global community. International organisations, non-governmental organisations (NGOs), individual countries and groupings of countries all have a part to play in addressing the issues faced by many African countries. There is no single silver bullet that can solve the complicated problems facing African people. Aid and support can come in many forms and what might be appropriate in one situation may not be suitable in another. Sometimes immediate short-term emergency aid is essential, while at other times a prolonged programme of long-term support and aid is required. There is even debate as to whether aid is an appropriate way to help Africa – does it support or does it create reliance (see pages 163–5)?

Types of aid

Bilateral aid

Figure 4.14 **The UK Government gives aid to the government of Ethiopia**

Bilateral aid is government-to-government assistance, where one country gives aid directly to another. The aid is usually long term and part of a programme of development. It can take the form of emergency assistance at times when disaster strikes. Increasingly, aid comes without strings attached, though much assistance still comes in the form of tied aid (see page 149).

Multilateral aid

Figure 4.15 **The flags of the EU and the UN**

Multilateral aid is aid provided by multinational organisations such as the United Nations (UN), the European Union (EU) or the African Union (AU). It has the advantage that it is not usually tied and these organisations can operate on a large scale because of their economic power.

Non-governmental organisation (NGO) aid

This is provided by voluntary organisations such as Save the Children, ActionAid, Oxfam, Mary's Meals and SCIAF (Scottish Catholic International Aid Fund). Often NGOs will target particular groups, such as children, or will provide specialist services. They are motivated by humanitarian concern and have no political ties.

Tied aid

Tied aid refers to aid given to a country but with conditions attached. The aid is conditional on the recipient country purchasing goods and services from the donor country. Tied aid has been a target of fierce criticism. It is estimated that tying aid can increase the prices of the goods and services by up to 25 per cent.

Criticisms of tied aid

- It favours companies in the donor country rather than the recipient country.
- Spending on goods and services takes place in the donor country, not in the recipient country.

- It can increase the costs of aid programmes because the best price is ignored in favour of buying from the donor country.
- It excludes and discourages companies and businesses in the recipient country from participating so local people do not benefit.
- It results in an over-reliance on knowledge, technology and spare parts from the donor country. Self-reliance is discouraged, leading to aid dependency.

Fifteen years ago, many aid donors pledged to end tied aid. The UK formally untied all development assistance in 2001, with the justification that 'tied aid reduces value for money' and tends to lead to inappropriate and expensive projects that do little to tackle the needs of the poorest. However, the UN has identified that a large majority of its members continue to tie aid. Much of this aid money is referred to as 'boomerang aid' – funds that flow to developing countries return immediately to donor countries. The USA makes sure that 80 cents in every dollar is returned home (see case study below).

The benefits of non-tied aid

- Competitive tendering is encouraged, attracting bids from local companies.
- It assists the development of the private sector in recipient countries, thereby creating more jobs.
- Local ownership is encouraged.

Case study: Tied aid – US food aid

The USA is the largest donor of international humanitarian aid, contributing roughly $8 billion in emergency food aid since 2010. But a significant portion of that food aid is 'tied', which means the food must be sourced from US suppliers and transported on US ships, even if cheaper alternatives exist. The benefits of tying go to companies in the US at the expense of aid recipients. For example, the Cargo Preference Act of 1954 dictates that 75 per cent of all US food aid must be shipped on private US commercial vessels, on which 75 per cent of the crew are US citizens. These policies translate into big gains for US shipping interests. The US might report a food aid shipment of $5 million to Ethiopia but $3.5 million of this is actually consumed by freight and logistics costs – in other words, profit for US companies.

- The value of aid is worth more to the recipient.
- Dependency on outside support is reduced, so self-sufficiency is more likely.

What makes aid 'good aid'?

Good aid is targeted at the people most in need and is not tied. It involves local people who are consulted about possible solutions. It is monitored to ensure that it is delivering what was intended and goes hand in hand with improving good governance in the recipient country. Ultimately, good aid should address the issues that hamper development so that, in the future, the recipient country becomes self-sufficient and capable of dealing with the social and economic hurdles that get in the way of development.

UK aid to African countries

Figure 4.16 **The office for the Department for International Development**

The Department for International Development (DFID) is the part of the UK Government that is responsible for Britain's aid to developing countries. The focus of the department is to promote development in the developing world, particularly in countries where people are suffering from extreme poverty. The department is led by a Cabinet Minister. DFID works with charities, businesses and international organisations such as the World Bank and the UN in working towards achieving the Sustainable Development Goals (SDGs; see pages 155–6).

An example of the work of DFID is in combating one of Africa's biggest killers, malaria. In 2000, only two-thirds of Ethiopians had access to health services. Rural areas in particular suffered from a lack of medical facilities and health workers. Since 2010, the Health Extension Programme, the flagship programme of the Ethiopian Ministry of Health, has aimed to extend health care with a primary focus on reducing malaria cases. DFID funding is currently supporting more than 3900 health extension workers to deliver health services to around 9 million people in Ethiopia. Additionally, the DFID is supporting the Health Extension Programme through a financial contribution to the government of Ethiopia, which pays for the delivery of services.

Fact file

Department for International Development aid statistics

- The UK Government has made a commitment to invest 0.7 per cent of gross national income (GNI) on official development assistance. The GNI target of 0.7 per cent is recommended and encouraged by the United Nations.
- In 2018 bilateral spend for DFID was £9.2 billion, which makes up around 64 per cent of DFID aid, while multilateral spend was £5.2 billion.

- In 2018, DFID spent £10.9 billion on aid to poorer countries.
- In 2018 Africa received £2.9 billion.
- The top three recipients of UK bilateral aid in 2018 were Pakistan (£331 million), Ethiopia (£301 million) and Nigeria (£297 million). The amount to these countries accounted for 20.6 per cent of total country-specific UK bilateral aid.
- The Democratic Republic of Congo moved into the top ten recipients of UK bilateral aid, as spend increased from £166 million

Fact file (continued)

in 2017 to £204 million in 2018 in response to escalating humanitarian crises.

- In 2018, the International Development Association received the largest amount of DFID multilateral assistance (£1.3 billion).

- Much of the finance donated by DFID comes with political conditions. The receiving country must be committed to tackling poverty, upholding human rights and must manage public money wisely.

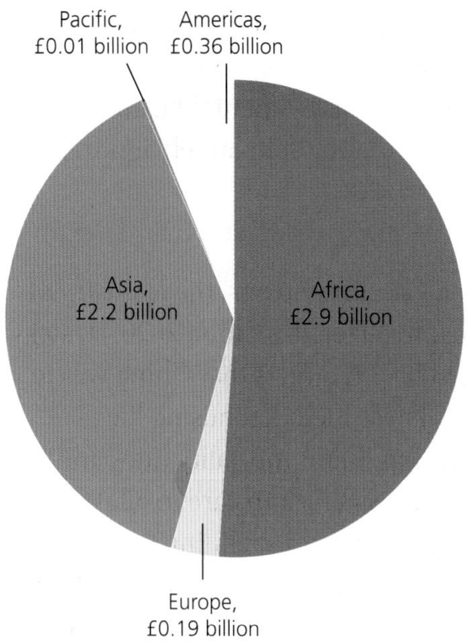

How successful is DFID?

The UN recommends, and its members have agreed, that 0.7 per cent of GNI should be allocated to overseas aid. However, some countries contribute more, for example, Denmark, Sweden, Finland and Luxembourg give more than Britain. While being among the richest countries in the world, Britain is around the middle in terms of the contributions it gives in aid, leading some to say Britain should give more. Concerns have been expressed that former British colonies are given preference when it comes to deciding which

Pacific, £0.01 billion

Americas, £0.36 billion

Asia, £2.2 billion

Africa, £2.9 billion

Europe, £0.19 billion

Figure 4.17 **Regional breakdown of UK bilateral aid spending, 2018**

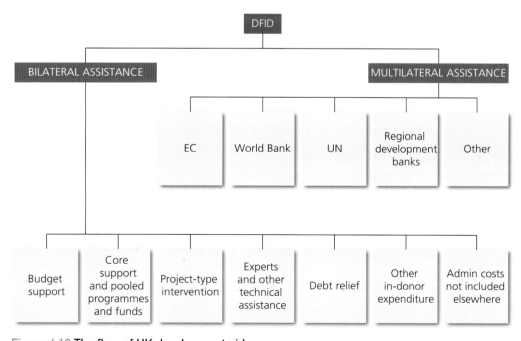

Figure 4.18 **The flow of UK development aid**

countries in Africa should receive aid. In addition, it is claimed that aid is used to control the internal affairs of African countries through political conditions. Necessarily, any government has to be selective when deciding which countries will receive aid, meaning that, however good the intentions are, many countries will not be helped.

ICT task

Visit the DFID's aid tracker to find out how the UK invests in developing countries at **http://devtracker.dfid.gov.uk**

Scottish aid to African countries

The Scottish Government's International Development Strategy seeks to build upon both the historical and contemporary relationships that exist between Scotland and the developing world, even although Scotland's financial contribution is included as part of UK aid. The Scottish Government's £10 million fund focuses on four countries around the world. The Scottish Government has a partnership agreement with the government of Malawi and around half of funding goes to projects in that country. From 2018–23, there are 11 funded projects happening in Malawi focusing on improving health and education in the country. In addition, the Scottish Government provides emergency humanitarian funding in response to crises. In 2018, £300,000 was donated in emergency aid for people affected by conflict in Syria, Yemen and South Sudan. The funding was distributed equally between British Red Cross (Syria), Mercy Corps (Yemen) and Tearfund (South Sudan) to provide urgent food, water, shelter, sanitation and health support. The Scottish Government is also funding projects in sub-Saharan Africa through the Climate Justice Fund.

Case study: Scottish Government multilateral aid

Organisation: Tearfund (a charity)

Project title: Water and Climate Justice in Malawi (£499,694)

This project seeks to support the better management of water resources and helps empower communities to hold duty bearers accountable for those resources. In terms of impact, the project leads to the improved socio-economic standing of the targeted households by reducing the number of people suffering from waterborne diseases. The project achieves three main aims:

- increased availability of clean and safe water
- increased water resource governance at district and community level
- households in targeted communities will employ strategies to adapt to climate change to improve water resource management.

Source: adapted from gov.scot

Show your understanding

1 Explain the various types of aid.
2 Why is tied aid controversial? Make reference to the case study of US food aid.
3 Outline the work of the DFID – make use of the fact file.
4 Has the UK been successful in providing aid to those in need?
5 Describe the provision of aid by the Scottish Government.

12-mark question

Evaluate the success of an individual country's response to a world issue you have studied.

Multilateral responses to development issues

The European Union

The European Development Fund (EDF) is the main instrument for European Union (EU) aid to Africa. It is managed by the European Commission (EC) but is not part of the EC budget. The EDF sets a budget over a multi-annual period with the current budget covering 2014–20.

The budget is around £24 billion. In 2000, the Cotonou Agreement was signed, which is a 20-year programme for delivering aid to African countries. During the first five years, the EU supported African governments to create a balanced economy, expand the private sector and improve social services in the countries covered by the agreement. Another continued objective is to integrate African states into the global economy.

The EC funds most African aid programmes in four stages. Indicative programmes identify overall priorities before money is allocated via commitments to specific projects. Then contracts with third parties to deliver projects are agreed through individual commitments. Payments are then made to the contractors for the delivery of projects. In delivering aid, the EC faces many challenges. This includes dealing with the world's very poorest countries, many of which have weak government structures and shaky economic policies. The EC must make best use of European taxpayers' money by ensuring that anti-poverty programmes are tailor-made to meet local needs and that they deliver concrete, lasting results.

Case study: EU aid and the Democratic Republic of the Congo

The Democratic Republic of the Congo (DRC) is a vast country with immense economic resources. From 1998 until 2003 it was at the centre of what some observers called 'Africa's world war'. This five-year conflict pitted government forces, supported by Angola, Namibia and Zimbabwe, against rebels backed by Uganda and Rwanda. This has left DRC in the grip of a humanitarian crisis that still goes on today. The EU's approach is to help rebuild the country politically (governance) and physically (transport infrastructure and health care). The EU also supports regional initiatives and measures to protect the environment. The multi-annual indicative programme in the DRC for the current spending round has budgeted £450 million for these priorities.

Figure 4.19 The location of the DRC

The EU's activities in the DRC also involve cross-cutting issues such as democracy, good governance, human rights, the rights of children and indigenous peoples, gender equality, long-term environmental protection and the fight against HIV/AIDS.

The African Union

Figure 4.20 **The logo of the African Union**

In 2002, the African Union (AU) was established. The AU seeks to create a strong and united Africa, with particular attention paid to the needs of women and young people. Peace and security are viewed as essential elements in creating development and a united Africa. Its official vision is to create 'an integrated, prosperous and peaceful Africa, driven by its own citizens and representing a dynamic force in the global arena'. However, many have challenged its success in realising this vision.

Aims of the AU

- To eliminate the remaining problems left by colonialism.
- To seek to unite African states in a common cause, creating solidarity among African countries.
- To accelerate economic development by co-ordinating and intensifying co-operation.
- To protect individual African states and their right to run their own affairs.
- To promote and encourage international co-operation, especially within the United Nations.
- To promote and defend African concerns on a variety of issues relevant to African people.

Has the AU been effective in resolving development issues?

The AU has had some successes over the last 17 years. In dealing with political corruption and dishonesty, AU observer missions are now sent as a matter of routine to cover elections in all member states, in accordance with the African Charter on Democracy, Elections and Governance (2007). Furthermore, there has been a significant fall in conflicts and coups, and an increased number of successful elections in the region in the past decade, suggesting the AU has added value to Africa's 'political performance'.

Perhaps the most significant development has been the creation of the Peace and Security Council, designed to address regional conflicts in Africa that are the cause of so much poverty and suffering. Africa is therefore aiming to take responsibility for addressing its own security problems rather than relying on outside intervention, which has often been inadequate or unsuccessful. In 2019, terrorist groups seized control of territory in Somalia, and the AU intervened with a military response to fight the terrorist threat.

The AU faces huge challenges in Africa. It is a comparatively new organisation and is still finding its way. It has struggled to boost the African economy in any great way, with poor internal trade still a major barrier to development. Despite numerous protocols to facilitate the free movement of goods and people across borders, the AU's record in stimulating the removal of trade barriers between countries in the union is less than impressive and the value of intra-African trade is still abysmally low as a percentage of total trade. Proposals for an African central bank and an African monetary union (like the euro) are still on the drawing board, as vested interests and concerns about sovereignty hold back the necessary political will to drive the process. There is no doubt the AU has been beneficial but it could still do better.

The United Nations

The United Nations (UN) plays a significant role in attempting to deal with development issues in Africa. One of the main aims of the UN is to co-operate in order to promote economic and social progress throughout the world and it is this aim that guides the work of the specialised agencies through which aid and assistance are channelled. The UN Declaration of Human Rights describes the rights that the citizens of all members should enjoy.

Millennium Development Goals

In September 2000 at the United Nations Millennium Summit, nearly 190 countries signed up to a range of goals and targets designed to reduce world poverty and hunger and improve life for people in developing countries. The goals were practical in nature and designed to encourage the international community to stop talking about making a difference and join together to start taking action. Eight precise targets were drawn up that the countries involved had to aim to meet in a specified time – before 2015. The idea of setting a time limit to achieve the goals meant that those involved and those benefiting from assistance had a clear goal to reach. However, when we look at the Millennium Development Goals (MDGs) in more detail, it can be understood why some criticised them for being too modest and unambitious. For example, the targets to address extreme poverty and hunger stated that by 2015 the number of people living on less than $1 a day and the proportion of people suffering from hunger would be halved. Without doubt this meant progress, but not to the extent required. Other MDGs were more ambitious, such as ensuring that by 2015 all children would be able to complete a full course in primary education.

Fact file

The eight MDGs

- Eradicate extreme poverty and hunger.
- Achieve universal primary education.
- Promote gender equality and empower women.
- Reduce child mortality.
- Improve maternal health.
- Combat HIV and AIDS, malaria and other diseases.
- Ensure environmental sustainability.
- Develop a global partnership for development.

Sustainable Development Goals

Over the 15-year term some excellent progress was made in attempting to realise the eight MDGs. However, ultimately, most of the goals were not reached. This led to severe criticism and questions being asked about the worthiness of the goals. The successful MDGs include the halting and reversing of the spread of HIV/AIDS, halving the number of people in extreme poverty and halving the proportion of people without access to basic sanitation. This sounds impressive but in reality 22 per cent of people still live in extreme poverty and over 30 per cent of people cannot access basic sanitation. The other goals have not been reached, which has led to the drafting of a new set of 17 goals that are running from 2015 until 2030. The goals rework, build upon and add to the original MDGs and are called the Sustainable Development Goals (SDGs). The targets include fully eradicating extreme poverty and, regarding hunger, call for doubling agricultural productivity and the incomes of small-scale farmers. The health targets include ending preventable deaths of newborns and children under five years old. The SDGs are more extensive and less 'headline' focused, which may mean they are more achievable over the time period. Only time will tell.

Added Value idea

Research the SDGs. Looking at their progress in a specific African country would be a good way to focus your work.

A selection of the 17 SDGs

1 End poverty in all its forms everywhere.
2 End hunger, achieve food security and improve nutrition.
3 Ensure healthy lives and promote well-being for all at all ages.
4 Ensure inclusive and equitable quality education and promote life-long learning opportunities.
5 Achieve gender equality and empower all women and girls.
6 Ensure availability and sustainable management of water and sanitation for all.
7 Build infrastructure, promote inclusive and sustainable industrialisation and foster innovation.
8 Reduce inequality within and among countries.
9 Make cities and human settlements inclusive, safe, resilient and sustainable.
10 Take urgent action to combat climate change and its impacts.

The work of the United Nations agencies and NGOs

The work of specialised UN agencies

The UN plays a significant role in attempting to deal with development issues in Africa. When the UN was established in 1945 one of its main aims was to encourage countries to work together to improve the lives of human beings all around the world. Nowhere is this required more than in many African countries. The UN operates a series of specialised agencies that work to deliver multilateral aid and assistance. Each agency has a particular focus and remit when it comes to meeting the needs of developing nations.

It is through the variety of agencies as well as in working with member states and other organisations that the UN attempts to meet the targets set in the Sustainable Development Goals. We will analyse the work of several UN agencies and look at how they attempt to resolve development issues in Africa.

The United Nations Children's Fund

Figure 4.21 **The logo of UNICEF**

The United Nations Children's Fund (UNICEF) is a huge agency that focuses on the needs of children and their mothers. UNICEF deals with providing emergency aid when disasters strike and will provide specialist assistance with a particular focus on helping children and women. In addition, UNICEF takes on long-term projects such as supporting governments to build and equip health systems, train health workers and provide food and clean water, so every child can be as healthy as possible.

Furthermore, UNICEF is the world's largest distributor of vaccines to the developing world. It supplies vaccines for 36 per cent of the world's children in over 190 countries. UNICEF also works to support families and communities to care for children and protect them against exploitation and abuse. The UN Convention on the Rights of the Child sets out the basic rights every child around the world is entitled to – UNICEF works to make sure these rights are fulfilled.

The World Health Organization

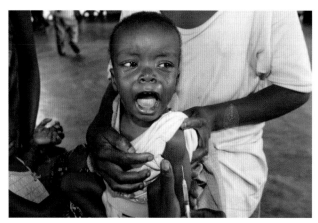

Figure 4.22 **WHO immunisation programme in Liberia**

Case study: The work of UNICEF – assistance to South Sudan

South Sudan is one of the world's poorest counties. It has been blighted by conflict since its independence in 2011. Since the conflict started more than 4 million people have fled their homes, with 2.47 million taking refuge in neighbouring countries. Close to 200,000 people are living in six UN 'protection of civilians' sites across the country. Seven million people need humanitarian assistance, most of whom face acute food shortages. Also, around 70% of children are out of regular schooling.

Addressing the situation regarding education, UNICEF works closely with the Ministry of General Education and Instruction (MoGEI) and approximately 30 implementing partners to address the challenges facing education in South Sudan. The long-term, countrywide presence and experience of UNICEF has greatly facilitated implementation of innovative, effective and context-specific education interventions through its strong network of partnerships. UNICEF's government-led approach involves working in close cooperation with national and state education ministries, giving them 'ownership' and responsibility over such areas as the payment of government teachers' salaries and providing supervision of teachers and head teachers. UNICEF has also set up nearly 300 temporary learning spaces/classrooms to help children access an education where no school exists or has been destroyed.

Source: UNICEF South Sudan

Case study: UNICEF project work – improving access to water and sanitation in rural schools in Tanzania

Schools with inadequate water and sanitation facilities usually have the poorest attendance records and highest dropout rates. In Tanzania, 89 per cent of schools do not have adequate water or sanitation facilities. A study in Tanzania showed a 12 per cent increase in school attendance when water was available within 15 minutes compared to more than half an hour away. Girls often have to walk long distances to fetch water and firewood in the early morning. After such an arduous chore, they may arrive late and tired at school. Being 'needed at home' is a major reason why children, especially girls from poor families, drop out of school. Providing water closer to homes increases girls' free time and boosts their school attendance. When girls get older they are often forced to skip classes or drop out of school because there are no separate toilets for them that guarantee a ⇨

Case study (continued)

minimum of privacy. Providing water, sanitation and hygiene facilities in schools is a cost-effective intervention that can significantly reduce hygiene-related diseases, increase student attendance and learning achievements, and contribute to dignity and gender equality.

UNICEF provided 25 rural schools with safe drinking water points, separate toilets for boys and girls and hand-washing facilities to benefit at least 25,000 school children. Hygiene education also encourages children to act as agents of change and promote improved hygiene practices at home and in their wider community.

Some of the work done by the World Health Organization (WHO) is visible and familiar: the response teams sent to contain outbreaks of diseases, the emergency assistance to people affected by disasters, or the mass immunisation campaigns that protect the world's children from killer diseases. Other work is visible because the diseases being addressed – HIV/AIDS, tuberculosis or malaria – have such a high profile for global health. However, some work undertaken by WHO is largely invisible, such as setting standards to help maintain the quality of medicines and vaccines. WHO specifically aims to reach the most disadvantaged and vulnerable groups. These groups are often hidden, living in remote rural areas in countries such as Mali or Burkina Faso. From 2000 to 2015, WHO was tasked with meeting three of the Millennium Development Goals and will continue to strive to reduce child mortality, maternal death in childbirth and the spread of HIV/AIDS. WHO also has work to do in relation to the new Sustainable Development Goals. It has a responsibility for helping meet the various health related goals such as SDG 3 – 'Good Health and Wellbeing' and its various sub-targets. With particular regard to Africa, the fight against HIV/AIDS has been WHO's priority focus for the past three decades, with HIV rates finally beginning to fall throughout the continent.

Case study: WHO and the Ebola virus epidemic of 2014

Ebola is a viral illness and the initial symptoms can include a sudden fever, intense weakness, muscle pain and a sore throat. Subsequent stages are vomiting, diarrhoea and – in some cases – both internal and external bleeding. The disease infects humans through close contact with infected animals. It then spreads between humans by direct contact with infected blood, bodily fluids or organs, or indirectly through contact with contaminated environments. Ebola has a high fatality rate of around 60 per cent and there is currently no licensed treatment or vaccine. In 2014, the virus broke out in Western Africa with WHO declaring in September 2014 that the Ebola virus was an 'international health emergency'.

In Liberia, Sierra Leone and Guinea, three of the world's poorest countries, Ebola caused the already threadbare health-care systems to almost collapse. Hospitals were in disarray as supplies ran out and as staff abandoned posts after watching their colleagues succumb to the virus. WHO deployed teams of experts to West African countries, including epidemiologists to work with countries in surveillance and monitoring of the outbreak and medical experts to support mobile field labs for early confirmation of Ebola cases. WHO also deployed clinical management experts to help health-care facilities to treat affected patients. Lastly, WHO set up logistics to dispatch equipment and materials and gave national and international advice to citizens on how to avoid contracting the disease.

The World Food Programme

Figure 4.23 **A bag of Pakistani rice, donated by Germany, for Laos in south-east Asia, as part of the World Food Programme**

Acute hunger and starvation are often highlighted on our TV screens. We see adverts from charities asking us to donate money to finance food aid to famine-struck countries. The World Food Programme (WFP) is the world's largest humanitarian agency, fighting hunger worldwide. Each year, on average, the WFP feeds more than 90 million people in more than 70 countries. In recent years, the number of hungry people in the world has grown to almost 1 billion, which means that one person in seven does not get enough food to be healthy and lead an active life. Of those hungry people, 265 million live in sub-Saharan Africa. The WFP is on the front line, using food assistance to help break the cycle of hunger at its roots.

Fact file

The extent of hunger and starvation in Africa

- 24.8 per cent of the population in sub-Saharan Africa are hungry.
- 38.8 per cent of Burundi's population are hungry.
- Almost one in three of the world's hungry live in sub-Saharan Africa.
- 23 million school-age children attend classes hungry every day.
- In every minute of every day, six children die of hunger in Africa.
- Hunger kills more people in Africa than AIDS, malaria and TB combined.
- Undernourished children lose their curiosity and motivation and millions do not carry on with their education as a consequence.
- For the cost of 6p a child can be fed in school for a day in Africa.
- Women are much more affected by hunger than men. Seven out of ten of the world's hungry are women and girls.

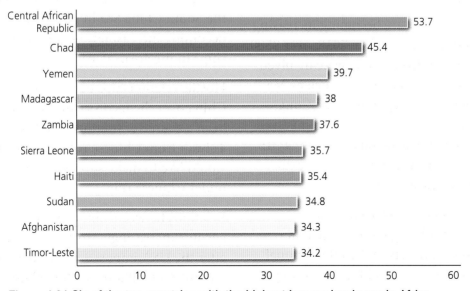

Figure 4.24 **Six of the ten countries with the highest hunger levels are in Africa**
Source: Global Hunger Index, 2019

The work of non-governmental organisations

Non-governmental organisations (NGOs) raise money from voluntary and private sources to fund projects in developing countries. They are free from government interference and can determine for themselves what their aims and policies are. They provide emergency relief at times of crisis and are most obviously in the public eye at these times when they are involved in high-profile fundraising, for example, during the famine in South Sudan.

NGOs work in partnership with other bodies providing short-term and long-term aid. There are literally hundreds of NGOs. Some, such as Save the Children, provide specifically targeted aid to groups, while others, such as Oxfam, act on a broader scale. By focusing on the work of two NGOs, a fuller picture of the role and work of NGOs generally will unfold.

Mary's Meals

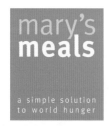

Figure 4.25 **The logo for Mary's Meals**

Mary's Meals is a Scottish charity that provides international aid to several countries around the globe. The charity sets up school feeding programmes in some of the world's poorest communities, where hunger and poverty prevent children from gaining an education. Mary's Meals provides one meal per day in a place of learning to attract chronically hungry children into a classroom where they receive an education that can, in the future, be their ladder out of poverty. Mary's Meals began feeding 200 children in Malawi in 2002 and is now feeding around 1.5 million children across 18 countries. In addition to this, many of the schools where Mary's Meals provide food have a school garden, which encourages the children to learn about agriculture. The produce of the garden (e.g. cabbage, peppers, avocado, pineapples) goes to supplementing the children's lunches. The children are also taught the importance of hand washing before eating, and Mary's Meals supplies soap to each school.

Mary's Meals is mainly financed through fundraising by supporters of the charity. Money is also received in donations from churches, businesses and other contributors. Mary's Meals has several charity shops across Scotland that help to fund the school feeding programmes.

ICT task

Watch the *Generation Hope* film at **www. marysmeals.org.uk**, a documentary that explores the work of Mary's Meals and gives an insight into the lives of children coping with the realities of extreme poverty.

Case study: Mary's Meals in Liberia

Mary's Meals started working in Liberia delivering shipments of emergency aid during the devastating civil war that ended in 2003. The school feeding programme began in 2006 and has steadily grown to reach more than 121,000 children, making it Mary's Meals' second biggest project. After the civil war, schools re-opened and pupils started to catch up on years of missed education. Most of the schools receiving Mary's Meals in Liberia are in small villages in rural areas. Children are often too hungry to attend school, or are helping to find wild food (fruit and fish), and even if they do attend, they are too hungry to concentrate and learn.

Mary's Meals helps to relieve the burden for families and other community members, tackling child malnutrition and crucially encouraging children back to the classroom. The schools, communities and volunteers are key partners in the feeding programme. The schools and communities provide storage and management of supplies, daily record keeping, organisation of volunteers and daily meal preparation. Mary's Meals provides project management, financial oversight, purchase and delivery of food, equipment and training with support visits from field monitors twice a week.

Mary's Meals has a long-term commitment to feeding the children of Liberia and is planning to reach a further 40,000 children over the coming years.

Response to Ebola outbreak in Liberia and Western Africa

During the Ebola outbreak in 2014, Liberia was in a state of emergency with all schools closed to minimise the spread of the virus. This brought a halt to the standard delivery methods for the feeding programme Mary's Meals operates on a daily basis. However, Mary's Meals launched an emergency response to Ebola by distributing meals to children's homes and to embattled health-care workers, as well as those being treated in Ebola holding and treatment centres.

Source: adapted from marysmeals.org.uk

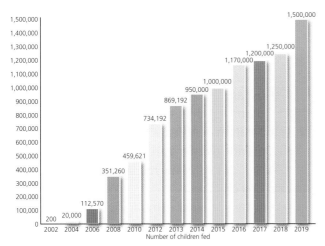

Figure 4.26 **Number of children fed a daily meal by Mary's Meals worldwide**

Source: marysmeals.org.uk

Oxfam

Oxfam has a general aim of fighting poverty all over the world. Oxfam focuses its work on vital issues to tackle the root causes of poverty, from life's basics – food, water, health and education – to complex questions around aid, climate change and human rights. With this extensive field of activity, Oxfam is one of the world's oldest and largest NGOs. Like other NGOs, Oxfam relies on private and voluntary donations; however, Oxfam also has a nationwide chain of charity shops in the UK that help with funding. Oxfam is also a pressure group with thousands of members in

Figure 4.27 **The logo for Oxfam**

the UK. As a pressure group, Oxfam works to improve the lives of many people around the globe, especially in developing countries in Africa. Political campaigning by NGOs is another way to help achieve development in Africa as well as more traditional aid-based methods.

Case study: Oxfam – Inequality and Poverty Campaign

Across the world, the gap between the rich and the rest is growing faster than ever. And this increasingly extreme inequality is destabilising economies, damaging societies and pushing more people into poverty. Oxfam is determined to change that world by mobilising the power of people against poverty. Oxfam is spearheading an online activist movement to bring about awareness among the general population that extreme inequality is not inevitable – it is the result of years of deliberate policies and rules that have been rigged in favour of the few. Oxfam also organised a letter-writing campaign aimed at getting its members and followers to send a letter or email to their MP to pressure elected representatives to challenge inequality.

Source: adapted from Oxfam.org.uk

Figure 4.28 An online viral campaign by Oxfam to raise awareness about wealth inequality across the world

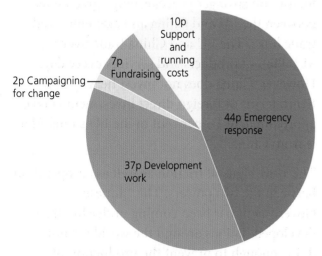

Figure 4.29 **For every £1 donated to Oxfam in 2019 …**

Source: Oxfam.org.uk

Show your understanding

1 How are NGOs financed?
2 Outline the different varieties of NGOs operating in Africa.
3 Describe the aims and work done by Mary's Meals. Make reference to the case study on Liberia.
4 Why are political campaigns a useful method for bringing about development in Africa? Refer to the Oxfam case study.

Show your understanding (continued)

12-mark question

Analyse the actions taken by international organisations to resolve a world issue you have studied.

20-mark question

International organisations have been successful in resolving a significant world issue.

Discuss with reference to a world issue you have studied.

How successful are NGOs?

The issues affecting Africa's development are immense and dwarf the resources of all NGOs, let alone one particular NGO. However, at their best, NGOs can make a striking and important contribution to improving the lives and futures of many African people. The examples in the preceding case studies show how lives have been changed for the better. For example, without Mary's Meals 1.5 million more children in the world would go hungry every day.

Needless to say, NGOs have their shortcomings. One growing concern is the so-called 'compassion fatigue' felt by the public as they are asked to donate to yet another important cause. Some NGOs are accused of spending too much on administration, which can put people off donating. Other NGOs are well meaning, but lack expertise and fall short of the standards expected of an aid organisation. In comparison to the UN and international governments, individual NGOs operate on a small scale and consequently their impact is inevitably limited.

There are numerous examples of superb work being done by various organisations, but their

impact in addressing the multiple causes that impede development is on a small scale. In addition, many NGOs target particular groups so their success can only be measured within the narrow framework in which they work. NGOs are one part of the jigsaw that is the possible solution to addressing the issues surrounding Africa's development.

Criticisms and controversies of NGOs

Some NGOs, like Oxfam, genuinely contribute to development. However, others are sometimes ideologically biased or religiously committed and promote their particular views. Many NGOs promote Western values such as women's liberation, human rights, civil rights, the protection of minorities, freedom and equality. Not everyone finds these liberal values acceptable and they may clash with traditional views.

NGOs are self-appointed and answer only to themselves. They are unelected and cannot be voted out. They frequently attempt to tell those who are elected democratically, and those who voted them into office, how to organise their countries.

NGOs in places like Sudan, Somalia and Zimbabwe have become the preferred agencies for delivering Western aid. According to the Red Cross, more money goes through NGOs than through the World Bank. Their power over food, medicines and funds creates the power of an alternative government and sometimes corruption takes place.

Is aid the way forward to assist Africa's development?

The great aid debate

Over the past 50 years there has been a general school of thought that those in developing countries should be entitled to aid from richer countries. Indeed, the developed world has seen it as a moral obligation to donate aid to those countries, mainly in Africa, that require support and assistance. However, more recently some academics have questioned the merits of development aid and cited that aid is actually detrimental to developing counties.

Development aid can be a controversial debate, with differing views of how this impacts the countries who receive it.

Aid is counter-productive

Richard Dowden, former executive director of the Royal African Society

Dowden argues a radical view claiming that aid is not the answer to Africa's problems. He concedes that humanitarian relief will always be needed when a disaster hits a country; however, he questions the view that aid can transform societies. At best, he argues, aid can only accelerate a process that is already under way. He explains that nearly $1 trillion has been spent on aid to Africa since the 1960s but the situation now for African people is not much better. Much aid was spent without consultation with local people and what are left are abandoned and useless projects.

Africa is a continent in which countries were created artificially by colonial powers and have not produced effective governments.

This means that aid providers have had to work alongside bad governance, making it impossible to deliver the development needed. Dowden highlights the fact that South Africa and Botswana have better-run governments and do not need aid. On the other hand, where governments have collapsed, such as in Somalia, it is impossible to put development aid into action effectively. The countries in the middle, such as Mozambique, have become aid dependent and have had their self-reliance undermined. Dowden argues that good governance is the essential component to facilitate development. Only by African governments raising appropriate taxes and spending them wisely can development take place. Short-term aid to assist countries moving in this direction may be appropriate, but otherwise aid will be wasted. The people themselves must undertake development.

Aid works

The use of aid and its resulting impact is tracked as much as possible, and many argue that these statistics depict a promising story. For example, *The Guardian* reported 'a growing flood of data shows that death rates in many poor countries are falling sharply, and that aid-supported programmes for healthcare delivery have played a key role. Aid works; it saves lives.' In 2000, as well as fighting tuberculosis and AIDS epidemics, malaria was a major threat to lives across Africa.

However, with the help of aid, the number of children dying from malaria has been 'cut from a peak of around 1 million in 2004 to around 700,000 by 2010'. While the fight against malaria continues, many argue that these statistics should encourage and strengthen the resolve to commit to providing aid to those in need. Those who advocate for aid and the resulting benefits worry about the opposing claims being made, with fears that this threatens the current funding they see as vital to help bring people out of poverty. ⇨

As well describing the vital work in saving lives aid can do during humanitarian disasters, the charity ActionAid UK details how aid is spent effectively to help long-term change in developing countries. They explain that 'aid goes a lot further than meeting basic needs. It helps tackle entrenched inequality and empowers people to claim their rights.' For example, in recent years, aid has helped give millions of women access to modern methods of family planning. Aid is also vital for increasing access to education, which can create previously impossible opportunities. Both of these examples give people, particularly women, greater autonomy over their lives and improve the prospects for them and their families. On a large scale, the positive long-term changes brought about with the help of aid has the additional benefit of helping international development across the globe and so has a positive impact on UK trade as well.

Development summarised for the twenty-first century

No one agency, charity or government can solve the problems confronting many African countries. The social, economic and political factors that explain Africa's development issues are complicated and cannot be addressed satisfactorily by short-term solutions.

Huge levels of international debt, corrupt or inefficient governments, trade that favours developed nations, not to mention the power of international corporations, the devastation caused by HIV/AIDS and desperate poverty, must all be tackled. This will require an effort of will and commitment by governments unparalleled in scope. Currently, admirable work is being undertaken by a variety of providers, but each has its limits and shortcomings. The Sustainable Development Goals, which will run until 2030, may take us a long way to creating a fully developed world – but progress will need to be better than the development goals we initiated at the millennium.

Show your understanding

1 What are the limitations and criticisms of NGOs?
2 a) Provide arguments for and against the view that aid is the best way to assist African countries to develop.
  b) Overall, which view do you support? Give detailed reasons to support your view.

Added Value idea

There is considerable controversy surrounding development aid. You could centre your research on the merits and drawbacks of aid, coming to a conclusion about whether the UK should increase or cut back aid to developing nations.

> Welcome to the revised Curriculum for Excellence (CfE) Higher Modern Studies!

Free-standing units at SCQF level 6

Students, who for whatever reason may not be proceeding to the exam itself, may be entered and assessed for the free-standing unit in International Issues, which no longer forms part of the exam.

The skills and knowledge that will be assessed are outlined in outcomes 1 and 2:

Outcome 1

- Use a range of sources of information to draw and support conclusions about international issues, focusing on either a major world power or a significant world issue.

Outcome 2

- Draw on factual and theoretical knowledge and understanding of international issues, focusing on either a major world power or a significant world issue.

Higher course assessment

The course assessment is made up of two components:

- two question papers with questions from each of the three sections and skill activities (80 marks)
- the Higher assignment (30 marks).

The marks awarded for the question papers and the assignment are added together and an overall mark indicates pass or fail. The course award is graded A to D.

The question papers

Question paper 1 has three sections:

- Section 1: Democracy in Scotland and the UK
  You will answer one essay from a choice of **three** (12 or 20 marks).
- Section 2: Social Issues in the UK
  You will answer one essay from a choice of **two** from your **chosen study** (12 or 20 marks).
- Section 3: International Issues
  You will answer one essay from a choice of **two** from your **chosen study** (12 or 20 marks).

You will have 1 hour and 45 minutes to answer the two 20-mark questions and one 12-mark question.

Question paper 2 has three mandatory questions as outlined below.

You will have 1 hour and 15 minutes to answer the two 10-mark questions and one 8-mark question.

What types of questions will I need to answer in question paper 2?

There are three types of skills questions that you will have practised in class. These are:

1 Using between two and four sources of information to detect and explain the degree of objectivity of a given statement (10 marks).

2 Using between two and four sources of information to identify what conclusions can be drawn (10 marks).

3 Using sources of information to evaluate their reliability (8 marks).

In the knowledge section of the exam you will answer four types of questions. Examples of the style of questions are given below.

> **Evaluate** the effectiveness of parliamentary representatives in holding the government to account. (**12 marks**)
>
> **Analyse** the impact of crime on society. (**12 marks**)
>
> **To what extent** does a world power you have studied have influence in international relations? (**20 marks**)
>
> International organisations have been successful in resolving a significant world issue. **Discuss** with reference to a world issue you have studied. (**20 marks**)

For an example of some source-based questions, have a look at SQA's Specimen Question Paper on the (CfE) Higher Modern Studies page of their website: **www.sqa.org.uk/sqa/47924.html**.

The assignment

The assignment is worth 30 marks out of a total of 110 marks for the course, and contributes 27 per cent of the total marks for the course.

The assignment task is to research a Modern Studies issue with alternative views. You will use your two one-sided A4 sheets (Modern Studies research evidence) to support you in presenting the findings of your research. The duration of the write-up is 1 hour and 30 minutes.

The assignment applies research and decision-making skills in the context of a Modern Studies issue. You can choose a political, social or international issue. The information collected should display knowledge and understanding of the topic or issue chosen. SQA recommends that you should devote about 8 hours for the research stage, including preparation time for the production of evidence.

The results of the research will be written up under controlled assessment conditions and must be completed within 1 hour and 30 minutes. Your Modern Studies research evidence recorded on up to two single-sided sheets of A4 will consist of materials collected during the research stage of the assignment. The allocation of marks is based on the following success criteria.

1 Identifying and demonstrating knowledge and understanding of the issue about which a decision is to be made, including alternative courses of action

You should choose a decision about which there are alternative views, for example:

To recommend or reject the continuation of the death penalty in the USA

or

To recommend or reject the continuation of positive discrimination in favour of black South Africans

You should agree an issue to research with your teacher. It has to relate to one or more of the issues that you have studied in your course:

- Democracy in Scotland and the United Kingdom
- Social Issues in the United Kingdom
- International Issues.

2 Analysing and synthesising information from a range of sources including use of specified resources

You will research a wide range of sources to widen your knowledge and understanding of the issue and to provide contrasting views on your chosen issue. By linking information from a variety of sources and viewpoints, you will be able to enrich and synthesise the arguments that are developed in your report. Remember it is important to provide balance in your report and to consider the arguments against your final decision/recommendation.

3 Evaluating the usefulness and reliability of a range of sources of information

You will comment on the background and nature of the source. Does it provide only one point of view, are its findings up to date and are its comments still relevant today?

4 Communicating information using the convention of a report

Remember you are *not* writing an essay. Your report style should include:

- a title
- a formal style that refers to evidence rather than personal opinion
- section headings breaking up the information to present evidence and contrasting arguments in a clear and logical structure
- references to the evidence you have used, especially the research evidence referred to in your A4 sheets
- a statement of the decision you have reached based on the evidence provided.

5 Reaching a decision, supported by evidence, about the issue

Your decision should be based on your research evidence and your own background knowledge of the issue.

Possible International Issues titles for your assignment

- Should the death penalty be abolished in the USA?
- Should positive discrimination legislation in favour of black South Africans be abolished in South Africa?
- Should the European Union continue to enlarge?
- Should NATO forces be based in Ukraine?
- Should the electoral college be abolished?

Research methods

In Modern Studies we look at a range of political, social and international issues that affect everyone's lives. Many of these issues are based on evidence gathered by research carried out by a whole series of people and organisations – from the government to charities.

How do I carry out a piece of research?

When researching a topic in Modern Studies, it is important to consider where you will get your information from. In the twenty-first century, you have access to huge amounts of information at your fingertips on the internet. However, you need to be conscious of its accuracy and the likelihood of it containing bias and exaggeration.

Figure 5.1 **Gathering evidence by research**

Where do I gather information from?

The information gathered from research can be broken down into two parts – primary information and secondary information – and both provide qualitative and quantitative information.

Primary information

Primary information is evidence that you have gathered by yourself and is unique to your personal research. The ways in which you gather primary evidence can vary greatly. Here are some examples:

- surveys/questionnaires
- interviews
- emails
- letters
- focus groups
- field studies.

Secondary information

Secondary information is evidence that you have gathered from research carried out by others. You should use it to help support your personal (primary) research. There are vast amounts of secondary information available. Here are some examples:

- newspapers, magazines and books
- official statistics
- internet search engines and websites
- television and radio programmes
- mobile phone apps
- social media such as Twitter
- library research.

Qualitative and quantitative research

Qualitative research is more focused on how people feel, what their thoughts are and why they make certain choices or decisions. Focus group meetings or one-to-one interviews are typical forms of qualitative research. On the other hand, quantitative research largely uses methods such as questionnaires and surveys with set questions and tick-box answers. It can collate a large amount of data that can be analysed easily and conclusions formulated. Table 5.1 compares the two types of research.

Table 5.1 **Qualitative and quantitative research**

	Qualitative research	**Quantitative research**
Objective	To gain an understanding of underlying reasons and motivations To cover prevalent trends in thought and opinion To provide insights into the setting of a problem, generating ideas and/or a hypothesis for later quantitative research	To quantify data and generalise results to the population of interest To measure the incidence of various views and opinions in a chosen sample Sometimes followed by qualitative research, which is used to explore some findings further
Sample	Usually a small number of non-representative cases. Respondents selected to fulfil a given quota	Usually a large number of cases representing the population of interest. Randomly selected respondents
Data collection	Unstructured or semi-structured techniques, e.g. individual depth interviews or group discussions	Structured techniques such as online questionnaires, on-street or telephone interviews
Data analysis	Non-statistical	Statistical data is usually in the form of tabulations (tabs). Findings are conclusive and usually descriptive in nature
Outcome	Exploratory and/or investigative Findings are not conclusive and cannot be used to make generalisations about the population of interest. Develop a sound base for further decision-making	Used to recommend a final course of action

Source: www.snapsurveys.com/qualitative-quantitative-research